GAME CHANGER

FROM PIXELS TO PITCHES

Karl W Newton

First published in paperback by
Michael Terence Publishing in 2024
www.mtp.agency

ISBN 9781800948273

Cover design (AI)
Michael Terence Publishing

Michael Terence
Publishing

1

From Virtual to Reality

In the small town of Swanford, just outside of the bustling city of Manchester, where the air is thick with the scent of freshly brewed coffee, vibrant music, the smoke of industry and the hum of football chatter, there lived a man called Adam Wells. He was a man of many talents, but his true passion lay in the digital realm of football management.

As Adam led his Rigsby Town team to European Cup success, he asked himself if his skill in managing virtual football clubs could make him a successful football manager in real life.

Adam Wells had always felt invincible in the dim glow of his computer screen. As the mastermind behind countless virtual victories in the intricate world of Ultimate Manager, he wielded power, strategy, and finesse with the click of a mouse.

Adam's latest achievement unfolded before his eyes as he gazed at his laptop screen. He saw Rigbsy Town capture the European Cup to complete a historic treble, having already captured their domestic cup and won the league.

Earlier that day, Adam had seen the news that Swanford Town Football Club had sacked their long-serving manager, Mark Booth, following a disastrous season to this point. Swanford found themselves in the relegation zone of the top division, three points from safety with just four games of the season remaining.

As Adam sat in his living room, sipping on a steaming latte and staring at his laptop screen, he decided to apply for the job, a real-life football manager position. The thought of it sent a shiver of excitement down his spine, and he knew that this was the challenge he had been waiting for.

As Adam saved and closed the game before opening his word processor, he realised that the world of real-life football management vastly differed from the virtual one he was accustomed to. There was no margin for error, no save points, and no easy ways to undo mistakes.

This was a world where the stakes were high, and the pressure was immense.

But Adam was determined. He spent countless hours studying the game, analysing tactics, and learning the ins and outs of football management; surely it wouldn't be that difficult to transfer those skills from the virtual realm to reality.

Swanford's decision to dismiss Mark Booth had come off the back of four straight defeats, the most recent being a 4-0 defeat to fierce local rivals Bridwal in which they were thoroughly outplayed and failed to register a single shot on goal. Mark had been the manager of Swanford Town for fifteen years and, during that time, had transformed them from an unspectacular team in the third division to a stable top-flight team, winning two domestic cups along the way.

Before Mark's time at the club, Swanford Town had been seen as a little working-class club from a few miles outside of Manchester with a reasonably unimpressive history featuring three minor cup competition trophies and five lower league promotions. The club's finest hour came in nineteen-fifty-seven when, as a third-tier club, they reached the national cup semi-final against top-flight champions Wrexford AFC and were winning and heading to the final, until a last-minute equalising goal, which transpired to have been offside from Wrexford. Consequently, following that sucker punch, Swanford failed to pick their heads back up and nearly conceded twice in extra time before losing the game on penalty kicks.

Now, though, they were looking for a new manager to keep them safe from relegation. The club had made it known that they were accepting applications for the role by receiving CVs sent to the club via email.

Adam started his CV with his name and date of birth, the fourteenth of May, nineteen-eighty-five, before the usual contact details such as email address, phone number and postal address. The following section was for Adam to detail his experience relevant to the role.

Adam started with his time at Eastwood Town. When Adam began at Eastwood, they were struggling in the seventh tier of English football; in ten years, Adam propelled them into winners of the top-flight league, winning several cups along the way. Adam's crowning glory in managing Eastwood Town was in his last match when he won the European Cup with them.

Adam then detailed his time managing his country, during which he won the World Cup twice consecutively.

Last but not least, Adam detailed his time as manager of Rigsby Town, where, during three years, he transformed the club from an unspectacular mid-table team in a relegation battle to league, domestic cup and European cup winners in a historic treble-winning season.

Although Adam's experience read spectacularly, it was all on Ultimate Manager, and Adam had never played professional football, let alone coached or managed it.

Adam closed his CV with a personal statement that read; I am fully aware that my CV will read as farcical and unsuitable given that my only experience detailed is on the video game Ultimate Manager. However, please note that the realism and accuracy of the game have been recognised in studies and the news recently, highlighting its use by pro clubs to try out tactical approaches and scout players. I am confident in my tactical knowledge, leadership and man-management skills and fully believe that, in the first instance, I can help your great club survive relegation before helping to build a bright new future and reach new heights within the game.

After a final spelling and grammar check, Adam emailed his CV to the club and thought, I've no chance, and the club probably won't even acknowledge my application, let alone reply. But you won't win the lottery if you don't buy a ticket, as my Granddad used to say.

A week passed, which only re-affirmed Adam's belief until Thursday afternoon at three pm. Adam was sitting playing Ultimate Manager, planning for the season ahead with Rigsby and the mammoth task of following on from the previous season's triumph. Adam was fully immersed in the game when his mobile phone rang, piercing the silence. Adam recognised the number as the generic number of Swanford Town's main switchboard. With much curiosity, Adam answered the phone.

"Hello, is that Adam?" a hyperactive voice asked. Adam recognised the voice. It was that of Swanford Town chairman Scott Brewer.

2

Scott Brewer

Scott Brewer had been chairman of Swanford for nine months now, having inherited the club from the previous chairman of thirty years, Donald Brewer, his father.

Donald was popular throughout the club, from the fans and playing staff to the receptionists and tea ladies. Over thirty years, Don, as he preferred to be known, transformed the club from a small, bankrupt, non-league team into a giant top-flight football club worth an estimated hundred and eighty-four million pounds.

Don was a larger-than-life character around the club and town who came across as a loveable, approachable father figure to generations of Swanford fans who felt like they knew him as a close friend or family member.

Don was a gentle giant standing at six-foot-three and weighing twenty-three stone with a hand like a bunch of bananas. Don had made his money as a young, ambitious local factory owner in Swanford for twenty-five years, increasing the town's economy and providing employment and opportunities for thousands of Swanford residents. Don had built the factory into a vast organisation worth hundreds of thousands of pounds by the time he was forty-five.

After firstly receiving a very generous offer to sell the factory and then secondly seeing that his local boyhood football club needed a new owner as they were bankrupt and on the verge of going out of existence, Don decided to sell the factory at a considerable profit and purchase Swanford Town football club. Scott, his only child, had now inherited the club and taken the reins as a hands-on chairman following the death of beloved Don, his father, in a car accident following a heart attack at the wheel aged seventy-five. Don's death came as a shock to everyone as he was a very youthful, fit and energetic seventy-five and had been around the club only that afternoon.

His death plunged the club and town of Swanford into mourning. His funeral was attended by hundreds who followed a procession through the town streets, lined to the rafters with fans young and old, as well as many others who knew and loved him. Out of the dust of the rubble of Don's loss now came his son Scott, who branded himself the next generation of chairman for this club, which he intended to make a forward-thinking, world-class flagship football club of the future.

Scott was somewhat of a showman and social media influencer who wanted to stamp his mark on the club and step out of his dad's enormous shadow. Unlike his dad, Scott was an unopposing five-foot-five and a mere thirty-two years old. Scott classed himself as a man of fashion, being on trend and living a lavish lifestyle in keeping with how he'd never wanted for anything in his life. He was used to only the finer things life offered, having always been spoilt by his father. Scott was always seen in a pair of flash-looking designer jeans and trainers with either a designer shirt or t-shirt, an overcoat and a watch worth thousands that his dad had brought him for his thirtieth birthday. In keeping with this image, Scott had a short haircut with a lengthy flicked-up quiff and blonde highlights.

"Hi, is that Adam?" Scott had opened the telephone call with.

"Yes, it is," said Adam, "That's Scott Brewer, isn't it?" Adam asked.

"Sure is," replied Scott, "How's it going?"

After a split second of disbelief that this self-professed social media celebrity was on the other end of his phone, Adam replied, "I'm good, thank you."

"Good," Scott replied. Look, I'm calling you because I've got your CV in front of me. Is it a joke or a hoax, or are you serious about applying for the job?"

"Yes, I'm serious, never more so. I believe I can do this and deserve to be considered as much as anyone else," Adam replied.

"Ok, so in that case, Adam, I would love to offer you the opportunity to come in and see me and the board of directors for a formal job interview. Is that something you'd be up for, mate?" Scott inquired.

"Absolutely, yes, please. I'd be honoured," replied Adam.

"Ok, sweet," replied Scott, "How about next Monday the eighth at two pm?"

"Yes, of course, I'll be there," replied Adam.

"Ok, sound. I'll email you the details now, and I'll see you there," Scott replied before terminating the telephone call.

Shortly after, Adam received an email from Scott confirming the interview time and date: Monday, April eighth, at two pm at the Swanford Community Stadium. Furthermore, Adam was instructed to report to the reception of the Donald Brewer stand, the club's main stand, newly named in tribute to their former chairman.

The next day, after the initial shock and excitement subsided, Adam realised that the interview was in four days, the other side of the weekend. With that in mind, Adam decided that to appear serious in his interview and hopefully impress the board; he should prepare a presentation outlining his vision and tactical knowledge and detailing the changes he would make tactically to ensure the club's survival.

Adam decided to start by analysing and breaking down Mark's tactics so far this season in detail. Mark was a veteran of the game, having been a manager at several different clubs and levels over his twenty-five-year career and a player for thirty years before his dismissal from Swanford Town.

Mark was from a generation that swore by the classic four-four-two tactic, and he moulded his Swanford team in that image. Although a proven successful tactic historically, most famously as the tactic that had won England the World Cup in nineteen-sixty-six, the game in the modern age had now developed so much that the tactic was no longer effective and had not aged well. Without being disrespectful to Swanford's longest-serving and most successful manager, a man who enjoyed much success at the club as a player and captain, firmly earning the title of club legend, Adam briefly highlighted via photos and video clips the flaws in the four-four-two system and how this had cost Swanford points this season so far.

Next, Adam analysed the available players for selection, highlighting under-par performances, players who would be surplus to requirements under his management, and assets to the team's performance.

3

Monday 8th April

Monday, the eighth of April, at ten am, Adam was standing in the shower staring into the abyss of a daydream as the hot water beat down upon him like a wild rain storm. Adam was in his own world running through the day ahead in his mind, full of anxiety and nerves that everything would go wrong or worse still, he would be told that inviting him for an interview was just a wind-up to see if he'd actually attend and then he would be laughed out of there. After ten minutes, Adam exited the shower and proceeded to the mirror above the bathroom sink to shave and do his hair.

Adam stood at an average height of five-foot-seven with a slightly rounded build, evidence of his poor eating habits and lack of exercise. His hair was light brown, expertly styled into a short, sharp cut with shaved sides and back. A neatly groomed ginger beard adorned his jawline, contrasting against the brown of his hair. He carefully chose his outfit for the day, a stylish ash grey suit tailored to perfection and accompanied by a crisp white shirt and a black and white striped tie, representing the club's colours. After putting on his freshly shined black shoes, he grabbed his bag containing a water bottle and his laptop before heading out for a relaxing coffee before the upcoming interview at the ground.

Adam made his way through the familiar streets of Swanford, his feet carrying him to his favourite coffee shop just under a mile from his house. The sign outside read Coffee Club, a name that had become as much of a comfort to Adam as the warm drinks served inside. From the moment he first stepped through its doors seven years ago, Adam had been drawn to the place by the inviting atmosphere and delicious beverages. He knew it was all thanks to Barbara Smith, known affectionately as Barb's, who had been running the shop since its inception.

As Adam pushed open the door, a wave of warmth hit him like a hug from an old friend. The scent of freshly brewed coffee mingled with the crackling of the log fire in the corner, making him feel instantly at ease.

The shop's interior had a shabby chic charm, with handcrafted furniture and upcycled decorations adorning every corner.

Barb beamed at Adam from behind the counter, her black hair pulled back into a tidy ponytail and her bronzed skin glowing. "Hi, ya love. How are you today?" she greeted him in her motherly tone.

"I'm good, thanks, Barb's. How are you?" Adam replied with a smile.

"You know me, babes," Barb's chuckled, "I can't grumble. No bugger listens if I do."

As Adam ordered a large flat white with two sugars, Barbs couldn't help but comment on his appearance. "You're looking smart today, babes. What are you up to?" she inquired.

"I have a job interview," Adam answered hesitantly, knowing that this interview was top secret and he couldn't share any details with anyone.

"Good luck, hun. Let me know how it goes when I see ya next" Barbs wished him well before he retreated to a quiet corner of the shop with his coffee.

Sipping on his hot beverage, Adam couldn't shake off the nervousness that was creeping up on him. He felt like a condemned man as he thought of the highly qualified and proven football managers being linked to the job he was interviewing for. But he took deep breaths and tried to calm his nerves, knowing that Barb and her coffee shop were always there to offer him comfort and support.

After Adam's much-needed caffeine boost, he grabbed his bag and proceeded to make the seven-mile trip through the streets of Swanford to the home of the Swans, The Swanford Community Stadium on the Swans Park campus. The campus was home to the men's, women's and academy teams, club shops and offices.

The campus was relatively new; the club had moved there three years ago, having left their home of a hundred and twenty-five years, the Swanbowl, which was tired and worn out and needed replacement to spring the club forward into the next generation.

The new stadium had a generic modern stadium look. It had complete wrap-around stands with no gaps and held a capacity crowd of sixty thousand. The stadium also offered facilities for hospitality guests in executive state-of-the-art boxes.

The club's previous home, The Swanbowl, only had a capacity of eighteen thousand and was not fit for purpose in the modern age. It was in the centre of town, a stone's throw from the train and bus stations. The long-serving home of the Swans was much adored by fans of the club for its history and memories, as well as its ideal transport access.

It was met with mass scepticism when it was announced that the club would move to the new campus. The scepticism was only furthered by the revelation that the new campus with the stadium at the heart of it was to be built on an unused ninety-acre piece of land on the very outskirts of town with no travel links. The club acted quickly to address this by creating the club's own train station and train line to link the club to the town centre and providing free match day shuttle buses for ticket holders from the town centre to the ground. The club also offered four multi-storey car parks, one for each stand, with hospitality guests and club officials parking on the main car park in front of reception in the west stand, now known as the Donald Brewer stand. Furthermore, the campus was located just off the motorway junction for Swanford and only three miles from the local airport.

Adam did not want to risk the train running late or being busy and humid, causing him to sweat, so he took a taxi ride to the ground, dropping him at reception on the big main car park. Above the reception door in the centre of the stand was a giant LED display of the club's logo, striking in size and of an evening lit up. It could be seen as a beacon of light from a distance away, leading fans to their sanctuary, church, and home.

Adam proceeded to report to reception, where he was asked to take a seat while the receptionist phoned Scott in the board room to let him know that he had arrived. Shortly after, Scott appeared at the top of the grand staircase with a larger-than-life smile. He bounced down the stairs toward Adam to greet him and shook his hand before saying, "Hello, mate. How are you doing? Good, yeah?"

"Yes, I'm well, thanks, if not a touch nervous, but yes, good other than that," Adam replied.

"Sweet," replied Scott, "Let's get you up to the boardroom, shall we?" he continued.

"Sure," replied Adam.

As Adam followed Scott up the flight of stairs, which, given Adam's nerves, felt like ascending Mount Everest, Scott engaged Adam in small talk.

"So, did you get here ok, Adam? Did you drive in?" Scott asked.

"Yes, it wasn't too bad, thank you," Adam replied, "I'm afraid I don't drive at the moment, so I got a taxi. Does that go against me as a candidate? Do you need someone who can drive?" he asked.

"Of course not. Don't be daft," Scott replied, "It doesn't matter at all. We have club chaperones, etc. It will be fine should we choose to employ you, so don't stress it, bud."

"Phew, thank you," replied Adam, "Don't misunderstand, though, I do drive. I am licensed, it's just that I've been unemployed for a while, and money has been tight, so I haven't been able to afford a car," Adam explained.

"Sweet, then," Scott responded, "That's nice and easy. We'll just sort you out a company car, no worries, bud."

"My gosh, really? Thank you so much," said Adam.

As Scott and Adam approached the boardroom on the third floor, they could hear disgruntled and angry voices debating, which got louder and more audible with each step toward the room. As they approached the door, Adam could hear the conversation vividly.

"What the hell is this, some kind of joke? Scott hasn't got a clue what he is doing. This is appalling and will ensure and confirm our relegation. The press will have an absolute field day with this. We will be an absolute laughing stock. Don would never have allowed this. He'd be spinning in his grave." Upon hearing the conversation, a ghostly white look came over Adam's face; he looked upset and even more nervous than he was already feeling. Having spotted this, Scott acted to reassure him.

"Don't worry, dude. It'll be fine," he said calmly, "I believe in you and what you can bring. These blokes are dinosaurs who have been here since my Dad took over and think backwards. I'm forward-thinking and wouldn't have you here if I didn't think it could work. Ultimately, despite their advice, the decision is mine to make, so relax, take a deep breath, and just be you, yeah, mate?" Scott explained.

"Ok, thanks, let's do this," Adam replied.

As Scott and Adam walked through the big, heavy boardroom door, they were greeted by a grand, old, thick-looking table with six chairs around it. Four of the seats were already filled, two on each side, by the members of the club's board. Scott proceeded to sit at the head of the table and invited Adam to sit at the other end facing him, which he duly did.

Adam took a moment to take in his surroundings. To his left were floor-to-ceiling windows with sliding French doors, and the room length overlooked the stadium and pitch. Behind Scott at the other end of the table was a framed signed club home shirt with a large flat-screen TV and a laptop shelf underneath it, the matching away shirt being opposite it, behind him. To the right, at the far end of the room, was the door Adam and Scott had walked through moments earlier to enter the room. The rest of that wall was filled with the club's achievements, detailed along a timeline, a visual record of the club's history and ups and downs over the years. The table they sat at had a telephone in the middle and a speaker and microphone, presumably used for conference calls, and the board and Scott sat around it, facing him intently. Everyone at the table had a pad of paper, a pen, and a glass of iced water laid out for them, and the jugs for refilling them were located by the telephone in the centre of the table.

4

The Interview

"Welcome, Adam. How are you doing? Do you need anything or want to ask anything before we get started?" Scott began.

"I am good, thank you, and no, I am fine cheers," Adam replied.

Scott went on to introduce the four board members in attendance. "Adam, four of our board members will assist me as club chairman in conducting this interview. Messrs Kerr, Stein, Lennon and Taylor have been at the club for several years. They will be part of the decision-making process in appointing our new manager."

"Ok, nice to meet you all," replied Adam, taking a deep breath to feel relaxed and ready for the opening question.

"So, Adam, what made you apply for the manager role here at Swanford Town?" Scott asked.

"That is simple, Mr Brewer," replied Adam, "It has always been my dream to be a football manager, and this opportunity at my local club offers a fantastic opportunity to do so."

Board member Mr Stein gave off a big tut and sigh before interjecting, "For god's sake, Scott, this is a real football club with real-life consequences. It isn't a computer game. You can't reload it and try again if it goes wrong. Adam, you say it's a dream come true, this is no make-a-wish project, it's a real-life club with people's livelihoods on the line."

Before Adam could respond, Scott replied, "Yes, thank you, Mr Stein. Leave the question asking and talking to me as chairman, please." "Right," continued Scott, "Beings as we were so rudely interrupted by Mr Stein, let's look at his concern. This is a real-life football club, unlike the computer game in which all your experience is based. What makes you think you can carry that experience into real life and succeed here at this club?"

With a confident smile, Adam reassuringly answered, "The game is more than just a video game. Clubs like yours, I'm sure, use it as an asset to scout players and try out, as well as analyse tactics. The game is now at such an advanced, realistic level. I am confident that the tactical knowledge I have through years of learning on the game is transferable to the real-life game and make me an asset to this club in its push for survival in the league."

"Ok, thank you," replied Scott. Scott took a moment to pause before asking his next question. "As I am sure you are aware, this club finds itself three points from safety in the relegation zone, with four games of the season left. We need this club to survive and stay in this division. How do you intend to achieve this?"

"If I may," replied Adam, "I have prepared a presentation detailing this. If I can link my laptop to the TV on the wall over there, I'd like to show it to you, please?"

"Of course you can, that would be great," replied Scott.

Adam started his presentation after taking his laptop out of his bag and plugging it into the TV. "It is my observation that the old faithful four-four-two tactical approach that Mark Booth used is no longer practical in this division and the game overall at all levels. It has led to a subsidence in performances and results. Following a complete evaluation of the players' true abilities on the training pitch, I intend to adopt a positive tactical approach with the team playing on the front foot and with urgency and a high press.

Ultimately, we must hit the ground running and get the necessary results in these final four games. Therefore, we have no choice but to attack these games fully and leave absolutely nothing on the pitch. If we are to succumb to relegation, it won't be for want of trying, and we will do so by fighting with everything we have as well as energy and determination. You will also notice I have highlighted some players within the ranks who would be surplus to requirements under my tactical approach moving forward into next season, should there be one. But do not be mistaken, the only focus for now will be survival and survival alone. Nothing else matters," Adam explained.

Scott looked impressed, although the board members were less so. "Thank you, Adam. That was a fantastic presentation, and I agree we need a positive attacking tactic to get results, so that's music to my ears" Scott said.

Next on the agenda was coaching. "Adam, do you have any coaching experience or coaching badges?" Scott asked.

Adam replied, "No, I don't, sorry," with a worried look on his face, worried that this would highlight his inability to do this job.

"Not to worry, dude. Don't look so worried," replied Scott, "We have a team of fully qualified and experienced coaches here at the club who can look after that side of things, with you directing them as per your approach and desires. It's not a problem." Adam looked hugely relieved. After a sip of his iced water, Scott continued, "Right, final question, bud, are there any changes you feel need to be made to the coaching staff? I imagine probably not, aside from who you want as your assistant manager. You can either keep the current one or hire your own."

Adam took a moment to think over his answer before replying, "I have heard that one club man, club legend and former captain, Mike Jones, is out of work and open to coaching here at what he classes to be his club. I think Mike would bring the passion and desire of the fans, being one himself. Mike would also bring leadership and experience to this set of players. Mike is a similar age to me and has a similar belief tactically to me from what I've seen of his coaching to date and have heard him speak about during recent punditry appearances. I'd love him to help me as my assistant manager if you can make it happen," Adam replied.

"Ok, sure," replied Scott, "Should we choose to appoint you, we will look into the possibility of that for you." After glancing at his board members, who were uninterested and unimpressed while shaking their heads with folded arms, Scott said, "Right, Adam, that's all I want to ask you for now. Thanks for coming today. I will contact you at some point over the next three days, bud, to let you know the outcome."

Scott stood to shake Adam's hand before showing him out of the board room. Adam returned down the stairs to reception before taking a seat on the same sofa he had waited on before the interview, upon which he pulled out his phone to use the taxi app to order a taxi.

Once home, Adam spent the rest of the afternoon relaxing and watching mundane television while reflecting on his job interview. He initially thought he'd messed things up by appearing too nervous. Furthermore, he couldn't put to the back of his mind the voices of discontent and disbelief he'd heard upon approaching the board room and then directly from Mr Stein. Next, his mind turned to how much superior to him in experience and real-life ability the other two candidates, whom it was rumoured were being interviewed for the role, were and how this meant he couldn't be taken seriously as a candidate for the role.

The other two rumoured candidates were Steve May and Wayne Livingstone. Steve May was a young manager at thirty-seven and had a point to prove within the game, having been fired from his previous role at Bremont United. Steve had won many plaudits in his eighteen-month tenure at Bremont for his attacking and upbeat brand of football, which led the club to a league cup trophy win in his first entire season in charge, the club's first trophy in fifty years. Steve had been relieved of his duties at Bremont before the start of the current season, with the official reason being given as the club not feeling Steve could push the club to the next level, that of challenging for European cup spots and even a league title. However, intense speculation and rumour suggested that Steve was fired following a heated bust-up with the clubs' tyrannical chairman Sam Michaels over his refusal to shell out a club record transfer fee and wage for a thirty-one-year-old once superstar, but now well past his best striker, Jamie Murray.

In comparison, the other candidate, Wayne Livingstone, was a veteran of the game at the age of sixty and had been in football coaching and management for twenty-five years, having enjoyed a playing career twenty years previous to that and being in a football academy before that. Wayne had exclusively only managed in the top two flights of English football; a luxury afforded him by his ability, success and track record. The only exception to this was three years managing the national side, during which he won the Euros and reached a World Cup final before resigning, feeling he could do no more and wanting to return to day-to-day club management. In Wayne's time as a manager at various clubs, his record featured nine top-flight league trophies, two second-flight titles with promotion to the top flight, ten national cup trophies, eight league trophy wins, three European cup wins and seven manager of the year awards. Amid the rumours and speculation in the press, it was felt that there was no way Wayne would consider taking a chance on Swanford and that no amount of money or promises could lure him into the role.

As for Steve, the clubs' ambition and Steve's ability to save them were heavily questioned. That aside, it was increasingly felt that he would ultimately be appointed to the role. It was speculated that this might be on an interim basis for the season's final four games, with a view to a permanent role subject to results.

Some media sources speculated that there might be a third candidate in the running, although they had no idea who, with one outlet even guessing that it could be Mike Jones.

As the clock struck four pm, Adam turned his thoughts to his dinner and making it. Before he could begin, his phone ringing stopped him, and it was a mobile number he did not recognise. Upon answering it, Adam was greeted by a flustered-sounding Scott.

"Hello mate, I'm a pain, I know. You've already seen enough of me for one day. You seemed nervous earlier. How are you feeling now? A bit more relaxed, hopefully?" Scott asked.

"Hi Scott, Yes, I was, but I'm ok now, chilled in fact," he continued, "Scott, please do me a favour. If this is that, sorry, not on this occasion phone call, please spit it out and put me out of my misery," Adam asked.

After a brief pause, Scott replied, "Not at all, bud. I want to talk to you further about it all, though. Are you free this evening?" Scott asked.

"Yes, I think so," replied Adam, "Why?" he asked curiously.

"I've got a thing to attend that you can attend with me, and we can talk on the go. Is that ok?" Scott asked.

"Of course," replied Adam, "Where is it and what time?" he inquired.

"I'll fill you in later," Scott replied, "All you need to know for now is to get yourself back to the club for half past five, and we will travel from there. Dress to impress."

"Bloody hell, Scott, that's only an hour and a half," replied Adam, "But that's ok, I guess. See you there."

After hanging up the phone, Adam rushed to his bedroom and wardrobe to get ready, as he was due at the club in just an hour and a half. Scott's details were vague, and the brief was to dress to impress. He wondered if that meant a suit and tie or just smart casual. Adam didn't know where to begin. Ultimately, he opted for intelligent casual: a black shirt with the top button open and sleeves rolled up to the elbow. A pair of dark blue designer jeans and camel suede boots accompanied the smart-looking shirt. All of this was complimented by a black leather jacket and an expensive watch left to him by his late Granddad, which he always wore on big occasions for luck.

5

Up and Away

Adam arrived back at the ground at five fifteen and reported to reception. He stated that he was here to meet with Scott to travel to an event. The receptionist replied, "Oh yes, Adam, is it?"

"Yes, that's right," Adam replied.

The receptionist continued, "I'm not sure if Scott is down at pitch level yet, but follow me, and I'll show you down there, where you can be briefed so you're ready to go once Scott arrives."

Intrigued, Adam followed the receptionist through the seemingly endless winding corridors of the Swanford Community Stadium. After about five minutes, he followed the receptionist down the players' tunnel, out into the stadium, and onto the pitch.

The first thing that struck Adam was the sheer size of the stadium. The second thing that hit him was a helicopter grounded on the centre circle of the pitch. Before Adam could enquire about the aircraft, the receptionist explained, "I can't see Scott down here. I'm sure he will be soon. In the meantime, let's get you over to the helicopter, get you ready for the flight, and have you briefed by the pilot."

"Hold on. You're telling me Scott and I are travelling to this event in the helicopter?" Adam asked.

"Yes, of course," replied the receptionist, "Did you not know? It's the quickest way to get to London, and Scott loves his chopper" She smirked.

"Oh, ok. Let's go then, I guess," Adam replied. With that, the receptionist escorted Adam to the helicopter and introduced him to the pilot for the flight.

"Hi, I'm David, your pilot for today's flight to London and then back again. Soon, I will be warming her up, ready for us to take off at exactly five-forty-five for our roughly one-hour, maybe just-over flight. Upon arrival in London, we will land on a helipad in the form of a local rugby club. From there, a taxi will meet you and Mr Brewer to take you to the event."

Overwhelmed, Adam replied, "Ok, brilliant." A few short minutes later, during which Adam couldn't stop staring at the now very loud helicopter as its engine warmed up, Scott appeared full of life with all the energy of an atom bomb instantly taking over the space he occupied with his presence.

"Evening Adam, you well? She's a beauty, isn't she?" Scott said, joining Adam in glancing at the helicopter.

"Hi Scott, she sure is," Adam remarked, "I'm good, I think, other than wondering what all this is about. Helicopter flight? An event in London?" he continued, still in surreal disbelief at the unfolding situation he found himself in.

"All in good time, my man," Scott replied, "All in good time," Scott continued, "For now, let's get on board this beauty and get strapped in, and then I'll explain en route," Scott said.

"Ok, sure," replied Adam as they climbed aboard the helicopter and strapped themselves in before the engine sprung into life. The helicopter took off slowly, rising out of the stadium and into the sky, making all below it shrink in visual size, eventually looking like a tiny model village below.

Suddenly, Adam heard a voice through the headset he'd been asked to wear. It was Scott. "Hey, dude, are you ok? I can relax now that we are in the air. I always get nervous on takeoff. You good?" he asked.

"Yeah, I'm ok," replied Adam, "I'm just wondering where we are going and what all this is about, to be honest," Adam explained.

"Yeah, sorry I was vague. It was all so rushed. I completely forgot about this event. I intended to take you for dinner in town, but we'll go to this thing first and then grab a bite afterwards. Is that ok?" Scott asked.

"Yeah, that's fine," Adam replied, "What's the event?"

"It's some league managers meeting, come new media deal launch event thing. There normally all quite boring, and to be honest, I really can't be arsed, but as chairman of the club, I'm obligated to attend," Scott explained. He continued, "I can't stand talking on these headsets. It's too noisy up here. Let's kick back and enjoy the flight for now, and we'll talk more when we are on the ground. That ok?" he asked.

"Sure, ok," Adam replied. Adam sat back and took in the flight with all the awe and wonder of a child on Christmas morning. The flight went over the city lights of Birmingham and the Midlands, then the Cotswolds and Chilterns countryside, before the bright lights of London emerged from the dark. Soon after, the helicopter slowly descended towards its north London helipad, otherwise used as a local rugby club pitch. Once the helicopter had landed, Scott and Adam were safely ushered off it and into a slick black people carrier, ready to be transported to the event in the centre of London.

Once the journey began, Scott spoke again. "So now we can talk. Let me explain why I wanted your company this evening," he said, "Adam, I want you as our next manager. I knew it before the interview. Still, the dinosaur board wanted to see you for themselves, follow protocol, etc. I know it's daunting, and we have a lot to discuss and finalise, but for now, I want you to know that the offer is on the table. Enjoy tonight's event and mull it over. Are you ready? Do you want to do this and risk how much it will turn your life upside down? After the event, we will get some proper food, given that the food at the event is that fine small portion stuff and won't fill us at all. At that point, we can discuss it at length. Is that ok?" he asked.

Stuck for words, Adam replied, "Sure, yeah, ok, wow, sure will do."

Half an hour or so later, Scott and Adam's chauffeur pulled up to a posh hotel, the destination for tonight's event. Adam didn't know anybody in attendance, although he did recognise many of the managers from other league clubs and some media pundits. Nobody in attendance knew who he was and assumed, as he was crutched next to Scott all evening like a loyal puppy to its owner, that he was Scott's PA.

The event went smoothly and without note. It was just the usual corporate networking type thing. It consisted of a sit-down three-course meal followed by a presentation and some speeches to launch a new media coverage deal for the league.

Scott seemed relieved and satisfied at the event's conclusion, which was hardly surprising as he appeared as captivated as someone watching paint dry for the whole evening. "Right, let's get out of here," Scott exclaimed, "And go get a proper bit of food. Is curry good with you, bud?"

"Spot on," replied Adam.

Scott led Adam back to the people carrier and waiting driver. Upon getting into the vehicle, he stated, "Driver, we are going for a curry, you know the usual spot, yeah?"

"No problem, Mr Brewer. We'll be there in ten," the driver replied. Ten minutes later, they pulled up to a lavish Indian restaurant called Akrams. The first thing that struck Adam as he got out of the vehicle was the beautiful smell emanating from the restaurant, an aroma so intense that he salivated slightly as he could taste the scent on the back of his throat.

As they entered the restaurant, Scott, a regular, was greeted by the staff's warm smiles. "Hello, Mr Brewer. It's good to see you again. Table for two?" Mr Akram, the restaurant's owner, asked.

"How are you, big man?" Scott replied, "Yes, please," he said, shaking Mr Akram's hand.

Seated at a private table, Scott and Adam settled into their seats, and the ambience enveloped them in a warm and inviting atmosphere. Soft, golden light from ornate lanterns cast intricate patterns on the walls. At the same time, the gentle strains of traditional Indian music played in the background, creating a soothing backdrop for their conversation.

Scott and Adam sat across from each other, the table adorned with crisp white linens and gleaming silverware. Their anticipation was evident as they perused the menu. The aroma of exotic spices wafted through the air, igniting their appetites and setting the stage for culinary and business exploration.

With menus in hand, they conversed, discussing the evening and Adam's potential appointment as the new Swanford manager. Amidst the murmur of diners and the clinking of cutlery, their voices carried an air of focused determination, interspersed with occasional laughter and nods of agreement. As they deliberated over their meal choices, they shared recommendations and preferences, bonding over their mutual appreciation for Indian cuisine. Their rapport blossomed amidst the culinary adventure unfolding before them, each dish promising a new sensory delight and serving as a catalyst for their burgeoning partnership.

As the waiter approached the table to take their order, Adam and Scott exchanged knowing glances, their excitement visible. With their selections made and the promise of a fruitful discussion ahead, they raised their glasses in a silent toast, eager to embark on this journey together over a delicious Indian meal. As the waiter brought complimentary poppodums to the table for them to pick at while they waited for their food, the small talk stopped, and the business conversation began.

"So, did you think about what I said earlier?" Scott asked.

"Yes, I did," replied Adam, "I would love the job. However, I do feel there are several issues to discuss and address," Adam stated.

"Indeed, there are, but the fact that you want the job is a great starting point. It means neither of us is wasting each other's time," Scott replied.

Shortly after, the curries arrived at the table, and a silence fell over both Adam and Scott as they ate and savoured the flavours of their beautifully cooked dishes. Scott had chosen a chicken vindaloo with extra spice, pilau rice, and Peshwari naan bread. On the other hand, Adam opted for a lamb saagwala with garlic and coriander naan bread and a side of chips.

Once they had finished their meals, Scott suggested they order a bottle of red wine to discuss matters over.

"I'll stick to the water, please, Scott," Adam interjected.

"Are you sure, mate? The vintage here is the best I've ever had. It's not to be missed," Scott replied.

"Honestly, I'm ok. I'll take your word for it. I'm fine with my water, thank you though," Adam replied.

"All the more for me then," Scott stated gleefully.

Once the bottle arrived at the table and a glass was poured, Scott began. "So first things first, we will sign you up until the end of the season, which is four games. Given the severity of the situation in terms of potential relegation, we can not look any further than that at this moment in time. The salary we are offering is twenty and a half thousand pounds per week, which reflects your lack of experience and the fact that some of your roles will be delegated and shared with other members of staff. This salary is competitive and in line with the current average manager earnings in the league. Upon completing the short-term deal, should you keep the club up, you will automatically be rewarded with a minimum of a one-year contract. Terms for this will be discussed at the time. Furthermore, if you ensure the club survive, you will be rewarded with a bonus payment of half a million pounds. How does all that sound?" Scott asked.

"Most agreeable, yes," Adam replied. Internally, Adam was pinching himself at such a great offer but decided it wise to maintain his professional-looking poker face for now.

"Great," replied Scott.

After briefly shaking hands to seal a gentleman's agreement on Adam becoming the new manager and a sip of his wine, Scott continued with the finer details. "So in terms of coaching, I would propose, to suit the criteria for coaches with their badges coaching the players, that you leave the coaching of players in training to your team of coaches and assistant manager who will feed back performance levels to you, for you to select a team for matches. This will only be the case for the next four games. Should we survive and you become a permanent manager, we expect you to have your badges, so we will get you through the courses at an intensive speed as part of your role. Regarding your assistant manager, we took on board your desire for it to be Mike Jones, and after a lengthy phone call and much negotiation this afternoon, he has agreed to take the role until at least the end of the season. It would be best if you leaned on his advice about tactics, team talks, etc. Does all that sound ok?" Scott asked.

"Perfect, yes," replied Adam, delighted with the terms on offer.

After a toilet break and a quick phone call to his driver and helicopter team to arrange the journey home, Scott re-joined Adam. He concluded, "I will need to get our media department to brief and train you for what's to come, which is something I will link you in with when you meet me at the ground to sign your contract and do the new manager reveal photos and press conference, ok?" Scott asked.

"Yes, that's great, thank you," replied Adam. Little did he know that this curry conclave would begin a new, life-changing era for him and the football club.

Shortly after, Scott and Adam sat comfortably in the plush leather seats of Scott's private helicopter. The blades whirled above, creating a rhythmic hum that drowned out the noise below. The journey home was a moment of reflection for both men.

Mr Brewer, an excited newly appointed chairman determined to stamp his mark on the club and leave his legacy, had gone against his board's advice in selecting Adam. Scott knew the decision would be met with scepticism from the players, fans and pundits alike. As they soared through the night sky, Scott knew that this was a gamble, but his desire for Swanford to be a forward-thinking club upon which he would stamp his mark drove this decision, and now he knew he would have to stand by his choice.

The helicopter provided a serene escape from the chaos of what had happened over the last twenty-four hours for Adam. The atmosphere was calm inside, allowing the two men to converse candidly. Adam shared his vision for the team tactically, speaking passionately about his coaching philosophy and his aim to get the squad to play with fight and desire in an attempt to get the points to ensure their safety in the division short term. Scott listened intently, nodding in agreement as he absorbed every word. He admired Adam's drive and passion, recognising that he had found a manager who would stop at nothing to keep the club up. Scott knew this was a high-stakes gamble with the club's future on the line.

As the helicopter glided through the sky, the lights of the towns and cities twinkled below, casting a magical glow. It was a moment of clarity for both men, a shared understanding that they were embarking on a journey together, united by a common goal. The challenges ahead seemed insignificant in the face of their unwavering desire. The conversation gradually shifted to personal anecdotes and shared experiences. They laughed and exchanged stories, forging a bond extending beyond the football pitch. Scott realised that he had found a manager and a friend who shared his passion and commitment to the club.

As the helicopter descended towards the club's training ground, the excitement in the air was palpable. The journey had ended, but a new chapter was about to begin. Scott and Adam stepped out onto the training pitch, ready to face the challenges that awaited them. Scott led Adam to a car parked in the car park of the training ground. "Adam, I'm delighted I've appointed you, and I hope you have had a good evening with me. Thanks for coming. My driver will now drop you home, and I expect to see you at the stadium tomorrow morning at eleven o'clock sharp to tie everything up before I unveil you as our new manager. Is that ok with you?" Scott asked.

"Definitely, and thank you so much for this opportunity and a wonderful evening. I'll be there at eleven am sharp," Adam replied.

"Brilliant, see you there, bud," replied Scott.

As Adam lay in bed drifting off that night, he had to pinch himself to ensure that this day had not been a dream. In twelve hours, he had gone from a nervous outside long shot to interviewing for the job as Swanford manager and now their new manager with a monumental, almost impossible task on his hands. Furthermore, throughout the twelve hours, he'd been on a helicopter flight to London and back and had eaten at one of London's finest Indian restaurants. Surreal didn't even begin to cover it.

6

First Day

The following day, Adam was awoken at seven am by his radio alarm clock tuned into Sports Radio. As Adam stirred and woke, his attention was brought to the radio and a lively-sounding presenter who seemed excited by the day's breaking news story.

"Good morning, Riley James here. It is believed Swanford have found their new manager, and it's shocking. We are led to believe from an inside anonymous source that it is a completely unknown man named Adam Wells, whose only experience is playing the video game Ultimate Manager. Is this some kind of joke, or is it just someone getting their facts wrong? Who knows? We'll be taking your calls on this next while we await comment from the club."

Adam was in shock. How on earth had this information been leaked? His next concern was how the public, and more importantly, the fans, would react. Adam grabbed a coffee and sat down in anticipation of the telephone calls to the radio station, a chance to gauge the public reaction.

The presenter came back on the air following some adverts. "Ok, let's go to caller number one about the Swanford news. Hello, who's that, please?" he asked.

"Morning Riley, I'm a big Swanford fan. I've been a season ticket holder for twenty years now. I didn't realise it was April Fool's Day again. Is this a joke? If this is true, what are Scott Brewer and the club playing at? This is an insane suicidal move and will only confirm our relegation," the fan declared.

"Thank you, buddy. I hear what you are saying, and it's a valid point. Next caller?" Riley, the radio show host, replied.

"Morning Riley, I hope Scott Brewer or the club are listening as I would like to read a statement from me and the official supporters club. We wish to express our deep concern and frustration regarding the rumoured appointment of an unknown and unheard-of manager as the new leader of our beloved club. As passionate fans, we feel compelled to voice our disappointment and seek clarification on this decision. First and foremost, we want to emphasise that our intention is not to criticise or undermine the club's management. However, the lack of transparency and information surrounding this appointment has left many of us perplexed and concerned about our team's future direction and safety. As loyal supporters, we invest our time, emotions, and resources into the success of our club. We expect the management to make decisions in the best interest of the team's progress and success and, therefore, survival in this division.

While we understand that sometimes unconventional choices can yield positive results, the club must communicate the rationale behind such decisions to maintain the trust and confidence of the fanbase. Please address these concerns and provide us with more information about the new managers' background, qualifications, and vision for the team. It would greatly alleviate the anxiety and scepticism that many of us currently feel. Furthermore, we urge the club's management to consider engaging with us, the fanbase, through open forums to address our concerns directly. This would demonstrate a commitment to transparency and allow for a constructive dialogue between the club and its supporters. Our club has a rich history and a passionate fanbase that deserves to be involved in decisions that impact its future. By fostering open communication and addressing our concerns, the club can strengthen its relationship with the fans and ensure a united front moving forward," the fan concluded.

"Ok, thank you very much for that," Riley replied, "Swanford and, in particular, Scott Brewer, are you listening? Do you have anything to respond to the speculation with?" Riley asked.

Adam had heard enough to fill him with even more anxiety than he was already feeling ahead of his first day, so he turned off the radio and proceeded to shower, get himself ready, and dress for the day ahead.

Ten am and the taxi that Adam had ordered to take him to the club arrived. It was time for him to set out. A short way into the taxi journey, the driver attempted to engage Adam in small talk. "Off to the football club, are you? Hoping for a glimpse of what is going on there today," he inquired, "Madness, isn't it? What are they playing at? Employing an unknown who has no experience other than on a video game, surely they will go down now won't they?" he continued.

"Hopefully not, but we will have to wait and see, I guess," Adam replied.

As the taxi approached the stadium, Adam spotted that the car park was full and that there was some bustling commotion. As the cab pulled into the car park and drove through the crowds to the reception entrance, Adam was blinded by the flash of cameras that greeted the car, anticipating it being his arrival at the club. As the taxi stopped outside the reception entrance, it soon became surrounded by journalists and photographers, swarming to the car like moths to a flame.

Taking a deep breath, Adam adjusted his tie and straightened his suit, ensuring he looked presentable for the occasion. He took another deep breath and exited the car, rushing into reception through a precession of flashing photographers' lights and journalists calling out, "Adam, are you the new manager?" "Is this a hoax?" and "Have you any comments for us, especially the fans, at this time?"

Adam stepped into reception, where Scott greeted him. "Let's get you out of the glare of the circus out there. Follow me, mate," Scott said.

As they reached the chairman's office, Adam paused to collect his thoughts. He knew this meeting would forever change his life and the club's future. As they entered the office, Scott said, "Morning, Adam. I'm thrilled to have you on board as our new manager. Please, have a seat." Adam shook Scott's hand, feeling a surge of confidence. He took his seat, ready for whatever was to come next.

"You must be wondering what today will look like," Scott said. "First things first, we start this whole thing by you signing your contract in the presence of the club's lawyer, Laura Smith, who will witness the signing. She is due to arrive at half eleven. Following that, I will take you on a tour of the ground en route to the club shop, where we will get you kitted out with clubwear.

Following that and some lunch, we have a meeting with the media department and your new media advisor and PA Sarah Baker-Jones, which will include the taking of your official unveiling photographs and video message for the fans. Following that will be the new manager's unveiling press conference, which is scheduled for five pm. Finally, you will have a private meeting at six pm with your new assistant manager, Mike Jones, who is spending today at the training ground meeting the other members of your coaching team and the players, whom he will be assessing and evaluating whilst they train today. Is all that ok with you?" Scott asked.

"That's a crazy busy first day, but yes, let's do it," Adam declared.

Scott's office was a spacious, elegant room with large windows overlooking the football pitch. Behind his desk, which Scott sat proudly behind, was a painted portrait of his dad, Donald. On Scott's desk was a photo of him and his dad on the pitch at the opening of the new stadium. Shortly after quarter past eleven, a smartly dressed, official-looking female with short jet-black hair entered the office.

"Hey Laura, how are you doing? Have you got the paperwork?" Scott asked, greeting her warmly.

"Of course," remarked Laura, "And I'll thank you to call me Ms Smith, please. Is this the guy?" she inquired.

"Sure is," replied Scott, "Ms Smith, may I introduce you to Adam Wells, our new manager. Adam, this is Ms Smith, the club's lawyer" Scott made the introductions.

Adam stood up before shaking Ms Smith's hand. "Pleased to meet you," he exclaimed. It was now time to get down to business. Scott sat behind his desk with Adam, and Ms Smith sat across from them. Placing a thick document on the table in front of Adam, Ms Smith explained, "Adam, please take a few moments to look through and review the contract we have drawn up as per your verbal agreement with Scott yesterday evening. It also details the terms and conditions of your employment. Once you're happy with it, let us know, and we can begin signing the contract on the formal side of matters."

Taking just over five minutes, before taking a deep breath, Adam replied, "I appreciate the thoroughness of this contract. It's evident that the club takes its commitments seriously."

Ms Smith replied, "Indeed, Adam. We believe in setting clear expectations and providing a solid foundation for our working relationship." The three engaged in a detailed discussion, with Ms Smith explaining the contract terms and addressing Adam's queries. The conversation was professional and respectful, with a mutual understanding of the importance of transparency and clarity.

After a thorough discussion, Adam was satisfied with the situation and declared, "I'm ready to sign the contract and commit myself fully to this wonderful club."

With that, Ms Smith handed Adam a pen, and he signed the contract. Shortly after, Scott signed his part of the contract with a smile on his face and declared, "Congratulations, Adam. We're thrilled to have you as our new football manager officially. We believe you have the tactical knowledge, vision, and desire to guide this club to safety and beyond."

Adam gratefully replied, "Thank you, Scott. I won't let you down. I'm eager to get started and work closely with the team to achieve that goal."

The room filled with optimism and renewed energy as Scott and Adam shook hands, sealing their partnership. "Right then," declared Ms Smith, "I have other business to attend to, so now that we are done here, I will leave you two to your bromance. I will email you both a copy of the contract within the next few hours for your records."

Scott shook Laura's hand and thanked her before showing her out of his office. He turned to Adam and said, "Right then, bud, are we good to go? Shall I show you around your new home?"

"Sure, let's go," replied Adam. Adam was excited to have an access all areas tour of the state-of-the-art stadium. As Scott and Adam passed through the club reception to begin the walk around the stadium, Scott declared, "I'll be showing you around our beloved home, a place that already in the club's recent history holds countless memories and embodies the spirit of our club." Scott began sharing the history of how this state-of-the-art stadium came to be. He pointed out the four stands, three of which were named in tribute to three of the club's most successful individuals.

The North Stand was named after Geoff Joyce, the club's all-time top goalscorer with two hundred and ninety goals in three hundred and two appearances.

The East Stand was named after Ian Gates, who served the club for fifty years. He started as a youth player before playing for and captaining the side. Eventually, Ian became player-manager and, soon after, full manager of the club.

The South Stand was named in tribute to Kevin Woods, who was club captain before World War II and never returned home from battle after losing his life in combat at the age of twenty-two.

The West Stand, the main stand that housed the club's reception, the players' tunnel, and the manager dugouts, had recently been named the Donald Brewer Stand in tribute to the deceased long-serving chairman. Scott's pride at pointing this out was evident as he recounted the job his dad did building up this great club from the brink of non-existence to the glorious club that it is today, a club that he had now inherited.

Moving deeper into the stadium, the tour entered the players' tunnel. Scott explained how this tunnel had witnessed the nerves and excitement of countless players before they stepped onto the hallowed turf. He emphasised the importance of creating an environment that inspires and motivates the team to give their best in every match.

Next, Adam was led to the home team's dressing room. Scott explained that this was where pre-match strategies would be discussed, team talks would be given, and the camaraderie among players would be fostered. He stressed the significance of building a united team, reminding Adam that success on the pitch was a collective effort.

Leaving the dressing room, Adam and Scott returned to the pitch. The lush green grass stretched out before Adam, who stared out towards the stands, mesmerised as the stadium's atmosphere seemed to come alive.

Scott shared stories of memorable matches, epic comebacks, and the crowd's roar that echoed through the stands. He emphasised the importance of creating a winning culture and instilling a sense of pride in the players representing the club on this pitch.

As they walked back up the tunnel and out of the emergency exit onto the car park, the tour ended with the club shop coming into view. Adam couldn't help but feel a renewed sense of purpose. Scott's passion for the club was infectious, and Adam felt inspired to lead the team to safety and hopefully new heights following that. Adam thanked Scott for the insightful tour, expressing his gratitude for the opportunity to be a part of such a storied institution.

"Remember Adam," Scott said, his voice filled with conviction, "This stadium is more than just bricks and mortar. It's a symbol of our club's legacy and the dreams of our fans. As the manager, you have the power to shape the future of this great club in the next four games. I have faith in your abilities, and I'm confident that together, we will achieve our short-term and hopefully long-term goals too." Adam followed Scott into the club shop with those words echoing in his mind.

Upon entrance to the club shop, Adam was greeted by an ample open space stocked as far as the eye could see, with all the merchandise that any club fan could wish for. From replica kits to homeware and pin badges, it was clear that the club was dedicated to offering every merchandise option possible to increase its profits. Scott introduced Adam to the staff behind the counters, especially the store manager, Cecilia Jackson, known affectionately as Pat.

"Hey Pat, this is Mr Adam Wells, our new first-team manager. I've brought him down to pick out any uniform items he wants and anything else he feels he needs. Please charge all of it to the club."

"Sure," replied Pat.

Scott then encouraged Adam to look around and pick out any training and match-day clothing he may need and any stationery items he wanted. These items were on the club as part of his job role. Adam started by picking out the club's training shirt, matching tracksuit, baseball-style cap, and woolly hat for the colder days. Next, Adam picked out an oversized, long club puffer jacket before moving to the formal section of the shop. He already had his suit and shirt but wanted to offset it with an official club tie on match day: white with black stripes and the club's logo.

Finally, Adam picked out two club notebooks with leather covers embossed with the club's logo and a pack of pens bearing the club's logo. After taking the items to the till to be processed, Adam followed Scott out of the club shop before returning to reception.

As they made their way toward reception, they walked past the flashing cameras and voices of journalists still waiting on a club announcement or comment on the speculation of Adam being the new manager. As they walked past them, Scott briefly commented, "Alright, lads and lasses, calm down. All will be revealed at the five pm press conference. See you there."

Once inside the reception, Scott led Adam to the club's media department for his first official briefing and to meet the media manager, Sarah Baker-Jones. The room was filled with a team of professionals, each equipped with cameras, microphones, and notepads. This meeting would set the tone for Adam's relationship with the media throughout his tenure.

Adam greeted the media department professionally, acknowledging their presence and expressing gratitude for their support in promoting the club's activities. Adam understood the importance of maintaining a positive and transparent relationship with the media, as they would play a crucial role in shaping public perception of him, the team and, therefore, the club.

The head of the media department, Sarah Baker-Jones, began the briefing by introducing the team members and explaining their respective roles. Sarah was twenty-eight and had been at the club for ten years, joining as an apprentice after leaving college. She had worked her way up through the ranks at the club before being appointed as the club's media manager just under two years ago. She stood at five foot with a petite build and was always well-presented in the finest designer gear and a glow-up, which came from a beauty regime she worked hard on and often shared on social media with tutorial videos. Her hair was long and striking, platinum blonde in colour.

The media team emphasised the importance of effective communication and the need to align their messages with the club's values and objectives. They also highlighted the significance of maintaining a consistent and professional image on and off the pitch. During the briefing, Adam listened attentively alongside the odd look toward and nod of acknowledgement with Scott. He took notes and asked clarifying questions when necessary. Adam wanted to ensure he fully understood the club's and media department's expectations and guidelines. He recognised that his words and actions would be scrutinised, and conveying the right message to the public and the fans was crucial.

After a brief pause, Sarah said, "Right now, onto our first pressing matter, before the photos and video we are taking to unveil you on the club's website and social media, these!" she remarked before slamming down several of today's newspapers. Offering the back pages of the papers for Adam and Scott to look at, she explained, "Seems someone within the club tipped off the press as to your helicopter trip yesterday with Scott and your appointment as the club's new manager. See this picture," she said.

Adam looked at the newspapers closely, all bearing pictures of him arriving at the club yesterday and then getting into the helicopter with Scott. After a brief second of shock, Adam remarked, "Well, that explains the radio call-in speculation this morning and the angry calls in response to the rumour."

"Indeed," replied Sarah, "We are aware of that too." Adam was advised not to engage with the media and to allow the club's press release and the upcoming press conference to do the talking. The media department then provided valuable advice on handling the forthcoming press conference and any more moving forward. Adam was also advised on other interviews, social media interactions, and conduct. Sarah stressed the importance of being prepared, staying composed, and delivering clear and concise messages. She also emphasised the need to be respectful towards journalists and to address any controversies or sensitive topics with tact and diplomacy, referring them to the media department for comment if he didn't feel comfortable at any time.

Finally, as the meeting concluded, Adam expressed his gratitude for the media department's guidance and assured them of his commitment to working closely with them.

Following the meeting, Adam was asked to be photographed and recorded on video for his unveiling as the new manager. He was first taken into the stands to pose for a photo with the stadium and pitch behind him while holding a club scarf. Next, he was taken into a well-lit room to give a new manager unveiling video interview.

Adam expressed his delight at being trusted with this opportunity. He asked the fans to overlook his apparent lack of experience and have faith in his tactical knowledge from the computer game. He stated that he ultimately wanted to and believed he could do what the fans wanted in the short term: keep them up. Finally, Adam asked the fans to be the twelfth man and make a difference in the short-term fate of this wonderful club.

Adam felt a sense of responsibility and excitement as he left the media department. He knew that the press and fan reaction would be challenging. Still, with the support and guidance of the media department, he was confident in his ability to navigate the complexities and effectively communicate the club's vision and aspirations.

Five o'clock soon came around, and it was time for the club, namely Scott, to unveil Adam as their new manager. This would be an intense and hostile affair, full of questions and scepticism, given Adam's lack of real-life experience. As Scott and Adam entered the press briefing room, the noise was deafening, with the sound of voices and clicking cameras accompanied by a barrage of blinding camera flashes. The atmosphere in the room was tense as journalists eagerly waited for the unveiling of Swanford Town Football Club's new manager and to see if the rumours were true. Scott stood at the podium, ready to introduce the man he believed would lead the team safely from the looming threat of relegation.

"Good afternoon, ladies and gentlemen," Scott began, his voice projecting confidence. "Thank you all for being here today as we announce an exciting new chapter for Swanford Town Football Club. After careful consideration, I have found the perfect candidate to take charge of our team until at least the end of this season, with the number one objective being to keep the club in this division."

Cameras flashed, and reporters leaned forward, eager to catch a glimpse of the man who would be entrusted with the club's immediate future. Adam stepped onto the stage. He exuded a calm demeanour, seemingly unfazed by the hostile environment that awaited him, even though he was a nervous wreck. As Adam took his place beside Scott, the room erupted with a barrage of questions. Journalists, eager to challenge the decision, fired inquiries from all directions.

"Adam, what makes you think you're the right person for this job?" a reporter shouted, his tone sceptical.

Adam paused momentarily, gathering his thoughts before responding, "Thank you for your question. I understand that there may be doubts surrounding my appointment, but I firmly believe in my abilities and the potential of this team. I am confident that my tactics and attacking, hard-working approach alongside the work and knowledge of my assistant manager Mike Jones will bring positive changes to Swanford Town Football Club, ensuring the club's survival."

Next up was what was a visibly angry journalist, angry about Adam's appointment. "Riley James here from Sports Radio. Many of you will have heard highlights from my phone in show this morning. Many fans and I are unhappy about this appointment, which only begs the question, is this some kind of joke?" he brutally opened with. "Scott, what are you thinking? In terms of the club surviving, this is a suicidal move. No disrespect to you, Adam. I'm sure you are a nice enough guy, and if anyone were offered this opportunity, especially pay-wise, they would take it, but this is pure fantasy. It is never going to work. There is a reason why experienced coaches and managers are appointed into roles, and it's because you need that experience and knowledge. I'm sorry, I don't pack any punches. I am known for saying it as I see it, but it is sometimes somewhat brutal. Simply put, this will not work. Mark my words, Swanford are going to be relegated without a shadow of a doubt, and I'll bet that with anyone," he stated.

After a gasp of shock at Riley's scathing assessment of the situation and a deep breath, Adam replied, "You are on Riley. How about a five hundred pound bet? The proceeds will go to the local children's hospital charity. If we stay up, you pay it, and if we go down, I'll pay it."

After a moment's contemplation, Riley replied, "You might as well write the cheque now, mate. You are on!" he continued, "If there is any way this is going to work, Adam and Scott, you need the fans on board, and they are not. If anything, they are horrified at this decision."

The room erupted with murmurs and raised voices as journalists challenged Adam's appointment. The questions ranged from his tactical choices to his ability to handle the pressure of managing a club with high risks and expectations.

Adam remained composed, addressing each question with professionalism and honesty. He acknowledged the press and the fans' concerns, emphasising his commitment to open communication and collaboration with the team and the fans. He expressed his desire to ensure safety on the pitch and to work tirelessly to bring success to Swanford Town Football Club moving forward. As the press conference continued, the initial hostility began to subside. Adam's calm and confident demeanour, coupled with his thoughtful responses, started to win over some of the sceptics in the room. Journalists began to see glimpses of the vision and passion that had led to his appointment.

By the end of the press conference, the atmosphere was split, and some journalists were cautiously optimistic after hearing Adam's confidence, vision, and passion. However, the room still had hostile, sceptical, unimpressed voices. As the press call ended and the journalists filed out of the room, their pens scribbling furiously, Adam and Scott exchanged a knowing glance. They understood the challenges ahead but were ready to face them together, united in their belief in the team's potential.

Following the press conference, Scott and Adam returned to Scott's office for a well-earned coffee and breather.

After a deep sip of his coffee and an even more profound sigh, Scott said, "That was intense, wasn't it? Bloody hell. I knew they'd be cynics, but that was much more than I anticipated," he said to a stunned and overwhelmed Adam, "Riley bloody James, what a twat. Did you see the press conference when I was officially named Dad's beneficiary? He called me a careless playboy playing football clubs with no consideration for the club's future, just the size of my wallet. I've never liked the bloke," he explained.

"It sounds like he will be a tricky customer, then. It's time to prove him wrong, I guess," Adam replied.

After a coffee break and some time to glance at the ensuing carnage on social media following the press conference and the unveiling of Adam as the new manager, Scott explained, "Shortly, Mike Jones will arrive for your meeting with him. You do not have an office here at the ground so I will set you guys up in the board room. You do have an office, it is at the training ground. Besides that, you have a small office in the home dressing room for a match day. Are you planning on being at the training ground and checking out your new office tomorrow?" he asked.

"Of course, yes. I know Mike is running training, but I plan to observe fully and work out of my office there. Is that ok?" Adam asked.

"Of course," replied Scott, "The job is yours, Adam. Perform within it however you see fit, bud," Scott replied.

Next, Scott led Adam to the board room and was joined by Mike for their meeting. "Hey Mike, good to see ya," Scott said, shaking his hand, "This is Adam I was telling you about, our new manager," he said before Adam and Mike shook hands. Upon seeing them shake hands, Scott said, "Right, I'll leave you two to it then," before exiting the room.

Mike was the quintessential embodiment of an authentic London cockney, having been born and raised in the bustling East End. Standing tall at six feet two inches with a skin-shaved bald head and a well-groomed bushy beard, his robust frame exuded confidence and strength from years of hard work and dedication in the gym since childhood.

His father had introduced him to boxing at the tender age of nine by taking him to a backstreet East End boxing gym that he went to, and from then on, Mike's passion for the sport only grew stronger. In his playing days, he was known for his imposing figure, often striking fear into his opponents with just one look. Even off the pitch, he commanded attention and respect wherever he went. To those who knew him well, Mike embodied all the qualities associated with being a proud East Ender, tough and determined, fiercely loyal to his roots. The spirit of the East End flowed through his veins, making him a force to be reckoned with, no matter what challenge came his way.

"Can I say something before we get down to it?" Mike asked.

"Of course," replied Adam.

"Like everyone else, I have major doubts about your appointment. However, I love this club dearly and am willing to put my doubts aside and work hard with you to achieve a goal that me you and the fans all have in common, safety. This club truly holds a special place in my heart, and under no circumstances do I want to see it go to ruin," Mike stated.

"I respect that, and thank you," replied Adam.

Mike explained that he had spent the day at the training ground meeting and evaluating the players at the club's disposal. "I'm intrigued," he asked, "I know I have my ideas, but what are your thoughts moving forward tactically?"

"I don't know the exact formation yet, Mike, but I do prefer to concentrate on having possession. If you stop the opposing team from having the ball, they can't score, right?" Adam explained.

"Correct," replied Mike.

"Furthermore, we need to win games fast, with time running out. We will need to be on the front foot and attack," Adam continued.

"Of course," replied Mike.

"Finally, I believe that football is a simple game. Defend well, keep your position, keep the ball, find your passes, and take your chances. We don't need to reinvent the wheel and overcomplicate things right now.

We need to do the basics well and keep the club up. Anything else can happen in the summer," Adam explained.

"Good," replied Mike, "I couldn't agree more. It's good to see we are on the same page."

After a brief pause, Mike explained, "So training today went well. We have a good squad of players available who can really play and are all pulling in the same direction. They are naturally fit and generally a good set of lads."

"That's music to my ears," replied Adam.

"I have to warn you, though," Mike stated, "Like me and the fans this morning, they were unhappy about your appointment and have their doubts. However, like me, they realise this is not about you, Scott, or your appointment. Only one thing matters, this club's safety, a common goal we all have to work toward," he explained.

Mike handed Adam a USB stick and explained, "On this stick, you'll find video footage of today's training session and the last two games from the first and under twenty-three teams. These are for you to have a watch of to help with your evaluation of the players in terms of selection," he said.

"Thank you. I'll have a watch of those as soon as," stated Adam.

Mike added, "Training starts at nine am daily, with players generally arriving from eight-thirty. If you want to watch the videos this evening, I suggest you, me and the coaches meet in your office at the training ground at seven-thirty tomorrow morning to discuss any thoughts and adjustments needed before briefing the players at five to nine pre-training. Does that sound good to you?" he asked.

"Of course, yes," Adam replied.

"Ok, great," replied Mike, "See you there." Mike shook Adam's hand as the meeting ended before exiting the board room.

Adam's first day was done agenda-wise, so he ordered a taxi to take him home before going to reception to leave the stadium. As Adam stepped through the front door of his home, he couldn't help but feel a mix of exhaustion and excitement. It had been a hectic first day at work, filled with meetings, introductions, and a whirlwind of information. Finally, he could take a moment to unwind and reflect on the challenges ahead.

Adam lived on New Road on the outskirts of town in a terraced two-up, two-down house that had been in his family since it was built. Adam's Great-Granddad had helped to build the house as a young bricklayer for a local building firm before purchasing it for himself upon its completion. He then lived in it his whole life until he died in nineteen-sixty, at which point he left it to Adam's Granddad, who lived there until he died in two thousand and fourteen. Upon his death, he left the house to Adam to ensure that he had a stable future ahead of him, a reflection of the tight bond Adam and his Granddad shared.

Adam made his way to his cosy living room, where the soft glow of the television beckoned him. He settled into his favourite armchair, ready to immerse himself in the world of football once again. Tonight, he focused on studying the team's performance in their last two matches and that of the under-twenty-three team. The screen came to life with a few clicks of the remote, displaying the familiar green pitch and the players in their vibrant jerseys.

Adam began by watching the first team's games. His analytical mind kicked into gear as he observed each movement, every pass, and every goal, mainly conceded but occasionally scored. He knew understanding the team's strengths and weaknesses was crucial to his success as a manager. As the footage played, Adam couldn't help but feel a sense of anticipation. He had heard about the team's recent struggles but was committed to turning things around. The players' drive and talent were evident, but some areas needed improvement. Adam made mental notes, jotting down observations and ideas to shape the team's training sessions and tactical approach.

The hours flew by as Adam meticulously analysed every play, rewinding and replaying key moments. He studied the team's formations, individual performances, and patterns of play. It was a meticulous process that he knew would provide valuable insights. Adam paused the video occasionally to jot down specific moments that caught his attention. He wanted to discuss these with his coaching staff, seeking their input and expertise. As the final whistle blew on the last match, Adam leaned back in his chair. He had gained a deeper understanding of the team's dynamics and identified areas for improvement. Armed with this knowledge, he was ready to devise strategies to maximise the team's potential.

Closing his notebook, Adam next turned his attention to the under twenty-three's games. The games were intense, with Swanford's team displaying their skills and passion. Adam observed the players' movements, analysing their technique, decision-making, and overall potential. He knew hidden gems could often be found in these games, where raw talent had yet to be polished.

Amidst the sea of young athletes, one player stood out. His name was Neil Cole, a lanky teenager aged seventeen with a natural grace and an uncanny ability to read the game. Neil's agility and speed were matched only by his composure on the ball. Adam's eyes followed him closely, captivated by the young player's every move. As the game progressed, Neil's talent became increasingly evident. This was backed up by three goals and five assists over the two games on video. Neil would constantly and effortlessly weave through defenders, displaying a level of skill and creativity that belied his age. Adam's excitement grew, realising he had stumbled upon a future superstar.

Adam had no hesitation in boldly writing Neil's name in his notebook, followed by three exclamation marks, intending to promote the lad into the first team tomorrow morning. Finally, Adam turned off the television, feeling renewed hope. The challenges ahead were immense, especially regarding the sceptics of his appointment, but he was confident in his ability to lead the team to safety.

Tomorrow would bring new opportunities, and he would be ready to face them head-on. With a contented sigh, Adam retired to his bedroom, knowing that a good night's rest would prepare him for the demanding days ahead. Adam, unable to sleep in silence, turned on his radio, which by default was tuned into Sports Radio, to drift off to sleep. The station was hosting back-to-back phone-ins from fans and ex-players of the club, slagging off the decision made by Scott and questioning Adam's credentials to manage the club. Adam kept visions of victory dancing in his mind, fuelled by his desire to keep the team in the division.

7

Getting Down to Business

The next day came like a train thundering down the track after a night filled with very little sleep and a lot of tossing and turning. It was six am, and the radio alarm pierced the silence like an air raid siren with very little change in the station's content. It was all about Swanford, Scott Brewer and his appointment. Although Adam allowed it to be background noise, all of a sudden, the radio show forced itself into the foreground of Adam's attention. He listened as Riley James, the presenter, spoke.

"Overnight, we received a statement from an anonymous source within the club. It reads as follows, regarding the appointment of Adam Wells as the new Swanford manager. As a pivotal first-team player at the club, I wish to state on record that I and many of the first-team players disapprove of this appointment. We find the idea of working for an inexperienced manager living out his video game fantasy laughable. If we are to adhere to his ways, we feel it will result in the club's relegation. We have a moral obligation to the fans of this great club, whom we love, to do our best to avoid that of our own accord. We will do that ourselves, not from some clown's instructions or directions."

After a short pause, indicating the end of the statement, Riley commented, "Oh dear, an unhappy dressing room from the start. There may be trouble ahead for Mr Wells," singing slightly in jest the words as they were also lyrics in a famous song.

A shocked Adam rose from his bed and allowed the radio to become background noise again before having an espresso coffee and jumping in the shower. Whilst in the shower, often a place for deep thought and contemplation, Adam second-guessed himself and his decision to take the job after hearing the statement from a source within the dressing room. After a few moments, the doubt subsided, and Adam stepped back out of the shower, a confident and driven man ready to face the day ahead of him. Adam was disappointed by the statement sent to the radio station, especially as he had yet to meet the players, so he was being judged before even making a first impression. Adam got changed into his club training gear and put on his giant club puffer jacket before leaving at six-forty-five to head to the club's training ground, nested within the club's sports campus.

Shortly after seven am, Adam arrived at an empty, quiet training ground amidst a cloud of fog and frost. The training ground operations manager greeted him on arrival, taken aback by how early he had arrived; he was the first on-site. Adam was shown to his office, where he used his coffee machine before firing up the company laptop, which had been left on his desk, along with a set of car keys presumably belonging to his new company vehicle.

Sitting back in his posh leather chair to ready himself for the meeting with Mike and the coaches at seven-thirty, Adam took a moment to take in his new surroundings. Adam sat behind a smart, modern, minimalistic desk against the far wall on the left. The wall behind the desk was filled above head height by whiteboards, and a flipchart was to the right of the desk. Opposite the desk on the right-hand wall was a three-seat leather sofa, above which a panoramic photo of the stadium filled the wall. The office's back wall had floor-to-ceiling French doors overlooking the training pitches with a small balcony outside the doors. Standing in front of the glass wall was a table upon which a coffee machine lay, accompanying refreshment options, and packs of various biscuits.

While Adam sat enjoying a calm before-the-storm moment of peace, his mind kept returning to the statement on the radio and how to deal with the issue. Shortly after, his office was bustling as the coaching team filed in, eager to meet him. The room was filled with a diverse group of individuals, each with their own unique expertise and role to play in the team's success.

Adam took a deep breath, reminding himself to stay calm and composed. He knew building a solid relationship with his coaches was crucial for the team's progress. Adam opened with "Good morning, team," ready to make a lasting impression, his voice projecting authority and warmth, "I am honoured to be here as the new manager, and I am excited to work alongside each of you," he continued. The room fell silent as the coaches turned their attention towards Adam. They were curious to see what kind of leader he would be and how he would approach his new role. "I believe that success is a collective effort," Adam continued, his eyes scanning the room, "Each of you plays a vital role in shaping the team's performance, both on and off the pitch. I am here to support you, to listen to your ideas, and to create an environment where we can all thrive."

Adam's words resonated with the staff, who felt a sense of unity and purpose. They could sense his genuine commitment to their growth and the team's success. "I would like to take this opportunity to get to know each of you better," Adam said, a friendly smile on his face, "I believe that understanding your strengths, passions, and aspirations will help us work together more effectively."

One by one, Adam invited each staff member to introduce themselves, sharing their name, role, and a brief overview of their experience. As each person spoke, Adam listened attentively, making mental notes of their unique skills and potential contributions. Throughout the introductions, Adam asked thoughtful questions, showing a genuine interest in each person's background and expertise.

After the introductions, Adam expressed his gratitude for the team's warm welcome. He emphasised the importance of open communication and encouraged everyone to share their ideas and concerns freely. "As we attempt to steer the club from relegation together, I want you to know that my door is always open," Adam said, his voice filled with sincerity, "I need your collective knowledge and skills to do the work on the training pitch given my lack of experience. I will guide you on what aspects of the game I would like the sessions to be based on. Together, I know that we can keep this club up."

It was now time to focus on the week ahead and brief the team. "So now to the task in hand, this first week's training," Adam opened with, "So design the schedules and sessions as you see fit, but this week I want to focus on retaining possession and finding our passes successfully, and then some work on both attack and defence. This will be alongside the usual strength and fitness work. Is that ok with you guys?"

"Of course," Mike, his assistant manager, replied, "Leave it with us."

After thanking the team for their cooperation, Adam requested that Mike send Neil Cole to his office upon his arrival.

A shy, reserved knock came at Adam's office door shortly after eight-thirty. Upon opening it, Adam was greeted by a nervous-looking Neil.

After guiding Neil into his office and inviting him to sit, Adam said, "Hi Neil, nice to meet you. I'm Adam, the new first team manager."

"Yes, I know who you are," Neil replied, "You're trending hard on social media right now," he declared.

"Oh, ok, cool, I guess," Adam replied, "I've called you in because last night I had the pleasure of watching your last two performances for the under-twenty-three side. I've gotta say I was majorly impressed," Adam remarked.

"Thank you, boss. I appreciate that," replied Neil.

"So Neil, how would you describe yourself as a player?" Adam asked.

"Well, I have been here since I was nine years old. I am a huge Swanford fan. I was born and raised in Swanford, and I love playing football. That could be in a park with my mates, or professionally, it's all the same. The ball at my feet is my happy place. Naturally, I like to play the ten role tucked behind the strikers. That way, there isn't as much pressure on me to score as a striker would have. I can be part of the attacking moves, supporting and assisting and occasionally being there to have a stab at goal myself. There have been times when I have slotted in deeper back in midfield, which I also enjoyed and contributed well as a team player. Although, if I had to play in any position, even goal, to realise my dream of playing for the club that I love and have my family, who are season ticket holders, watching and cheering me on, I'd do it," Neil explained.

With an impressed look, Adam replied, "That is stunning. What a great attitude and one I only wish I could have from every player at the club. I was super impressed when I watched you in the videos, even more so now, young man. So the reason I asked to see you is because I have made a decision. I want you to train with the first team immediately. The move is up to you and what you feel is best for your development. I want you to take a moment to decide if you'd be best staying in the under-twenty-three setup and playing every game and learning or whether you fancy the challenge of working and fighting for a place in the first team. It's whether you think the time is right. You're more than welcome to phone your family or agent for advice if you need to," Adam explained, giving Neil a few moments of shock to consider his next move.

After a few minutes of thinking it over and composing himself, Neil replied, "I want to take the opportunity, but I won't be just there as a work experience kid or to make up the numbers. I will show you and the underperforming players in the first team what I'm all about. I'm going to work tirelessly to make sure that I force myself into your plans and take this chance," Neil stated, his face laced with passion and desire.

"Brilliant," replied Adam, "Go get some breakfast and get ready to hit the pitch at nine am with the rest of the first team. Let's see what you can do."

It was eight-forty-five am, and Adam stepped out of his office, full of nerves yet appearing calm and authoritative. He was much like a swan on a lake, on the surface solid and majestic, although under the water's surface, paddling away like crazy. As he stepped into the canteen, he entered the centre of the big, light, spacious room, ready to address his troops for the first time. The players, finishing their breakfasts and clad in their training gear, gathered around, their eyes fixed on their new manager. Some wore expressions of curiosity, while others seemed sceptical. Adam took a deep breath, trying to exude confidence despite the butterflies in his stomach.

"Good morning, everyone," Adam began, his voice steady and composed, "I am honoured to be standing here as your new manager. My name is Adam, and I am excited to work with each of you."

Interrupting him, defender Kofi Adams stated, "We know who you are dickhead. You're all over the papers, radio and social media," he heckled. The players sniggered and exchanged glances, whispering amongst themselves. It was clear that they were unsure about their new leader.

Kofi was a beast of a defender. Solid at the back, strong and one of the team's most consistent performers in the three seasons he had been at the club. He stood at an imposing six-foot-one and was of mixed race with dreadlocks that reached halfway down his back and a lengthy beard. Kofi's father was of Jamaican origin. Kofi got his build and strength from his father, a tower of a man with a lion's heart, which he'd handed genetically to Kofi. As a result of his DNA, Kofi opted to represent the Jamaican national team proudly and, to date, had been capped for them fifty times.

Adam understood the scepticism, knowing that he had yet to prove himself in the world of football management outside of a video game. "Yes, thank you, Kofi, a bit of respect, please, lads. Your pros paid to do a job and follow your manager. I understand that some of you may have reservations about my lack of experience," he continued, addressing their unspoken concerns, "Still, I want you to know that I am here to learn and grow and ultimately achieve the common goal that we all have, to avoid relegation. None of us want to go down, hopefully mainly for the fans who pay their hard-earned money to follow us in their droves home and away, but also for ourselves. It won't look good on any of you if you have a relegation on your CVs." Adam paused, allowing his words to sink in. The players remained silent, their eyes fixed on him, waiting for him to prove himself worthy of their trust.

"I believe in the power of teamwork and unity," Adam continued, his voice filled with conviction, "Each of you brings unique skills and talents to this team, and it is my job to harness that potential. I will work tirelessly to create an environment where you can thrive and reach your full potential." Some players' eyes flickered with interest, while others remained sceptical. Adam knew gaining their trust would be difficult, but he was confident he could prove himself. "I am committed to open communication and transparency," he emphasised, "Your opinions and ideas matter to me. I want to hear your thoughts, concerns, and aspirations. Together, we will steer this club to safety."

The players exchanged glances again, this time with a hint of curiosity. Perhaps this new manager was capable and genuinely cared about their input and growth.

"In the coming days, I will assess the squad and its strengths and weaknesses by attending training sessions," Adam announced, "I will observe each of you closely before selecting a team for the first of our four matches on Sunday against Newborough. Mike and the other coaches will work with me to develop strategies that match our strengths and get the desired results and points."

As Adam concluded his speech, cautious optimism filled the air. The players, though still uncertain, were, for the most part, willing to give this new manager a chance. They understood that success would require their collective effort and trust in their management team of Adam and the experienced Mike Jones.

"Oh, finally," Adam declared, "Let's address the larger-than-life elephant in the room. The statement sent to Sports Radio. Which one of you was that?" he asked.

A deafening silence fell over the room, with the players looking expressionless. "Come on, whoever it was, you weren't shy in wording the statement and obviously have something to say. Grow some balls and own up!" Adam exclaimed.

"Fine! It was me, and I stand by every word. What of it?" a voice answered. It was the club captain and midfielder, Michael Knight. Michael was in the autumn of his career, having had a celebrated, if not troubled in parts, career playing at the very highest level, and was one of the club's star players.

A shocked Adam replied, "Fine. For the foreseeable future, you will train with the under-twenty-three squad. Go get acquainted with them and get ready for training."

A shocked Michael replied, "What on earth? You can't drop me and make me train with them. Do you know who I am?" Michael raged.

An assertive Adam stared him in the face and replied, "Under-twenty-threes, GO!"

Michael stormed out of the canteen with all the force of a tornado, destroying everything in his path before slamming out the door and screaming, "You twat, you'll regret this!"

The other players in the canteen looked visibly confused, shocked and angry. Adam, sliding his foot across the floor in a straight line in front of him, declared, "This is the line in the sand, lads. Any of you who aren't with me and Mike to act in the best interest of this club and the fans in doing our all to keep the club safe, this is your one chance to cross the line and join Michael in the under-twenty-threes. If not, I expect nothing less than a hundred and ten percent from you. Let's get on with it, and get on with training out on the grass and begin the hard work." Adam made a brave call: "Anyone wanna cross the line? Final call," he gave it a few brief moments, none of the players taking him up on the offer, "Good, let's go then," he said.

Finally, Adam added, "One final thing," putting his assuring arm around Neil, "This is Neil Cole. Many of you may have heard about his recent performances at under-twenty-three level. For the foreseeable future, he will be training with the first team. Please make him feel welcome."

Following the morning meeting, Adam followed the lads and Mike Jones out onto the training pitch to take his first steps towards building a team that would defy expectations. As the players started warming up and bracing themselves for a hard training session, Adam joined Mike and the other coaches at the side of the pitch, ready to evaluate the lads in action. The first part of training consisted of fitness work, allowing Adam to see the fitness levels and speed of the squad. One player stood out above the rest; he was built like a tank and the clear winner of the sprinting drills, leaving everyone else chasing his tail.

"Who is that?" Adam asked before Mike replied.

"That is Jay Donovan, his a wing-back. He is arguably the best in the league and has big clubs enquiring about buying him this coming summer should we go down. He is fast and gets up and down the wing at the speed of light, providing solid defensive skills with a pinpoint tackle timing-wise and then a pinpoint cross attacking at the other end. He is the complete player and a vital part of this team," he explained.

Next, the team practised their possession and passing skills; one player stood out as Adam watched: Kofi Adams. Kofi was composed on the ball, moved fast to receive passes and had the precision of a master marksman when finding a pass. Adam could see that he could be vital distribution-wise in playing out from the back to begin attacking moves. Adam also knew from the analysis tapes and season stats that Kofi had the best tackling success rates in the league and that the team had kept the most clean sheets when he played. It was also clear that Kofi was a vocal leader on the pitch, and Adam could see how hard he was working, giving everything even though it was only a training session.

After a short refreshment break, the team worked on their attacking plays. Mike instructed them that in this drill, they could only shoot in the box and take no less than six but no more than ten passes in each build-up. He added that breaking these rules would result in ten laps running around the pitch as a forfeit. The lads got down to work, and after a series of drills, Neil got his chance to shine and immediately imposed his hungry young talent onto the squad.

In his first attempt at the drill, he started the move by laying off a solid pass to Donovan before making a run toward the edge of the area. As the rest of the side made their passes and moves, Neil concentrated on his positioning and getting ready to make himself an option before calling for a pass. Now was his time. As Neil called for the pass, he took the ball down from a cross and, with his first touch, nutmegged it through the legs of Sam Reynolds, the defender, before turning him and leaving him to stumble over. Once he'd beaten Sam, entering the box, Neil rifled a shot off his right foot, which glided past the goalkeeper with the beautiful elegance of a bird in flight.

"Oh wow, just wow," remarked Mike and Adam in sync.

"That is stunning, well done Neil," Adam added, "You feel that lads?" he asked, "the bar just got raised."

"Ok, lads, lunch break," Mike declared, following a sharp firm whistle.

Sam Reynolds looked as angry as a bull staring at red before getting back to his feet and shoulder barging Neil, grunting, "Piss off back to nursery, twat."

Sam Reynolds was part of the furniture at Swanford after being at the club for the last seven seasons. At the peak of his career, he had signed for the club at the age of twenty-seven for a then-record fee as one of the best solid defenders in the country and for England as well. However, now he was thirty-four and well past his best. In truth, although the first name on Mark Booth's team sheet, Sam had become a liability over the last two seasons, especially this one. He was single-handedly the reason Swanford conceded so many goals this season, leading to sixteen defeats.

Sam was an old-school defender and a hard man of the game, but in recent years, he needed help to keep up with the pace and skill of the new generation of younger players in the game. He had become an aggressive and angry figurehead at the heart of Swanford's defensive line. As Adam watched, Sam struggled to meet the pace of the training session, leaving him to conclude that now would be the time for a change in the defensive line and dropping this Sam-shaped weakest link.

As training resumed after lunch, Adam requested that the coaches gather a promising eleven young under-twenty-three players for a half-hour each-way match between them and the first team. As Adam watched from the sideline, he wanted to see what talent was emerging from the youth setup and spot another Neil to bring some energy, hunger and passion to the first team. This was especially important as he now had two huge gaps in the side, in defence and midfield, to fill. From the first team, he wanted to see which players were up to the task and would step up for the club in its hour of need. Adam would also observe positional play and strengths and weaknesses to help him decide how this team could perform tactically. Adam was further hoping that a candidate to take over the captain's armband from Michael Knight would manifest itself.

Throughout the game, three things became clear about the first team. Firstly, their pass success rate was appalling and needed to be a lot better. If they couldn't find a teammate with the ball, they would never be able to retain possession and make attacking moves from which to score. Furthermore, they would be gifting opposing teams with possession and would likely be punished by their attacking moves. Nobody was running into space to be open for a pass, so passes were forced to players who were marked and unable to win the ball.

Secondly, they leaked more at the back than a burst pipe, conceding four goals during the game.

Thirdly, and most importantly, the team needed more confidence.

Two positives did arise from the game, though. Neil scored two goals effortlessly and assisted another amid the 4 - 4 draw, and Kofi Adams showed outstanding leadership at the back, which gave Adam the thought that he could be an ideal captain.

Overall, the week's training started on a less-than-impressive note. The players seemed disengaged and needed more energy and enthusiasm. Passes were sloppy, shots were off target, and the overall performance was far from what Adam had hoped for. It was clear that there was a lot of work to be done.

As training ended, Adam couldn't help but feel a mix of disappointment and frustration. He had envisioned a smooth transition into his new role, but instead, he found a team that seemed resistant to change. Doubts started to creep into his mind, questioning whether he had made the right decision in accepting this position. However, Adam was not one to back down easily. He knew that building a successful team required patience, perseverance, and the ability to navigate through the immediate challenges. He understood that change takes time, something they did not have, and that his decisions may only sometimes be popular. But he was determined to prove himself and turn things around.

Reflecting on the day's events, Adam realised that he needed to find a balance between implementing his ideas and respecting the experience and opinions of the players. He knew that earning their trust and respect would be crucial in gaining their commitment to his goal of keeping the club up. As he left the training pitch, Adam made a mental note to have a one-to-one conversation with Michael to explain his decision and reassure him that it was not personal. He understood the importance of maintaining a positive relationship with the club captain, as his influence could significantly impact the team dynamics.

As Adam went to his office to pack away for the day and then grab his new company car keys, he reflected further on the issue with Michael after deciding to demote him to the under-twenty-three team. It was a bold move, one that sent shockwaves through the squad. Adam knew that this decision would not be well-received by everyone, but he believed it was necessary to establish his authority and set a precedent for the team from day one.

As Adam entered the car park, the only indication of the company car lay in the manufacturer logo on the key fob. There were only two cars in the car park with that make. As Adam approached them, he pressed the keyfob to open the car, revealing which one was now his. It was a lovely black, brand-new-looking sports hatchback. As Adam opened the door and sat in the driver's seat, the unmistakable new car smell hit him, and he scanned the car's interior with amazement. The car was clad in the best, heated leather seats. It also had a huge digital screen interface, wireless phone and satnav features, and a dab radio player. This car exhumed luxury. As Adam looked toward the speedometer, a plastic card was covering it. Adam picked up the card to examine it; it was a fuel card that would charge the club for any petrol consumption needed.

While driving home in his new state-of-the-art company car, Adam's phone, linked to the car's speaker system via Bluetooth, began to ring. Adam answered the call, and a calm, professional-sounding female voice greeted him. "Hello, Adam. This is Mary, the receptionist from the training ground. I have a phone call for you. It is Mr Arthur Jenkyn-Jones, the football agent. Shall I put the call through?" Mary asked.

"Sure, go for it," Adam replied.

A moment later, a voice said, "Hi, is that Adam?"

"Yes, who's speaking, please?" Adam replied.

"Hi, this is Arthur Jenkyn-Jones. I am a football agent. I am calling because I represent your player, Michael Knight," Arthur explained.

"Oh yes, Michael, we've had quite the day," Adam replied.

"Yes about that," Arthur said, "What are you playing at? He is your star player and club captain. What were you thinking dropping him into the under-twenty-three squad? Are you mad? Do you want to get this club relegated?" Arthur asked.

After a pause to compose his response, Adam explained, "On the contrary, Arthur, my job and my aim is to steer this club to safety. As a new manager with no experience in real-life football and having my critics before I've even started, I need to take no crap and assert my authority from day one. With that in mind, once your client owned up to the statement sent to Sports Radio, making it clear he would be unprepared to back or follow me as his manager, I asserted my authority by immediately punishing him with a demotion to the under-twenty-three side. I also allowed anyone else sharing Michael's opinion to join him. I felt Michael's statement to the radio station was scathing, unjust, unprofessional and disruptive. I had no other choice than to react as I saw fit," Adam explained.

"I understand that," Arthur replied, "Furthermore, I advised Michael against sending the statement. He can be so hot-headed sometimes, and I'm afraid he won't listen to anyone when he is in that mood. A red mist comes over him. However, the fact remains that Michael is far from happy with how you have treated him, and you have made an enemy of him, which I can't help but feel will be your and the club's downfall. I need a solution to this problem and now. Is there any way you can make amends with Michael and get him back into first-team training tomorrow?" Arthur asked.

After a moment's contemplation, Adam replied, "Absolutely not. There is only one person who needs to apologise and make amends here, and it certainly is not me."

"Ok, fine," Arthur replied, "So, do I need to find a new club for my client? Perhaps firstly on a short-term one-month loan deal, given his need to be playing right now to stand a chance of being called up by England for the upcoming World Cup?" Arthur asked.

"Arthur," Adam replied, "Please do not misunderstand me. I admire Michael as a player, and I know that he is a huge part of the dressing room here and is integral to any success that this club can have. That said, I can not tolerate his behaviour, no matter how good he is as a player. I'd be open to peace talks if he could share my vision for the team and apologise to me and the fans publicly. The balls in his court," Adam stated.

"Ok, fine, I'll relay the message back to him," Arthur replied before hanging up on Adam.

Once Adam got home, he fixed himself some food before heading to bed. He was knackered and needed rest to reflect on the day's events. An early night would allow him to wake early the next day to do it all over again.

8

Thursday 11th April

The following day, Adam was awoken again by his radio alarm clock. After waking up, he adjusted and tuned his ears attentively to the background noise to hear, to his horror, more drama unfolding on air.

"Good morning. This is Riley James on Sports Radio if you're just joining us. Yesterday, the new Swanford manager took training for the first time in his fight to keep the Swans up, although according to an inside source, he doesn't take training. Instead, he lets his coaches do that while he watches. Reports suggest that this is an uphill struggle for Adam already, both on and off the pitch. Listen to this phone call we received overnight from club captain Michael Knight." After a brief pause, the audio played.

"Hi Michael, we don't usually hear from inside the camp, but we believe you have something to say," the radio presenter said.

"Yes, that's right," Michael replied, "Adam Wells, what a clown." Michael continued, "Firstly, let me make it known the statement yesterday was from me, something I shouldn't have done before meeting him. I apologise for that unprofessionalism, mainly to the fans. Before training yesterday morning, Adam asked who had sent that statement to the station, which I admitted to. Instantly he squared up to me and told me to piss off and train with the under-twenty-three squad and that I'd never play for the club again whilst he was manager. I was shocked as I have carried this team at times this season, and without me, I fear the club will go down, something I don't want the fans to experience as I have always had a good relationship with them," Michael explained.

As attention threw back to Riley in the studio, he declared, "A damning listen for Swanford fans this morning. What do you make of this? What are your thoughts on this situation?" Riley asked. "The lines are open. We're taking your calls on this now," he stated. "Oh, and just to add, we have, of course, made contact with the club, Adam and Scott Brewer, for comment on this, to no avail," he explained.

Adam was initially shocked, then angered by Michael's unprofessionalism in leaking an internal matter and lying about the manner of the incident. He felt this was a deliberate ploy to get the fans on his side against him as new manager.

Adam rose like a corpse from the dead, had a coffee, and left the house at eight am to head to the training ground. The day's training passed without incident, giving Adam more opportunities to evaluate the players before their first game in just three days.

Adam watched the afternoon defensive and goalkeeper drills and concluded that this was the side's weakest point by far. As training concluded, Adam retreated to his office to depict notes he had taken over the last two days, intending to start to plan his tactics. This would not be unlike a general standing at his map, planning his attacking moves ahead of the war, which would be the final four games of the season in this case.

Looking at the time, five thirty pm, Adam decided to stay at the training ground as there was an under-nineteen game at half-past six, before an under-twenty-threes game featuring first-team reserve players at half-past seven. Adam decided to take in these games to see all the players outside the first team at the club's disposal, hoping to discover capable players to throw into battle.

As Adam watched the under-nineteen game, it was clear that these lads were still developing and some way off the first team, except for one player, Ethan Fox. Ethan was playing as a defensive midfielder, just in front of the defence but behind the midfield. His role was as a vital first line of defence for the back line and essential in distribution to the midfield when it came to building attacks. Despite playing with all the maturity of a seasoned pro at his peak, Ethan was just sixteen. He stood six feet tall and was stocky in build. As a result, he was solid and commanding, the beating heart of everything the team did, and a vocal leader with exceptional vision. Repeatedly without fault, Ethan stopped attack after attack, reaching the defensive line before showing composure on the ball and picking out a pass moving forward.

As the game reached half-time, Adam approached Ethan, who, despite being a fearless leader on the pitch, was shy to talk to. "Ethan, you're smashing it, son. Tomorrow morning, please report for first team training. I'll let your coach know I've promoted you, ok?" Adam declared.

A stunned Ethan replied, "What, really? Wow, yes. Yes, please. Is this for real?"

Adam replied, "Sure is. See you bright and early."

Next, Adam watched the under-twenty-three side play, which included reserve players from the first team. Almost instantly, Michael Knight, who was in the team, spotted Adam on the sideline and threw him a look, which, if looks could kill was true, would deem Adam six foot under stone cold and full of rigour mortis before lip-syncing him an obscene name in anger whilst pointing his middle finger up at him. The game saw Michael perform faultlessly to prove a point to Adam.

Away from the Adam v Michael circus, one performance stood out above the rest: Louis Sims's. Louis was twenty and played as a winger. He stood just five feet tall and could have only been about nine stone wet through. He was a whippet, fast, with the acceleration of a greyhound out of the traps when running onto the ball. Time and time again, Louis would pick up the ball before dancing through defenders like an elegant ballerina, going through on goal and getting a shot away, scoring four goals.

The game finished 6-1 to Swanford thanks to Louis's goals. By a country mile, he was the man of the match and the difference between the two sides.

Louis recognised Adam and approached him at the end of the game, greeting him with "Welcome to the club, good luck, you sure are gonna need it."

Adam replied, "Yes, it seems that way, doesn't it?" Adam continued, "What a game you just had. Wow. Do you fancy training with the first team tomorrow?" he asked.

After a moment to think it over, Louis replied, "Yes, of course. See you there, gaffer. Thank you," he answered.

The days training and two games he'd watched had given Adam more food for thought and his plans for the team were slowly becoming more apparent.

9

Friday 12th April

Adam arrived at the training ground the following day with nervous optimism for the first game in just two days. Before training, Adam introduced Ethan and Louis to the team, explaining that they were joining the first team with immediate effect, and asked the squad to make them feel welcome and help them where needed to fit into the setup.

Training passed without incident, and Ethan and Louis integrated themselves into the team effortlessly as if they'd been in the first team for years. This even caused some senior first-team players to recognise their raw talent and remark on how impressive they were, along with Neil, who had continued to impress over the last two days. The youngsters were making an immediate impact and adding fresh, passionate energy to the squad.

Sarah Baker-Jones arrived at the training ground at two pm to meet with Adam, and they proceeded to his office.

After sitting down and feeling relaxed, Adam greeted Sarah, "Hey Sarah, how are you today?"

"Yeah, I'm all good, cheers. How are you settling in, boss?" Sarah asked.

"Yeah, not too bad, cheers. There have been a few rocky moments, but yeah, not bad. Thanks," Adam replied.

"Yeah, I heard about the Michael incident. It was a brave move on your part," she continued, "Let's start with that. As I see it, Michael and his agent, who has spoken about this to the national tabloid press, are acting unprofessionally regardless of your decision and handling of this matter. With that in mind, my immediate advice is not to bite and refuse to comment. In terms of that, at the forthcoming press conference, the press will push you to comment on it," Sarah explained. "As you know, you will conduct a pre-match press conference at three pm ahead of the Newborough match. The experienced press will try to draw you into tactical plans and team selection. Stay calm and assertive, and don't get drawn into it," she explained.

"Ok, got it," Adam replied.

As three pm approached, Adam, escorted by Sarah, went to the press briefing room to prepare for the press conference. Before entering the room, Adam took a deep, calming breath to conduct himself before entering the awaiting circus. The briefing room was bustling with noise and speculation before filling with white blinding lights and camera click noises as Adam approached the table, facing out toward the room and the prying eyes of the gathered media outlets.

Adam opened the press call by saying, "Hi guys, thanks for coming. I'm here to talk about Sunday's game against Newborough. I will now open the floor to questions." Instantly, gathered journalists put their hands up, "Ok, yes, please," Adam said, pointing at a hand on the front row.

"Hi, Super Sports TV here. Let's address the big news of the last couple of days. What do you have to say about the Michael Knight situation?" the journalist inquired.

After a deep sigh, Adam replied, "In short, nothing. I have no comment to make on the situation at this time. Furthermore, I am here to talk about the match on Sunday, and that alone," he explained.

"Ok, thank you," the journalist replied, "So about that, how can we expect to see the team line up and approach the game tactically?"

"Well, we have four huge games left," Adam replied, "There is no time for caution. We have to get points, and without revealing too much, I can assure fans that attack is the only option. We have to play with attacking urgency and aggression where needed. We have to fight for our survival in this division," Adam explained.

"Ok, thank you," the journalist replied.

After a pause, Adam picked out the next journalist in the crowd, pointed to him, and said, "Yes, please."

The journalist probed, "Hi, UK News here. Can we expect to see any changes in the starting eleven? There is speculation that you will adhere to fans' calls to drop Sam Reynolds and that some youth players have joined the first team setup," he inquired.

"I will not be revealing my team for Sunday, but I will confirm that I am considering our options, and, of late, things have not been working results-wise, so it is my job to make any changes I see fit to remedy that. I can confirm that three youth team players have been brought into the first team setup for selection consideration. Neil Cole, Ethan Fox, and Louis Sims. Their roles for the rest of the season remain to be seen. However, their talent is evident, and I believe they bring hunger, passion and determination to the group," Adam replied.

The journalist, taking notes as Adam spoke, replied, "Thank you."

Next up was Swanford Daily, whose reporter asked, "Newborough are on a run of three straight wins and are unbeaten in six games in their push for a European spot. This will be a tough away game. Do you believe your side has what it takes to get a much-needed result?"

Adam took a moment to consider his answer before replying, "Yes, I do. I believe in my ability, my coaches, and this team's ability to go into this and all four final games and secure the points we need to keep us up. If I didn't, what would be the point in me being here?" he asked.

Finally, Adam pointed to the familiar troublesome face of Riley James from Sports Radio. Riley sat with his arms folded and looked like he'd chewed a wasp, emanating negative and sceptical body language toward Adam. Adam sighed and remarked, "Finally, for today, hello again, Riley. What's your question?" he inquired.

Riley replied, "Is it fair to say that your first few days have shown that you are out of your depth here and that the club needs an experienced hand to guide them to safety?"

"Thanks, Riley," Adam replied, "Optimistic as ever I see. Yes, that may well be a fair comment. However, I have Mike Jones with me, who has a wealth of experience, and we are working together as a team toward keeping this club in the division. I would argue that regardless of lack of experience, I bring tactical knowledge and an approach, which, along with the professionalism of the playing squad who are being paid to do a job on the pitch, can make the point you have made an irrelevant factor in keeping this club up. Please make a note of this and quote me on it. I back myself, my coaches and the players to get the results needed to keep this club in this division, end of story!" Adam replied.

Adam wrapped up the press conference by thanking the attendees and leaving the room.

The final part of the day's agenda was Adam's meeting in his office with his coaching staff about the team's tactical approach to the upcoming games.

"Alright, let's get to it," Adam said, his voice low but commanding, "As I see it, we need a fresh approach. We need points, and we need them fast," he explained. "With that in mind, I have been considering our tactical approach moving forward. As I see it, we need to play with urgency, aggression, and attack games to get those points as soon as possible. We are weak at the back, which won't be fixed easily or overnight. We have to accept it, and with that in mind, our approach needs to be to attack and get points by outscoring our opponents. This is not without its issues, as it would appear that the team lacks confidence and goals, but I feel this can be fixed with some hard work on the training pitch. Any thoughts?" he asked, looking at the vacant faces of his coaching team.

After gathering his thoughts, Mike, his assistant manager, replied, "Yeah, I get that. It's brave, but we are cornered and have to fight, so that could work. Do you have any thoughts on formation, boss?" he asked.

Taking to his whiteboard to draw up his proposed formation, Adam replied, "I wanna setup with a four-three-three, which will turn into a two-three-five when in possession," he explained, illustrating his words with drawings of the formation and movement on the board, "In possession, both our inverted full-backs will push into midfield with one midfielder dropping deeper to support the defence as a defensive midfielder. The other two midfielders join the front line, with our central striker playing deeper in the false nine role. Our play will then be based around passing diamonds between forwards and midfield. We will aim to provide lots of passing options to work through the opponents and help us retain possession. If we keep the ball as much as possible, we cannot concede chances or goals or ultimately lose, right?" Adam asked.

"Correct. However, it is worth noting that the side has only kept three clean sheets all season, so that will be easier said than done in terms of not conceding goals," Mike replied.

Adam continued, "I want us to play out from the back with short, sensible, successful passes at a fast pace. In playing out from the back, I want our fullbacks to attempt to draw pressing opponents to one side of the pitch before passing to the other open side of the pitch to begin an attacking move. I cannot stress enough the vital role passing diamonds moving up the pitch will play. Any thoughts?" Adam asked.

"Good, I like it," Mike nodded, scribbling notes on his pad, "I mean, it's brave. It's the polar opposite of how the team has played until now. It will take some adjustment and getting used to, but it could just work," he said.

Adam turned to Amy, the defensive specialist. "Amy, your thoughts on shoring up the defence? Is there anything we can do to try and tighten things up? Will they be able to adapt to playing out from the back?"

"It's something we can work on for sure. Leave it with me," she suggested, her eyes scanning the tactical diagrams on the whiteboard.

"Excellent," Adam said with a surge of confidence.

There was a sense of unity in the room, a shared belief that they might be able to pull this off. The session continued, ideas flowing freely as they dissected every possible angle, each suggestion met with thoughtful nods or constructive criticism.

Time seemed to warp around them, the importance of their task narrowing their world down to this very room, where tactics and strategies were woven into a coherent plan that would, with hope and hard work, lead to the club's survival.

Adam concluded the meeting sometime later by saying, "OK, thanks, team. Tomorrow morning, please work through the tactic with the team, emphasising those passing diamonds and finding successful passes, before I assist in taking tomorrow afternoon's session with an idea I've had. Thanks, guys. Have a good evening."

10

Saturday 13th April

Saturday morning came, and Adam gathered the players on the training pitch, their faces a mixture of anticipation and apprehension. Adam stood at the centre of the pitch as the players gathered around him. "Today, we're going to work on something different. We're going to unleash our attacking prowess with tomorrow's and the remaining games in mind."

"We will work on our new tactical approach from nine to ten thirty. After a short drinks break, we will have a special session I've planned until noon. Following that and lunch, we will depart here at one pm to journey to our hotel in Newborough," Adam said.

Ready to explain the new tactical approach, Adam continued, "Alright, lads, listen up," Adam began, his voice booming across the pitch, "You've had your fair share of setbacks this season, but today marks a turning point. From now on, we're going to fight like lions on that pitch. We're going to attack with everything we've got," the players exchanged glances, their determination slowly igniting within them. They knew it was time to give their all, to prove their worth and save the club from relegation.

"Now, we are going to set up in a four-three-three that will turn into a two-three-five when in possession. Key to this system will be passing diamonds and playing with no fear," Adam explained, beckoning his team closer, "We need to be sharp, decisive, and calculated in our movements. It's not just about finding successful passes. It's about creating opportunities. We need quick, precise passing to carve through the opposition's defence. We will be playing out from the back. Our fullbacks will be crucial in drawing out our opponents and creating space for our midfielders and forwards."

The players nodded, their eyes reflecting a mix of curiosity and scepticism. But deep down, they knew that something had to change if they were going to turn their fortunes around. With that, Adam finished by urging, "Alright, lads, let's get started."

As the training session progressed, Adam's vision began to take shape. The inverted fullbacks pushed into midfield, creating overloads and confusing the opposition. The midfielders weaved intricate patterns of passes, carving through the defence like a hot knife through butter. And the forwards, invigorated by this new approach, displayed a hunger for goals that had been absent for far too long. Gradually, confidence seeped back into their veins. The players started to believe in themselves and each other again. They saw glimpses of what they could achieve when they played as a cohesive unit, united by a shared mission.

The players moved with newfound purpose, their passes crisp and accurate. The sound of boots meeting the ball echoed across the pitch as they practised the intricate patterns of their formation. They slowly began to embrace this new style of play. The passes flowed more freely, confidence building with each successful exchange. The attacking players grew bolder, running into dangerous positions and creating opportunities. Alongside the tactical training, Amy worked tirelessly with the defensive line, drilling them to play out from the back and tighten their positioning. She emphasised the importance of communication and trusting each other's abilities.

"Remember," Adam called out, raising his voice slightly over the sound of boots on grass, "We need to remain calm and confident on the ball. Trust in your abilities and look for those passing options within the diamonds."

As the session continued, Adam gradually observed a shift in the players' mindsets. Confidence grew within them as they realised they could outscore their opponents and secure crucial points. They started taking extra touches, seeking out their teammates rather than resorting to hopeful long balls. It was a small but significant step towards embracing the new tactical approach.

As the morning sun rose higher in the sky and the clock struck ten thirty, Adam called time on the session, exclaiming, "Brilliant lads, well done. That is great stuff. Go get some energy drinks, and I'll see you back out here in five for a special session I've planned."

Curiosity was rife among the players as they returned after their drinks break. Adam sat in the centre of the pitch, contemplating the finer details of his plan, his face focused on the task ahead. As the team gathered around him, Adam rose to his feet and greeted them with a smile. "Alright, lads," Adam called out with a grin, "Ready for round two?" he asked.

A chorus of affirmative responses echoed back. Adam clapped his hands together, an excited gleam in his eye that hadn't been there before. "Firstly, let me say that the first session was superb, well done. I don't expect us to become fluent in the new tactical approach instantly, it will take much hard work and training, especially next week. For now, though, I feel I saw enough to indicate that you understand the basics of it, which is encouraging for me and the coaches."

Adam started to explain his plan for the second session, which would involve attacking movements, shooting practice, and, hopefully, goal-scoring. Adam knew that goals had become a rarity for this side in recent months, leaving them bereft of confidence. He explained to the squad, "For this session, I have brought in three midfielders, three defenders, and a goalkeeper from the under-twenty-three team to play against you guys in this drill. Their task is as follows: shot stopping from the keeper, hard pressing and tough defending from the defence. Finally, the midfielders will work on retaining possession and pressing you hard when you are in possession. Your aim is to play through them and not only create opportunities for yourselves but crucially score goals, as many as possible. To make this a bit more interesting, I have planned for us all to have a team-building day with an activity before heading to a bar in town on our day off Monday. For each goal you score, one hundred pounds will go into the kitty for the day and food and drinks. Let's get ourselves a healthy budget and dine and drink like kings, shall we? I wanna see goals goals goals, think you can do that?" Adam asked, greeted by a mass joy of responses and smiles.

Adam knew that this session and plenty of goals would go a long way toward breeding confidence and smiles back into the squad. Adam barked one final instruction, "Under twenty-three players, stay on your feet. No hard tackles or fifty-fifties. Hustle on your feet but no fouls. I don't want any injuries."

The squad immediately moved into position, their eyes gleaming with competitiveness at the added challenge. The defenders from the under-twenty-three side instantly formed a compact line while the midfielders shuffled into position. Adam watched on from the sideline in excitement and hope.

The first few minutes brought little progress. The players circled like wolves around a herd, probing for weaknesses, but with little success. The under-twenty-three side showed surprising resilience and formed a solid defence. Shot after shot was blocked or saved by the young keeper, who seemed to be on fire. Adam watched silently as initial frustration appeared on some of his senior players' faces.

"Keep moving," Adam called across the pitch, clapping his hands together for emphasis, "Keep creating spaces, look for those diamonds, look for those pockets, keep shooting."

The shout seemed to jolt his team awake. They began to make more daring runs, passing quickly in diamonds to keep the under-twenty-three side guessing and unable to win the ball. The breakthrough finally came as one of the strikers managed to slip past two defenders to convert a cross into a goal. Cheers echoed around the training ground before being drowned out by the familiar thud of boots against leather again. After scoring their first goal, something shifted within the Swanford side. A spark had been ignited. In the next twenty minutes, they scored one goal after another. It wasn't just about scoring goals anymore. It was about doing it stylishly and ensuring they caught Adam's attention.

As the session drew toward an end and noon approached, a visibly exhausted but ecstatic team gathered around Adam again. There was cheering and some light banter about Monday's plans, expectations high for a great day followed by drinks and good food.

"I want you all to remember this feeling," Adam said over their laughter, his voice tinged with pride and satisfaction as he surveyed their faces, flushed with triumph and camaraderie, "The feeling of scoring, of winning. This is who we are. We are Swanford." His words were met with roars of approval and pounding heartbeats. The team was fired up, ready to do battle on the pitch, ready to take on the world, and prepared to save themselves from the threat of relegation.

"Right, time to get a well-earned break and have some lunch before you board the team coach, ready to depart at one pm. There is a list in the canteen detailing the match day squad and who is on the coach to travel. Finally, the bit you've all been waiting for, Mike, what are the scores on the board?" Adam asked.

"Boss, I can confirm that twenty-eight goals were scored, which gives us a total kitty of two-thousand-eight-hundred pounds for Monday."

Instantly, Adam interjected, "Make that three thousand. I'll put the other two hundred in out of my own pocket."

This news was greeted with elation-filled cheers from the squad. Adam watched them disperse toward the canteen, his heart filled with hope for the first time since he'd taken up the arduous task of managing this near-doomed side.

He had made them believe not just in him but also in their collective power as a team. Adam had always got victories on the virtual platform, but now, looking at his squad sharing banter and laughing together, Adam came to understand that the magic of football lay beyond just statistics and tactics; camaraderie was its true essence. For once, despite all their recent shortcomings, Adam felt hopeful about Swanford's chances in their desperate battle against relegation.

By one pm, all the players travelling as part of the matchday squad had taken their seats on the team coach, and they were all set to depart the training ground, bound for Newborough. Unbeknownst to the players, Adam had prepared a surprise. It was a motivational video playing on the big screen at the front of the coach. The video highlighted Swanford's most significant victories over the years. The video also featured ex-club legends' messages detailing the honour bestowed upon their shoulders playing for such a great club, reminding the players of their responsibilities ahead in this relegation battle and featuring good luck messages; the video was wonderfully put together by the club's media team at Adam's request.

As victory scenes played out on the screen, Adam could see eyes glisten and faces harden with resolve. Some even shed tears silently as old heroes relived their glory days wearing Swanford colours. Adam took this chance to make his way around the team coach, talking to each player individually, getting to know them beyond their roles on the pitch, and building a team and a family. A sense of unity and camaraderie started to take shape, and Adam could feel the difference in the atmosphere. It was no longer just about football; now it was about survival, about fighting for each other in the trenches of this relegation battle.

Once they reached the hotel at Newborough, just after two thirty, Adam stood at the front of the coach to address the players. "Right, lads, follow Mike. He will get you checked in with the hotel. Following that, I want you to go and get into your rooms, unpack, etc. We will meet at three thirty in the hotel basement at the swimming pool. See you there."

Shuffling off the team coach and following Mike, the players checked into the hotel before going to their rooms. Once settled in, the players arrived promptly at poolside at half-past three. The hotel's basement had been converted into a luxury spa and housed a large indoor heated pool with four hot tubs backing onto it, one at each corner of the pool. Furthermore, the far wall along the pool's side featured a large sauna and steam room.

The large indoor heated pool was filled with inflatable unicorns, a couple of inflatable balls and nets. The players' faces, clearly amused, waited on Adam's instructions. "Jump in, lads, don't be shy," Adam said, "For the next hour, have some fun before at half four, spending half an hour in the hot tub, sauna or steam room, whichever you'd prefer." The players jumped in the pool without hesitation, some even performing bombs or silly dives. Adam took a poolside seat, basking in the joy of watching the players, under pressure, let their hair down and enjoy themselves to lift their stress amid the relegation battle. As the time in the pool concluded an hour later, Adam left poolside, saying, "Enjoy your wind-down half hour. See you in the conference room for a team meeting at half six."

At half past six, the players gathered in the conference room. Adam and Mike stood before a projected screen. Adam had spent most of the previous night strategising based on whatever intel he and his coaches had gathered about Newborough and was eager to share his insights with the team.

He explained their opponents' strengths and weaknesses before discussing how they would approach the game. Finally, addressing the elephant in the room, "I'm sure you are all aware that there is a situation with our club captain, Mr Knight, at the moment. Michael has not travelled with us, and with that in mind, I want to add a second vice-captain alongside Sam," pointing at Sam Reynolds.

"I'm sure you will all agree that this next lad is also a true leader and more than up to the task. Kofi, it's you, mate," he explained, pointing out Kofi. All eyes turned to Kofi Adams before the whole room gave out a roar of approval and proceeded to stand and give the decision an ovation. Sam Reynolds quickly patted Kofi on the back in an approving gesture.

As Kofi was invited to the front of the room, where he exchanged handshakes with Adam and Mike, he gave a brief speech simply, declaring, "Thank you, gaffer, but this is not about Michael, Sam, or me. In these last four games, we are all gonna need to be captains. This is a collective effort. Let's go, Swans." The team buoyed up gave out another roar of approval.

The team meeting concluded with Adam stating, "I've just checked, and both our relegation rivals Cliffe and Wry lost today, so a positive result tomorrow will see us move closer to safety." As Adam delivered that encouraging news, he was interrupted by the first team coaches walking into the room carrying twenty pizza boxes between them. Adam closed the meeting on cue by saying, "Tuck in, lads, and enjoy. The hotel will bring out some sides and drinks shortly. After we've eaten, we will watch a movie together before I ask you all to retire to your rooms for a ten-pm bedtime. Bon appetit!"

With the team demolishing their way through their pizzas, Adam raised his drink for a toast, saying, "To Swanford! May we rise like phoenixes from our ashes and show the world that we're here to stay." The room erupted into cheers as glasses clinked, and they all repeated the toast.

The evening was spent in light-hearted banter and camaraderie, with everyone joking about how they'd spend the three-thousand-pound kitty. It was a beautiful night of bonding and reaffirming their faith in each other. Lying on his bed later that night, Adam smiled as he reflected on the day. He had managed to rejuvenate the team's spirits and create a bond crucial for the team's success. On the morrow, they would march onto the battlefield as one team, ready to fight tooth and nail to secure their place in the division. Tonight, though, Adam could hear them laughing from down the hall, and it wasn't the laughter of a team scared of relegation; it was the laughter of relaxation and positivity.

11

Match Day – Newborough Away

Breakfast came the next morning, and as the players gathered in the restaurant to start the day, they were greeted by Adam's team sheet for the game, which would kick off at half past four. Adam's selection began with the goalkeeper Barlow, who had been an ever-present in the side this season.

Across the backline was Donovan on the left and Turner on the right, with Kofi Adams captaining the side alongside Lambert in the centre. This was the same backline used all season except Lambert, who came in for Sam Reynolds.

In the middle of the park was Ethan Fox, who had impressed in training, meaning he'd earned his debut in the defensive midfield role with Price and Young in front of him in midfield.

Fletcher was on the left wing, and Davids was on the right. Hart played up front alone, hoping to add to his tally for the season, which currently stood at twelve goals, making him the season's top goal scorer.

The subs bench featured a mix of youth and experience, with Sam Reynolds still retaining his place in the squad and Neil Cole and Louis Sims making their debut outings in the match-day squad.

The team's reaction to seeing the team sheet was mixed. Overall, though, a positive vibe filled the room. Each player had confidence in Adam's selection, knowing he had a good sense for strategy and the players' abilities within this new tactical approach.

A gentle murmur of conversation filled the air as the players looked through Adam's choices, speculating how their opponents would react.

"Ethan Fox in midfield," one player remarked, "That's a game changer."

Turning to him, Kofi Adams nodded, "He's been a revelation in training. Quick on his feet, and he's got vision, too. It's his time to shine."

Players chatted together while finishing their breakfasts, their camaraderie strong. The coaching staff joined them soon after, looking confident and relaxed, which helped to lighten the atmosphere.

Following breakfast was a light training session where Adam and the coaches ran the team through some last-minute drills based on the new team formation, followed by a light jog around the local park. Despite the high stakes awaiting them later that afternoon, there were few signs of nerves from any squad member. They had trained hard all week and knew they had roles to play in this crucial match; all they could do was give everything they could to the cause. They were ready to leave the hotel bound for the stadium by half-past-two. Each player emerged from the hotel dressed smartly in their training gear. Coats were slung over shoulders against the brisk afternoon breeze as they loaded onto the bus.

As the bus pulled out of the hotel car park, the city rushed by in a blur of colour and noise. The hum of conversation on the bus had gradually petered out as they approached the stadium, each player lost in their own world of thoughts and strategies. Turner was going over moves in his head, mimicking actions with his hands. Hart was conversing deeply with Fletcher, discussing possible opportunities from the wings. Adam watched them all with a sense of pride, though he, too, had his pre-match nerves to contend with. As they approached the stadium, the captain for the day, Kofi Adams, stood up and addressed the team.

"Lads, I know we're all feeling it right now. But we've trained for this moment. We have prepared for this. Trust in that preparation and trust each other. We stand together."

Suddenly, the towering structure of the stadium, home to the mighty Newborough, loomed into view, the sight carrying a tangible sense of anticipation with it. It was an intimidating yet exhilarating sight. This was where their collective hard work would be put to the ultimate test. Adam noticed each player's eyes were locked onto the stadium and knew their minds were already on the game. He watched them from his vantage point at the front of the coach. No matter what happened later that day, he knew his team had each other's backs.

The bus pulled up outside the away team entrance of Newborough's home ground, a grand old stadium that had witnessed many historic games and monumental victories in its time, promptly at three pm. A wave of applause erupted from gathered away fans, a welcoming chorus that further bolstered every player's spirits. As they disembarked individually, each player acknowledged their cheers with nods and waves before disappearing into the stadium. As Adam got off the team bus, his phone rang; it was Scott.

"Hey, bruv, you ok?" Scott asked.

"Yes, not too bad, gaffer. I'm a bit nervous, but I'm ok. We've trained and prepared well," Adam replied.

"Look, sorry, I won't be there today. I've got my best mate's stag do in Miami, and I'm on my way there now. I just wanted to say good luck, though. You and the boys have got this," Scott said.

"Cheers, boss," Adam replied before the phone call was terminated.

After briefly walking out onto the pitch to check out its playing conditions and take in the stadium, the players made their way to the away dressing room to put their possessions into their lockers. Shortly after, they went onto the pitch again to do their pre-game warm-up at three-forty-five.

The warm-up was a well-practised dance of drills, stretching, and light jogging. The team moved as a unit, synced in their steps and breathing rhythm. Hart took some shots at the goal from different angles, receiving approving nods from Turner, who was also taking an occasional swing at goal himself. Fox curled some free kicks into the top corner, and Lambert nodded appreciatively. Fletcher and Davids completed their tricks and juggled the ball on the wings, drawing a few whistles. Amidst all this, Kofi Adams stood in the centre of the pitch, looking intently at each player, observing their movements for any sign of injury or discomfort but finding none. Each player was performing at their peak. They had trained hard, and it showed. At one point, Adam threw Kofi a thumbs-up from the sidelines, acknowledging that everything was going according to plan.

The warmup concluded with the whole team practising shots at goal, which was also an opportunity for Barlow to face some shots and practice making some saves. By quarter-past four, the warm-up was over, and the players walked toward the tunnel, which was surrounded to the right by an army of four thousand Swanford fans who cheered them off the pitch and into the tunnel in the hope of inspiring and encouraging the players for the task ahead.

Inside the dressing room, each player prepared himself for the game ahead. Boots were double-checked for perfect fit, and shin guards were firmly secured. Jerseys donned were soaked with hard-working sweat and pride, and deep breaths were taken to calm nerves.

The clock struck twenty-past-four, and Adam reached the whiteboard in the corner of the room facing the players to deliver his final pep talk before kickoff. "Remember," he began, "We play as we trained. There is no room for heroics or individual glory today. We win as a team, or we lose as a team." His gaze swept across each player, reinforcing his point.

"Hart," Adam said, pointing to the striker, "You're our arrow. Stay sharp and focused. Kofi and Lambert hold the fort down and control the game's pace. Let's face forward and play those diamond-passing sequences. Fletcher and David's speed and precision support Hart in forming a forward three, remember? And you, Fox," Adam looked at the debutant, "Just play your own game. Remember your training, see the pitch and read the game. You are the first line of defence, so try to win the ball before showing composure and picking a pass to start an attack. All of you play with urgency and aggression. We need to start fighting for the points that will keep us up. Do not under any circumstances lose possession in your half, also work tirelessly not to be breached and keep a clean sheet. If we can succeed at these two things, we stand a good chance of not only not losing but hopefully getting a win."

The players nodded in understanding; their eyes carried a glint of fighting spirit. At four-twenty-five, with a final clap from Adam and a rallying call from Kofi, the dressing room resonated with a unified roar as each player thumped his chest in response. Shortly after, the team walked out of the room and into the tunnel, lined up beside Newborough and the match officials before walking down the tunnel and onto the pitch. The afternoon sun glittering on the emerald green grass welcomed them as they took their positions. The whistle blew at exactly half-past-four as the grand old stadium excitedly shook. The chanting of fans in black and white rang out, drowning out the noise from the home crowd as the teams launched into action.

Swanford played on the front foot with great energy from kick-off, finding their diamond passing formations immediately. They moved forward, and Hart headed narrowly wide from a cross to almost instantly give Swanford the lead.

As the game wore on, the players grew in confidence. Lambert and Kofi quickly controlled the defence, expertly distributing the ball to Ethan Fox to set things up moving forward. The clock ticked by, and twenty minutes into the match, Swanford's aggressive style of play finally paid dividends.

Having made a successful interception in Swanford's half, Fox embarked on a charging run down the pitch, skilfully navigating his way through Newborough's midfield and defence before delivering a perfectly timed pass to Hart, who fired the ball into the back of the net. The Swanford section of the stadium erupted into cheers as if Swanford had just won the league while Hart ran towards Fox for a celebratory embrace. The celebrations were halted by the referee and linesman, who wanted the video assistant referee to check the goal for a possible offside. Ethan and Hart looked bemused as they knew they had timed everything perfectly. Watching on from the sideline, Adam was also adamant that it was onside.

Nevertheless, the check was being made as Adam, the players, and the Swanford fans waited for the verdict with bated breath. After what seemed like a lifetime, the referee blew his whistle to deliver the verdict; the goal stood. 0-1.

From there on in, Swanford's defence stood tall. Kofi and Lambert held their fort as instructed. Every attack from Newborough was dutifully quashed. Headers were won, tackles were clean, passes were found, and interceptions were timely. Like a seasoned veteran, Fox played his debut game, winning balls back and looking for intelligent passes to his attacking teammates.

Swanford had dominated the first half and played with the sort of precision and confidence of a team at the top of the table, not one in a desperate relegation battle. In truth, they should have led by two or three goals at halftime, not the one goal they found themselves with. Adam couldn't help but feel proud of his players, but he knew this wasn't over yet.

During their half-time team talk, he reminded them they hadn't won anything yet. "Fifty per cent is not one hundred per cent," Adam said sternly, "We must continue playing well and concentrate so as not to allow them back into this game. I want to see even more urgency in the second half to get this result over the line and take a crucial three points home with us."

From kick-off in the second half, Newborough came out re-energised and motivated to show their recent form and turn this game around. It felt as if the tides had turned dramatically. They quickly adapted their strategy, exploiting the weaknesses they had identified in Swanford's defence. Despite Swanford's best efforts to maintain their lead, a well-orchestrated and timed move allowed Newborough to level the scores as their striker ran onto a through ball to go one-on-one with the keeper before rounding him and slotting the ball into an empty net. 1-1.

The Newborough crowd went wild in encouragement for their side, firmly smelling Swanford's blood for them to now pounce upon like a great white shark. In contrast, a deafly fearful silence fell over the away end of the ground. Straight from the resumption of play, Newborough intercepted a Swanford pass to win back possession before executing another almost identical through pass to their striker, who once again went through on goal; this time, however, with Lambert to get through first. Lambert went to the striker and tracked him back into the box before unleashing a nervous and mistimed tackle. Penalty.

As the referee blew the whistle, signalling the penalty kick, the atmosphere in the stadium grew electric. The excitement was short-lived, however, as the referee once again wanted validation from the video assistant referee to confirm that it was the correct call, given the game's high stakes. Unfortunately for Lambert, the challenge looked even more horrific on the instant replay, and he now feared he might be sent off. The referee again blew his whistle and pointed to the penalty spot before asking Lambert to come over to him for a word.

The referee told Lambert to calm himself down before showing him a yellow card. Newborough's designated penalty taker stepped forward confidently, fully aware of the weight on his shoulders. Barlow, determined to make a crucial save, positioned himself between the goalposts, ready to defend his team's honour. With the crowd holding their breath, the Newborough player took a few steps back, preparing for the decisive moment. He focused his gaze on the goal, visualising the perfect trajectory for the ball. The tension was palpable as he sprinted towards the ball, striking it with precision and power. The ball soared through the air, evading Barlow's desperate dive. It found the back of the net, triggering an eruption of cheers from the Newborough supporters. 2-1.

The once jubilant Swanford away fans were now a complete contrast to the joyous fans in the first half, filled with looks of shock and disbelief. They'd fallen behind so quickly, so unexpectedly. They and the players were shell-shocked and dazed.

However, the game was far from over. Adam tried to rally his team on the sidelines, shouting instructions and encouragement across the pitch. The Swanford boys tried their best to recompose themselves, setting off in search of an equaliser, but Newborough were relentless.

Now leading by one goal, Newborough continued to press on, hungry for another goal. They were ruthless in attack and wouldn't take their foot off the pedal. The Swanford players, pale-faced and panting, had begun to lose their rhythm. Their passes were misplaced, their runs were half-hearted, and their defence was easily broken. Newborough were merciless in exploiting Swanford's disorientation; soon enough, they found the back of the net again. This time, a curling shot from outside the box by Newborough's midfielder caught Barlow off-balance. All he could do was watch as the ball sailed over his head into the top corner of the goal; there was nothing he could do but grimace in disbelief. 3-1

The game kicked off again, and again, Newborough went on the attack. Despite scoring three goals already, they seemed hungry for more. They exploited the shambolic state of Swanford's defence and effortlessly broke through their lines. A series of well-calculated passes led to the ball finding its way to their striker again, who neatly dodged Lambert's defensive effort and took a scorching shot that sailed past Barlow into the top right corner, 4-1.

Down and seemingly out with just under twenty minutes remaining, Swanford were in a state of shock and disbelief. Their heads had well and truly gone as they looked increasingly tired and defeated.

Out of nowhere, with fifteen minutes of play left, Swanford somehow managed to find an attacking rhythm again despite the odds stacked against them. Fox was instrumental in this resurgence; his relentless drive pushed Swanford forward and breathed some life back under their broken wings. However, Newborough's stalwart defence stood firm whenever an opportunity arose to take a shot at the goal until, in the eightieth minute, finding a combination of passes to set up a counter-attack, Newborough easily carved through Swanford to score again. 5-1.

With just three minutes left, Newborough struck again on another counterattack. Their striker was again at the heart of it all, setting up their midfielder for a delightful chip over Barlow, who was caught off his line for their sixth goal. 6-1.

The final whistle brought more relief than disappointment for Swanford. They were put out of their misery after a nightmare second half. As the players trudged off the pitch, the weight of the loss on their shoulders, they couldn't help but remember the crowd's roar just an hour ago. Now, they were met with boos from their fans, in contrast to that of the jubilation, joy and cheers of the Newborough fans, which rang out with a haunting echo as they made their way down the tunnel. It was a harsh lesson in how quickly fortunes can change in football.

The Swanford boys sat in stunned silence in the dressing room, the reality of their situation settling in. Adam paced up and down, a troubled look on his face. His inspiring halftime speech felt like a lifetime ago, and now he was grappling with the task of addressing a team that had lost so heavily. He stopped pacing, looking at the crushed faces of his players. He sighed deeply before beginning by saying, "Lads, what on earth was that?" As he looked at the expressionless faces of his squad, he continued, "Seriously, I'm speechless, truly I am. What on earth, lads?" He continued, "Let me say for now, tomorrow's jolly is cancelled! I want to see every one of you at the training ground tomorrow morning. We begin at nine am sharp in the briefing room. If you are even a minute late, I will fine you the day's wages. On the bus journey home and overnight, please think deeply about what happened in that second half. Go get showered and changed and onto the bus, we will talk more in the morning," he said, before throwing in anger his water bottle against the wall and storming out of the dressing room to the waiting Super Sports TV presenter for his post-match interview.

The TV presenter, a tall, slim woman with ice-blonde hair and an air of professionalism, stood by the dressing room door. She was known for her intelligent questions that left no room for evading or dodging by the interviewees. As Adam emerged from the dressing room, she stepped towards him, her cameraman following her lead.

"Adam," she began with an empathetic smile that didn't quite reach her eyes, "That was a disastrous second half. Despite an encouraging first half, what happened? Would it be fair to say that the team seemed disjointed in the second half, and Newborough capitalised on those openings?" she inquired.

Adam nodded, rubbing his temples as he tried to formulate his response. "Yes, I'm still not entirely sure what happened. The players and I are shocked. I felt that it was a Jekyll and Hyde performance. Let me say for now that the club will refund all travelling supporters their tickets and travel money, as that was unacceptable. Furthermore, each fan that travelled will receive a pie and a pint voucher by way of apology for the upcoming home game on Saturday against Cliffe."

Nodding, the presenter continued to quiz Adam. "As much as the fans will appreciate those gestures, do you have any words by way of explanation on this afternoon's performance and result for them?" she inquired.

"I will be making no comment at this time, sorry, other than to state the obvious, that being that we were miles off where we should have and needed to be, miles off. If and when there is anything further to say, the club will issue a press statement," Adam said.

The puzzled TV presenter replied, "Somehow, I don't think that's enough, Adam. Fans want answers."

"I refer you to my previous comment, thank you," re-iterated Adam.

Stubborn and unrelenting in her questioning, the presenter asked, "Would it be fair to say that you are in over your depth and relegation is inevitable?"

An angry Adam replied, "Oh, piss off, I'm sick of this now! The club have made their decision, I'm here, and that will be the case until the end of the season, so please let's change the record now and get on with it."

A stunned presenter watched as Adam stormed off onto the team coach without further comment. As Adam took his seat on the bus, raging with hurt and anger, he couldn't help but wonder if his conduct in the interview had been out of order. As the players shuffled onto the coach, Adam ignored them with a deadly silence before the coach pulled off the stadium car park and began the journey back to Swanford, with every mile feeling like a hundred. Adam gazed out of the window at the blinking city lights flying past. He was deep in thought, reflecting on their disastrous performance and trying to figure out how to get his team back on track.

Suddenly, in the silence, his phone ringing disturbed his thoughts; it was Scott. Adam took an age to answer the call, looking at his screen and fearing the worst. Surely, after that car crash of an afternoon, this story had finished before it had even begun. Adam was sure he would answer this call and be told he was sacked. Adam reluctantly pressed answer on his phone screen, where, to his surprise, he was greeted by a buoyant and intoxicated Scott, who was enjoying the stag do he was on.

"Now then, bruv, how are you?" Scott asked.

"Not happy, a mix of confusion, heartbreak and anger," Adam replied.

"Yeah, I get that, mate," Scott replied, "But listen, I have faith in you, and that hasn't changed. I can promise you that. That first half was superb. I've heard good things from the coaches about how training went this week and everything else you did to breed confidence into the squad. Inevitably, there will be a lot of speculation and calls for me to fire you. I will give you my word right now that this will not happen. This is only one result, and thankfully, both Cliffe and Wry lost, so the table still stands the same, which has let us off the hook. I have full faith in you as our manager, and anything you decide to do off the back of this afternoon in terms of ramifications has my full backing. Do what you see fit, knowing I've got your back, ok?" Scott asked.

"Of course, thank you, Scott. That truly means the world to me," Adam gratefully replied.

"No worries, bud," Scott replied, "Listen, I gotta dash, mate, it's my round, we'll catch up in the week," before hanging up.

After a few moments of relieved contemplation, Adam's phone rang again. This time, it was his PA and media manager, Sarah. "Hi Sarah, you ok?" he answered the call.

"Yes, I'm ok, thanks; how are you, more importantly?" she asked.

"Crap," Adam replied.

"Yes, I can well imagine," Sarah replied, "I'm calling because we have a problem in the shape of Michael Knight."

Sighing, Adam asked, "Why, what's he done now?"

"Well," said Sarah, "Unbeknown to us, he decided to join the Super Sports TV studio panel for this afternoon's game. In fairness to him, he tactfully chose not to be drawn into commenting on the current situation with you pre-kick-off. With us winning at halftime after a brilliant showing, he praised only his teammates. He refused to comment on the tactics and potential success of your appointment or your management of the club. However, after that second half, his vocal brakes came off, and he was scathing in his opinion of the second half display, your appointment and ability, and more importantly, the treatment he has received from you."

A disappointed and angry Adam replied, "Oh bloody hell! Had he consulted you for permission to make that appearance?" he asked.

"Absolutely not," Sarah explained, "We had no idea until he appeared on the screen."

An assertive Adam replied, "Fine. Inform him or his agent, whatever, that I expect him in my office at the training ground at eight am sharp tomorrow morning. Thanks."

"Ok, I will do," Sarah replied before hanging up.

Adam sat back in his seat, the rhythmic hum of the coach engine a sobering soundtrack to his tumultuous thoughts. The blinking city lights outside the window morphed into abstract streaks of colour as they sped along the motorway.

Every awkward conversation pointed insult and failed strategy ran through his mind repeatedly, like some torturous highlight reel from a game he wished he'd never played. Every so often, he would glance at his phone, half expecting another damning call or message, but the screen remained dark. The players were silent all around him, apart from the occasional whispers and stifled laughter. Occasionally, Adam would find himself nodding off, but he found no peace even in his sleep, his dreams filled with nightmares of an angry crowd chanting for his removal with Michael Knight leading the protest.

When they finally arrived back at their training ground in Swanford, Adam was the first one off the coach. He could feel the gazes of his team lingering on his back as he shuffled towards his car in the car park. The chilly night air did nothing to cool down his infuriation but seemed to numb him physically, just enough to maintain composure. Once inside his car, Adam let out a scream and a sigh that had been building up all day. He leaned back in his seat and pinched the bridge of his nose, struggling to keep at bay an encroaching headache. He refused to sink into desperation, though. This would not be the end for him, not yet anyway. Mentally preparing himself for what tomorrow might bring, he started his car and went home, leaving behind a trail of heated thoughts and unsaid words.

12

Monday 15th April

Adam was the first at the training ground the following day, just after seven thirty am, his eyes were heavy from lack of sleep, but his resolve hardened like steel. After grabbing a coffee from the canteen and setting up the team briefing room, Adam went to his office. He barely had time to settle into his chair when he heard the unmistakable sound of stomping boots echoing through the empty hallways. Michael Knight soon appeared at his office door, an expression of defiance plastered across his face.

"Eight am sharp," Adam remarked, getting up from his chair to meet him halfway, "I see you're a man of impeccable timekeeping," he continued.

"Indeed," Knight retorted before taking a seat, "I have never been late a day in my life," he stated.

"First time for everything," Adam shot back, matching his steely gaze.

The silence that followed was thick with tension as Adam re-took his seat behind his desk.

"You've made your thoughts on my management quite clear," Adam finally broke the silence with a stubborn look on his face, "I never asked for anyone's approval. Your job is to play football, and mine is to manage this team," he stated.

"Well then, maybe you should start doing your job," Knight replied, crossing his arms over his chest.

"I am doing my job," Adam replied calmly, not rising to Knight's bait, "And part of my job is to ensure that each player respects this club and its management." Adam was determined not to let this meeting erupt into an all-out war.

Knight quickly interrupted Adam, "Respect has to be earned, mate," he declared. After yesterday's appearance and words on TV, Adam was stunned by Michael's boldness and unremorseful manner. Adam stared at Knight. The meeting's atmosphere turned ice-cold, and the tension was unbearable.

"And so it shall be," Adam declared after a moment of silence. "I didn't call you here to argue with you. I called you here to tell you I am the club's manager, and that won't change until at least the end of the season. If you can't respect that, then maybe this isn't the club for you." Adam's words were stern and assertive, shocking Knight into silence.

Adam and Michael stared at each other, neither backing down from their stance. "So," Adam asked, "What on earth was yesterday about?"

"Well, I had nothing else to do, did I?" Michael replied, smirking.

"Any players wishing to undertake a media appearance such as that appearance on television have to do so with the club's permission, and you are no exception. Your behaviour in doing so without said permission constitutes misconduct and is highly unprofessional. Furthermore, making such comments as you did at full-time and after the match is disrespectful and unprofessional. Why did you do it?" Adam asked.

"I stand by every word that I said. I have my right to an opinion," Michael remarked.

"In light of your conduct and behaviour and blatant lack of remorse, I have decided that you will continue to be a player training with and at the disposal of the under-twenty-three squad. This will remain the case until you are ready to issue me with an apology and commit to the cause of helping the first team survive relegation. Furthermore, I expect a public apology from you, not only to me but also to your fellow teammates, the fans, and the club. On top of that, I am fining you two weeks' wages for your misconduct," Adam explained.

A shocked and angry-looking Michael replied, "What the hell! Two weeks' wages, that's bang out of line. That's two hundred thousand quid. As for your apologies, you can stick them where the sun doesn't shine. I'm going to speak to the real gaffer, Scott. He won't stand for this," Michael fumed.

"Oh, ok. Good luck with that," Adam replied, smiling, "I spoke to Scott after the game yesterday. I have his full backing to make whatever decisions I see fit."

Michael stood up and stormed out of the office, slamming the door behind him with an aggression that almost took the door off its hinges. As the door slammed behind Knight, Adam let out a sigh of relief. His focus could now turn to the team meeting he had called for at nine am and what he would say and discuss with the players after yesterday's disaster. Today was a new day.

Just as he started to plot his approach, there was a soft knock on the door. He called for the person to enter while seated in his chair. His assistant manager, Mike Jones, entered the room, his usual jovial expression replaced by a stern resolve.

Closing the door behind him and taking a seat, Mike glanced towards Adam and raised an eyebrow. "Did Knight show?" he asked.

Adam nodded briefly, rubbing the bridge of his nose. "I've dealt with it," he replied, not wanting to dwell on it anymore. Mike grunted in response, nodding as if he agreed with Adam's decision. It was his way of showing support without prying into Adam's affairs.

By half past eight, the team briefing room was slowly filling with players, all wearing hangdog expressions and radiating an air of unease. The memory of yesterday's defeat was still raw, a wound that continued to plague them no matter how hard they tried to ignore it.

Adam stood at the head of the room, coffee cup in hand, watching as his team shuffled in, nodding in acknowledgement as each player met his gaze. By nine am sharp, everyone had arrived. With a deep breath and a brief nod at Mike, Adam stepped forward to address the players.

"Morning, lads, we had a rough day yesterday, and I'm sure no one is proud of what went down," he began, "But dwelling on it isn't going to make it go away," he continued. "We need to break it down. Understand what went wrong and how we can prevent it from happening again. I won't and can't sugarcoat it. Yesterday's second half was not acceptable, in fact it was nothing short of crap. In the first half, we were superb, and how we only came in with one goal, not two or three, is beyond me. However, we were sloppy, disorganised and complacent in the second half. Generally, we were miles off," Adam said furiously.

A murmur ran through the gathering, recognition, perhaps even agreement. Few could deny that Adam's words rang true. Adam continued, "We're not here today to wallow in our defeat. We're here to learn from it, dissect what went wrong, and figure out how to rectify it moving forward."

Looking at the players, Adam asked, "Before we start, have any of you guys had a chance to reflect on the game? And have any thoughts or comments to share with us all?"

"Yes, gaffer, if I can, please?" Ethan Fox spoke up, "I feel like being the new player in the team and an inexperienced one, that this is my fault. I could have done better, and I apologise and understand if you're gonna drop me back down to the under twenty-threes," he said dejectedly.

"Ethan," Adam replied, "Let's have it right. To a man, every one of you was at sixes and sevens in that second half. Ethan, this isn't just on you. We win, and we lose as a team. Ethan, you're a cracking player who I've no doubt will be a star one day. Don't worry, I won't be dropping you," Adam assured him.

"Thanks, boss. That means a lot. I will work harder than ever to repay your faith in me and help this club survive" Ethan replied.

"Good lad," Adam replied.

Next to speak up was midfielder Price. "You should have changed things at halftime and made us more defensive. We needed that win, and you sending us out with an attacking approach in the second half made us vulnerable and cost us the game and the points," he uttered.

After thinking about his reply, Adam explained, "Yes maybe," he continued, "However, we are in a relegation battle. There is no time to be defensive. We are running out of games and time to get the points we need. I aimed to get a second, maybe even a third goal, before going defensive to ensure we came away with all three points. Perhaps I got that wrong, and I shouldn't have taken the gamble, and I'm sorry about that. However, I stand by the fact that there is no more time for caution in this current situation. We need points, and we need them fast, simple as that."

"Ok, gaffer, fair enough, thanks," Price replied, with a few other players nodding in agreement.

The next few hours were gruelling but necessary. Play by play, they dissected their mistakes from the previous day's match, particularly their second-half performance. They discussed their lack of formation on the pitch, how their defence was easily penetrated, and how they could not hold onto possession for any significant amount of time.

Adam didn't mince his words throughout the session. He pointed out the positives and praised the first-half performance before moving on to the second half and pointing out every mistake. He ensured every player knew where they stood with him and what was expected of them moving forward. Slowly but surely, the room filled with a new kind of energy, not exactly hopeful but resolute, a commitment to pull themselves back up in the face of defeat.

As Adam concluded the meeting, which at times was more like an autopsy, he knew his message had been received.

Finally, Adam decided to address Knight's continued absence. "I'm sure you're all aware of Mr Knight's behaviour over the last few days, as well as his media appearance and subsequent comments yesterday," he said, "For now, he will continue to be in the under-twenty-three squad. He needs some time to figure out where his loyalties lie and what his future at the club looks like. This is a team, and there's no place for his hostility or behaviour within it." The sentiment sounded harsh even to Adam's ears, but it needed to be said.

Finally, Adam closed the meeting by stating, "Take this away with you boys. The greatest test of courage on earth is to bear defeat without losing heart. We win as a team, and we lose as a team. We may have been knocked down yesterday, but life isn't about how often you get knocked down. It is about how often you get back up and stay in the fight. Enjoy the rest of your day off, and I'll see you at training in the morning, ready to work even harder than before for success." As the players started filing out of the room, Adam could only hope that today's actions would pave the way for better tomorrows for his Swanford side.

Adam's job was about more than just managing a team. It was about leading a group of individuals who shared a common goal. It was about learning to turn a crushing defeat into a stepping stone for future victories.

As the players left the briefing room, Adam called, "Barlow, Fox, Kofi and Hart, please stay behind for a moment." As the lads waited for further instruction, Adam welcomed Sarah and the media team into the room. "I've asked the media team to come down and record a video message from yourselves and me to apologise to the fans for yesterday and outline our intent to fight to save this great club here on in," Adam explained.

Kofi, looking motivated, replied, "That's a superb idea, gaffer. Let's do it, lads."

As the media team set up the cameras, microphones and a backdrop, Sarah turned to Adam and asked, "Adam, me, and the club secretary want to meet with you at three o'clock in your office, please. Is that ok with you?"

"Sure, see you there," Adam replied before Sarah, a busy woman, shuffled out of the room.

The players and Adam recorded their video messages, apologising for the previous day's poor showing in the second half. They then outlined their commitment to the cause and determination to do much better and give everything they had to keep this club up. After about forty-five minutes, the recording wrapped, and Adam thanked the players for their help before dismissing them for the day. "See you in the morning, lads," Adam remarked, gesturing to them goodbye as they left the room.

As Adam took a lunch break and reflected on the morning, he was pleased with the effort and commitment shown by all the players. He knew his words were harsh, but he also knew they were necessary. The team had to understand the gravity of their situation. It had been a gruelling day so far, and it was only halfway done. Adam grabbed a plate of steamed vegetables and grilled chicken, conscious of setting an example for his players. They needed as much discipline in their eating habits as in their playing.

As he sat eating, less than amused at how healthy his meal was, in contrast to his usual diet of fatty foods and takeaways, Adam scrolled through some emails on his phone. His mind was still racing from the team meeting. Just then, Adam received a message from Sarah informing him that the video message had been edited and was ready for release, pending his approval. Adam quickly watched it over, nodding to himself in satisfaction. This might be what they needed to regain their supporters' trust again. Adam told Sarah that the video was perfect, after which she informed him on their message feed that it would go out across the club's media feeds at four pm sharp.

With his lunch finished and little time left before the next meeting, Adam decided to take a break and clear his head in preparation. He headed for a short walk around Swanford's training grounds. The air was crisp, and the silence was refreshing. As Adam reached the far side pitch, he could see the under-twenty-three side training. Knight immediately caught his eye. The guy had potential, loads of it and was a star. However, his attitude posed a significant problem, and Adam felt that now he had committed to his approach in dealing with it, he must stick to his guns and not relent.

Adam returned to the club building and his office, ready for the coaching team's debriefing of yesterday's humbling and humiliating defeat. On his desk in front of him lay a scattering of notes, diagrams, statements, and statistics, the autopsy of yesterday's defeat yet the blueprint for future success. "Alright, team," Adam began, his voice firm, "We're here to analyse yesterday's game, particularly the second half, take responsibility for our mistakes, and learn. Let's get started."

Amy, the defensive coach, was the first to speak up. Amy was thirty years old, a curvy five-foot-two and had fiery short ginger hair, which perfectly complimented her fiery personality. She qualified as a coach at first university and then earned further FA & UEFA coaching badges in the following years. This was Amy's first professional job as a coach, a position she had held for three seasons. "Our defence was all over the place. Once they were breached, they completely crumbled. Out of formation, out of sync," Amy's honesty was one of her best qualities. It wasn't unkind. It was just straight to the point.

Adam nodded attentively, letting Amy's words sink in before replying, "We need to be solid at the back, as well as attacking and winning games. Every player must know their role and responsibilities on and off the ball. Can you please do any work with the defensive units this week to improve that?" Adam asked.

"Yes, leave it with me," Amy replied.

"Good, thank you," Adam said.

Next, Adam turned his attention to George, the attacking coach. George was fifty years old and a giant of a man, standing at six-foot-four. George, an ex-player at the top level of the game for over a decade, was a towering target man of a striker in his day. He was one of the game's great journeymen, both as a player and now as a coach. His short one, or two-season spells at each club he played for featured a season at Swanford in the nineteen-ninety-five to nineteen-ninety-six season. That season, he scored eighteen goals in twenty-three appearances as part of a promotion-winning Swanford side. George retired from the game in the early noughties and had worked as a coach at various levels of the game and clubs since. His current position as attacking coach at Swanford being the longest he had worked anywhere, having been in this job for six years now.

"What about our attack? That first half was good. Is it just me, or should we have not scored another goal or two? There were moments we had clear chances, but there seemed to be a lack of final execution," Adam said.

George rubbed his bushy, long, bearded chin thoughtfully before answering, "There's no denying we've got talented players, but I think their confidence took a hit after the first half. Once they miss a chance or two, they start doubting themselves. We need to work on their mental game as much as their physical."

Adam nodded in agreement. "Organising team-building exercises might boost their morale and confidence on the pitch. Maybe we should repeat Friday's exercise with the goal scoring," he suggested. The suggestion was met with nods of approval and murmurs of agreement around the room. It was settled then that, in the upcoming week of training, the focus would be on intensive defence and attack work, supplemented by building a stronger team spirit.

Next was Carlos, the fitness coach. Carlos was very slight in build, standing at just five-foot-five, and was originally from Spain. He had been at the club for four seasons now. He was initially appointed as a fitness coach and translator following the signing of Spanish international superstar striker Diego Lopez. Lopez's signing was a flop, and he left the club after just one season, but Carlos's exceptional fitness coaching had seen him retained by the club as a vital part of the coaching team. Carlos had been silent to this point. He often let the other coaches do most of the talking during these meetings. When it came to fitness, Carlos was a wealth of knowledge. He gestured to some charts on the table in front of him, "Our fitness levels are not up to par," he began in his thick Spanish accent, "During the second half, it looked like our lads were already running on fumes."

"Point taken," Adam said, acknowledging Carlos's input, "We should incorporate more endurance training into our routine then," he declared.

As the meeting approached its conclusion, Adam turned to Mike. "Mike, any input from my assistant manager?" he asked.

"Yeah," replied Mike, "I thought the first half we were superb. We showed all the benefits of Friday's session and other confidence and morale-boosting efforts. In the second half, however, I felt there was an overconfidence or complacency. The lads crumbled once we conceded the equaliser and then the second goal. In my experience, you need experience and leadership in those moments to rally the troops and keep them fighting. Kofi tried, but we needed Michael Knight out there. I'm not suggesting you bring him back and back down from your stance. I'd do no different. However, in his place, we need that kind of leader and experience out there," he explained.

Adam, taken aback by Mike's words, replied, "Absolutely, I agree. What do you suggest?" he asked.

"Well," Mike said, "There is a name that springs to mind, Shea McNamara. Shea is an ex-teammate, club legend and a friend. He is thirty-six and unofficially retired since being without a club as of the end of last season. That said, hear me out. If we can coax him back out of retirement, he has won nearly everything in the game and is a fearless leader and inspirational presence. I feel a three-game deal, even for his impact in training and around the camp, would be invaluable, especially as he has been doing his coaching badges," Mike explained.

"Do you have his number, Mike?" Adam asked.

"Of course I do, yeah. Shall I set up a meeting?" Mike asked.

"Absolutely," Adam replied, "Four o'clock today in my office, please."

"Consider it done," Mike replied.

Adam was quietly optimistic. Despite the defeat, this could be an opportunity in disguise, an opportunity for them to rectify their mistakes and make a comeback for their remaining matches. He looked around the room and was met with faces that mirrored his own determination. "Alright, everyone, let's get to work," he stated.

Adam's next meeting was with Sarah and the club secretary, Mr Broad. Their discussion centred around Adam's comments after yesterday's game regarding compensating the travelling fans for the dismal showing at Newborough. Adam, Sarah, and Mr Broad discussed the issue, as Adam was met with resistance from Sarah and Mr Broad.

Mr. Broad, an aged man with thinning hair and a permanent furrow on his brow, cast a wary glance at Adam. "I understand your intentions, Adam," he began cautiously, "But you must realise the financial implications such a move could have on the club."

"Ok," Adam replied firmly, "Explain it to me then, please."

"Adam, I understand you want to make a gesture to acknowledge the fan's disappointment, but such a gesture may backfire in the long run," Mr Broad began to explain, "You need to understand that we do not see all of the ticket sales money for an away match, a majority of the revenue made goes to the hosting side. We can't set an expectation that whenever things go south on the pitch, refunds will be issued. Furthermore, despite the club being a business and not one laden with financial resources, as it stands, the club is in quite a precarious financial situation," he explained.

Mr Broad continued, "Whether or not you believe it, this club faces the realistic prospect of relegation, which will only worsen the issue. Not to mention that if we survive, you and some of the playing staff will have substantial bonuses to be paid out. Additionally, the team will need significant investment to replace players leaving at the end of their contracts and make the improvements needed to ensure we don't struggle against relegation again next season."

"Thank you for explaining all that to me. Rest assured, I understand those factors, truly, I do," Adam replied.

"Adam," Sarah interjected, "Public relations is a very delicate matter. Your sentiments about compensating the travelling fans, including travel costs and a further pie and pint deal, were appreciated across social media platforms. Still, we need to ensure it's done in a manner that doesn't negatively impact the club financially."

Sarah continued, "We had four thousand travelling fans yesterday, and compensating them for their tickets and travel costs, as well as the pie and pint vouchers, could dent our budget significantly," she stated, her tone serious.

Adam nodded, taking in her words. "I get that," he replied, tapping his fingers pensively on the table, "But we need them on our side now more than ever. They travelled far and wide, braving the cold for us and, to say the very least, that second-half performance and the result was unacceptable."

Sarah cleared her throat nervously. As the club's media manager, she would have to manage this delicate situation with absolute precision. "Adam," she said tentatively, "Perhaps we should consider drafting a public apology instead? Something that acknowledges our performance and promises improvement for our loyal fans?"

Adam considered this suggestion but shook his head, "Words are cheap," he said grimly, "We've made promises before and failed to deliver on them. If we want to show our fans that we truly value their dedication, we need to demonstrate it in more tangible ways. Moreover, the video going out at four o'clock is a public apology," he paused before adding, "I believe covering the fan's expenses and making a future gesture is a better step in the right direction."

Against his better judgment, Mr. Broad agreed with Adam's conviction. Though it was unorthodox and financially risky, this could be what they needed, a grand gesture of good faith.

Sarah nodded slowly. She could already imagine the headline 'Unprecedented Move by Club Shows Dedication to Fans'. It would certainly make waves among their fanbase and throughout the football community.

Adam, nodding after winning the battle of wills, stated, "Look, I get the financial implications. With that in mind, I will get each player who featured to put five-hundred-pounds into the pot out of their wages to cover the cost needed. Any shortfall can be taken out of my wages, from which I will kickstart the donations with fifteen hundred quid."

"That is brilliant. Are you sure? Will the players be up for that?" Mr. Broad asked.

"Leave the players to me," Adam replied.

"It shows great consideration for the situation, and the knowledge that the players and you are footing the bill shows that this is a heartfelt and personal apology gesture. Bravo," Mr Broad said, as Sarah nodded with a smile.

The room fell silent as Mr Broad sighed heavily, his hand skimming through his greying hair. "Any other business from either of you?" he asked.

"Well," Adam remarked, "Following this meeting, I have a meeting with Shea McNamara, in which I intend to offer him a short-term player-coach role for these final three games, including a survival bonus. Can you please recommend the financial figures I have to play with in accordance with the current budget?" Adam asked.

"Let me get back to my office now and call accounts to look at the numbers, and I'll email you what we can do within half an hour. Is that ok?" Mr Broad asked.

"Of course, thank you for that," Adam replied.

"Were you going to tell me about this for the sake of the media department, press statement, unveiling media, etc?" Sarah interjected.

"I'm telling you now, any problems?" Adam replied.

"None. I just would have appreciated a bit of a heads-up. Don't worry, I'll get to work on the press release. What time shall I send the camera guys up here?" Sarah asked.

"Five o'clock, please, Sarah," Adam answered.

The meeting eventually drew to a close at quarter to four, with a consensus reached and a plan of action laid out, as Sarah and Mr Broad left Adam's office. Adam strummed his fingers on his desk, watching the clock tick towards four, eagerly awaiting Shea's arrival. The weight of what he had proposed began to sink in, and he questioned if he had been too impulsive. But as he thought about the disheartened faces of the fans after yesterday's match, their boos still ringing in his ears, he felt justified in his decision. He decided, therefore, to take this moment to inform the players of his decision by writing in the team group message feed.

'Guys, as we all know, yesterday was a letdown and completely unacceptable for our travelling fans. I've proposed a gesture of good faith for them from each of you who featured in the game. It requires you to contribute five hundred pounds out of your wages to make this happen. I'm kicking it off and leading by example with fifteen hundred pounds. Let's show our fans we're sorry and in this together. If you have a problem with this, please see me at training tomorrow, cheers'.

As he hit send, he leaned back in his chair and ran a hand through his hair, anxiously awaiting their response. He didn't have to wait long as the notifications began rolling in. A mixture of shock, camaraderie, and shared responsibility echoed in their replies, led by Kofi assuring Adam that they would all get behind this decision and willingly give the five hundred pounds to show the fans their remorse.

On the dot of four o'clock, the door to Adam's office creaked open, snapping him out of his thoughts. Mike stepped in first, a grim expression on his face, and behind him loomed Shea McNamara.

Shea was a true son of Schull, having been born and raised in the small town nestled in the southwest corner of Ireland. He possessed a thick Irish accent and stood at five-foot-five. He may have been considered slight in build, but his presence on the football pitch was anything but. His jet black locks cascaded down his back, tied into a top knot with shaved sides and back, a signature look that only added to his intimidating aura. Ten seasons as a player for Swanford had moulded him into a well-respected figure in the football community, adored by fans and looked up to by fellow players. His mere presence could boost team morale significantly. Many speculated that he would make an excellent coach, using his expertise and experience to guide future generations of footballers. Amongst his peers, Shea was known as a legend in his own right. Although retired from the game, he still possessed the energy and agility to jump back onto the pitch if needed. It wasn't, however, just his skills as a player that made him stand out. Shea's outgoing personality and contagious sense of humour made him a joker in the dressing room and a beloved member of any team he was part of. He always kept morale high and spirits lifted in the dressing room.

"Adam," Mike greeted, taking the seat opposite him, "Shea," he nodded towards the former player sitting beside him, "Shea, this is Adam" Mike made the introductions as the two shook hands over the desk.

Adam opened the conversation, "Firstly, thank you for coming on such short notice, Shea. It's an honour to meet you."

"Anything for this club," Shea stated. He continued, "Besides, my new hobbies aren't going well. I tried to teach my dog to play football with me, but it was no good. He's a boxer," Shea joked. "Say, Mr Wells, ask me about my sheepdog training," Shea remarked.

"How's the sheepdog training going, Shea?" Adam duly asked.

"Aye, it's brilliant! You wouldn't believe how well I'm trainin' the sheep," Shea boasted.

Mike raised a sceptical eyebrow, "Training sheep, Shea? You couldn't even train a fly to stay off your shoulder during a match!"

Shea slammed his fist on the table. "Ah, that's different! See, with the sheep, I can finally give a yellow card without gettin' sent off myself!"

The whole room laughed before Adam requested they get serious and down to business.

Without wasting time, Adam explained his proposition for Shea to join as a player-coach for the season's remaining three games, clearly spelling out what role he would play and what they would expect from him. Shea listened intently throughout, his piercing blue eyes never leaving Adam's. Once Adam was done speaking, Shea softened his look and said in a low voice, "I'd be lying if I said I wasn't interested in this proposition," he paused before adding cautiously, "And I'm willing to consider it subject to terms, what are you offering?" he asked.

Adam composed himself, taking one last look at the email from Mr Broad, which had now arrived, before replying, "Having spoken to the club secretary and him to accounts, we are in the position to offer you the following contract." He explained, "A four-week contract with a salary of fifty-thousand pounds per week alongside an appearance fee of a thousand pounds per game and a relegation survival bonus of a hundred thousand pounds."

After taking a moment to consider the terms, Shea countered, "That's a decent offer, but I want seventy-five thousand per week and a five-grand appearance fee, with a survival bonus of two hundred and fifty thousand."

"The best I can offer is sixty-five thousand per week and a two-grand appearance fee, alongside a hundred and fifty thousand pounds survival bonus," Adam replied.

Holding his hand out to shake Adam's, Shea replied, "Let the boogie see the woogie and the monkey see the nuts. You've got yourself a deal."

Laughing, Adam replied, "Brilliant, let's get it signed. Give me a second," he said, turning his attention to his laptop. Mr Broad had attached a contract template to his email for Adam to complete and get signed, with Mike being a witness to the signing. The fields for payment amounts had been left blank for Adam to fill out, which he did before printing it off. Grabbing the contract off his printer, Adam signed it before laying it on the desk in front of Shea, inviting him and Mike to sign it and seal the deal.

As Shea signed the contract, Adam declared, "This is brilliant. I just know that you can offer invaluable experience and leadership to the lads to help keep us up. Thank you for signing up to the cause." Relief washed over Adam as he leaned back into his chair. He was desperate to know one more thing, "Although the bulk of your work will be in coaching and generally being around the camp as a leader, what has your fitness and match sharpness been like since you retired last summer?" he asked.

"Well, there's life in the old dog yet, that's for sure" Shea replied. "Since my retirement, I've been training with and playing for my local semi-pro club in the seventh tier. I'm not at an elite level, but I can do a job. The older the fiddle, the sweeter the tune and all that. I'm not banjaxed just yet, and that's for sure."

"Brilliant," Adam replied. Despite their desperate situation, Adam felt an inkling of hope burgeoning within him, hoping that he and his coaching team, alongside Shea, might turn things around for the team and the club's devoted fans.

Once the media team joined them in the office, Shea posed for his unveiling photographs and recorded an accompanying interview video. Meanwhile, Sarah showed Adam her prepared press statement announcing Shea's arrival before it was released. Her concise and eloquent words perfectly expressed Shea's introduction as their returning hero as player-coach. As Sarah read the statement aloud, Adam could imagine the anticipation buzz lighting up the club's social media accounts and the local news headlines.

Adam nodded, "Excellent work, Sarah. Please release it once Shea's done his interview." Sarah smiled in return, her eyes gleaming with pride.

Whereas yesterday brought despair, today was shaping up to deliver hope. While Shea was occupied with the media team, Adam sought out Mike, who had disappeared after their meeting. He found him on the pitch, alone on the sidelines, staring into space. Mike looked up as Adam approached, both men exchanging glances that spoke volumes about their shared understanding of what was at stake.

"We made our choice," Adam began, voice low but steady, "Now we rally our troops and fight."

Mike nodded slowly before he replied, "Shea is a good lad, a great player and will make a difference, but we need more than a miracle to avoid relegation," Mike explained.

"A miracle," Adam mused aloud, a slow smile appearing on his face as he turned his gaze back towards the empty pitch, "Maybe that's exactly what we need," he said, optimism seeping into his voice as he envisioned each player giving everything they had on the pitch.

Mike stared across the pitch momentarily before smiling slightly, "If anyone can pull off a miracle, it's us with Shea in the camp," he said.

With renewed vigour, they walked back towards Adam's office just as Shea finished his promotional shots for the press release. He looked every inch the warrior they needed. Strong, experienced, and entirely unfazed by the task at hand. Confidence swelled within Adam, a feeling he hadn't felt in the last twenty-four hours. There were still several hurdles to cross and battles to face, but with Shea on their side and a newfound hope burning brightly within them all, things were finally starting to look up for their team. The season was far from over, and in this game of unpredictability and constant surprises, they had every intention of changing the narrative before the final whistle blew on the season.

13

Tuesday 16th April

As the week's training began on Tuesday, the team worked hard on the training pitch, with the coaches focusing on the areas for improvement identified in the coaches' meeting. The players and coaches worked meticulously with a steeled determination, committed to writing the wrongs of Sunday's second half, keen to ensure results would take a turn for the better, and guide the club to safety.

Before training began, Shea decided to address his new teammates for the first time. Shea stood in his Swanford training gear and aged football boots, prematurely grey hair breaking through the edges of his hair, which seemed at odds with his youthful grin. Gone was the clean-cut professional athlete of yesteryear; in his place stood a slightly frazzled-looking figure in a rumpled tracksuit that screamed Sunday league warrior more than top-flight footballer.

"Alright, lads," Shea bellowed, his voice surprisingly booming for his slight frame, "Gather round. This shirt must have shrunk in the machine, no? It fitted last time I wore it, fecks sake." A rumble of laughter echoed through the canteen, a wave of nervous energy dissipating as Shea's easy demeanour put them at ease. He raised an eyebrow, "Now then, for those of you who haven't heard of me or searched the internet for me yet, I'm Shea. I used to play for this great club, among others, and without offending anyone, a team that rhymes with cry, but let's say my career highlight wasn't that epic own goal against Dunstan."

Ethan Fox interjected, "Wait, are you that Shea? The one with the commentary guy screaming 'And Shea with a scorcher, into his own net!'?"

Shea grimaced theatrically, "The one and only. Though, technically, it was a 'defender-assisted wonder goal', but hey, at least it's memorable, right?" he laughed.

The players erupted in fresh peals of laughter. Ethan bounced on his toes, clearly starstruck, "Definitely, welcome aboard. What's your role then, coach or player?" he asked.

"I've seen your performances, kid; the thrill is mutual, Ethan," Shea remarked, "As for my role here, the contract reads player-coach. I envisage the bulk of my work being in assisting Adam and Mike in coaching you wonderful lot. However, Adam also asked me to be prepared to enter the fray and bring experience and leadership to the side on the pitch where needed. Just don't expect me to pull a rabbit out of a hat. I'm an ageing fecker but one on hand to mentor you to safety in this relegation survival bid."

Shea cleared his throat, "Alright, lads, it's time to get to work. Remember, there's a fine line between confidence and delusion. Let's aim for the former, shall we?"

A chorus of "Yes, Coach!" echoed through the squad. Shea surveyed the team with a hint of determination flickering amidst the humour. These weren't exactly world-beaters, but there was raw talent and a spark of something special in their eyes.

"Now," Shea continued, a playful smirk twisting his lips, "Who's up for some drills that won't involve me reenacting my own humiliation?"

The team erupted in cheers once more. With a good dose of humour, a sprinkle of self-deprecating charm, and a hint of tactical genius, Shea could help turn these Swanford Swans into something beautiful, or at the very least, a team that wouldn't be relegated.

Shea's impact on the camp was immediately evident, especially in his role as coach. He had been in a couple of relegation battles in his career and seemingly knew how to rally the troops and drill the players to improve the shortcomings that Sunday's performance had shown. His concise instructions and unerring focus on detail quickly gained respect, while his devotion to the cause was infectious. Every player rallied around Shea's guidance, attacking their training with renewed work rate. Once filled with a hushed sense of doom, the training ground now pulsated with energy.

Adam arrived home on Tuesday night and was in for a harrowing shock. As he walked through his door, his doormat held a padded envelope addressed to him. As he bent down to pick it up, he realised it did not have a stamp. Therefore, it had been hand-delivered.

The envelope had some weight to it and was bulged with some sort of small item. Adam carefully opened the envelope and pulled out a note. The note was typed, 'You are not welcome here. Stick to your stupid video games. Resign now and piss off, or the next one will be in you'.

'The next one will be in you', Adam wondered what this was about for a split second before tipping a bullet out of the envelope. The air around him seemed to suck the warmth from his body, replaced by a bone-chilling cold that spread from his fingertips to his core. His heart, a frantic drum solo in his chest, threatened to burst from his ribs. Time, once a steady march, fractured into a kaleidoscope of slow-motion moments as the cold whisper of wind snaking through the cracked window sent shivers down his spine, each a tiny hammer blow against his already crumbling composure.

But above the terror, a primal instinct clawed its way to the surface. This wasn't just a threat; it was a grotesque invitation. In the face of his fear, a fierce resolve ignited. This bullet was a challenge, a twisted test of his will. Burning with a cold fury, his eyes locked onto the metal messenger of death. This wasn't just a game anymore. This was a fight for his life, and Adam, with a deep breath that tasted faintly of iron, knew he had to fight back.

The silence in the room was a predator stalking Adam as he continued to stare at the bullet. Cold and metallic, fear threatened to clamp its icy grip around his heart. "Intimidate me?" he muttered, his voice challenging in the suffocating quiet. It wasn't as steady as he'd hoped, but there was a spark in his eyes, a flicker of defiance that refused to be extinguished.

Quitting wasn't an option. It never had been. This wasn't just a threat; it was a declaration of war. They wanted to break him, to make him cower. But Adam wasn't built that way. He would take this fear, this primal urge to run, and twist it into something else. He'd turn it into a weapon, fuel propelling him forward.

The game had changed, and the stakes raised. It wasn't just about winning anymore but about proving a point. Adam wouldn't let them win, not by a long shot. Adam straightened the fear, a knot in his gut, but a knot he could use. This bullet was a challenge, a dare, and Adam, a cornered fighter with his back against the wall, was ready to fight back. The game was on, and Adam was playing for keeps this time.

14

Wednesday 17th April

Wednesday morning came, and after very little sleep, Adam made his way to work with the envelope packed with its original contents. Adam's mind had raced throughout the night, halting any attempts to sleep as fear consumed him. Every slight noise, even the blow of the wind against his bedroom window, scared him into a panic, and he couldn't sleep for fear of letting his newly alert guard down. Adam feared that he might not wake again if he went to sleep.

As he made his way in, he decided to phone Sarah. As she answered, Adam got straight down to business, explaining, "Sarah, I received a death threat last night," he began with a slight tremor in his voice, "An envelope was hand-delivered to my house. It had a bullet inside."

There was a pause on the other end of the phone before Sarah finally replied, "Oh my god, Adam, are you alright?" she asked, her voice filled with concern.

Adam took a deep breath. "I'm good, Sarah, just shaken up," he paused before adding, "But I can't back down now. Not when the stakes are so high."

"Are you sure about this, Adam?" Sarah asked worriedly. "Maybe it might be wise to walk away. Somethings are more important than football."

"No, Sarah," Adam declared firmly, "I refuse to be bullied into retreating. This is not just about me anymore. It's about standing up against intimidation."

His resolve solidified as Adam ended the call and continued his journey towards the training ground. Within an hour of settling in at work, Scott appeared at his desk and ushered him into the briefing room for an urgent meeting. As Adam walked into the room, he was greeted by Sarah and a man in a suit and tie who introduced himself, "Hi Adam, I'm Shane Finn, and I'm head of Swanford Police."

Shaking his hand, Adam replied, "Adam Wells, pleased to meet you."

Shane was imposing, well-built, and six feet tall. His shoulders looked like his coat hanger had been left under his suit jacket. He had skin-bald hair, a tidy, well-groomed, thin beard, and brown eyes. Adam noticed that the back of his hands were covered in tattoos that didn't look like they stopped there; they probably extended up his forearms. His aura exuded that of a stern and professional man. Shane gestured to a chair, and Adam sat down, the leather cool against his back. Shane began the meeting by explaining, "We've been informed of the threat you received, Adam. We take such matters very seriously." The solemn expressions on Sarah and Scott's faces echoed the gravity in his voice.

"Yes, I understand," Adam responded. His tone was calm, but an undercurrent of fear caused his words to tremble slightly. As Adam placed the envelope on the table, it seemed to echo ominously in the quiet room. Sarah reached across the table, her fingers shaking slightly as she examined the envelope. Shane, too, leaned forward, his experienced eyes studying it thoroughly. Shane, Sarah and Scott examined its contents for some time, their faces in deep concentration. As Adam sat watching them, a steely edge settled over him. His gaze never wavered from the bullet as thoughts raced through his head about football, about the threats, about what he had to do next.

Shane finally broke the silence, "I'll take the envelope and the bullet for evidence now, and our labs will analyse it forensically for any clues," he explained, "We'll do everything we can our end, Adam. We won't let this go. We'll catch those responsible for this." Shane's words were firm and adamant, which was assuring.

"One thing worries me about this, though. The envelope was hand-delivered. This means the person who sent it knows where you live and is possibly also stalking you," Shane continued, "That leaves us with two options. We can temporarily place you in a hotel in a secluded area out of town or have your house guarded and monitored, which might help us catch the culprit and protect you. Which would you prefer?" he asked.

After a few moments of consideration, Adam replied, "I won't be driven out of my own home if I do that, they've won. Please let's go with the guarding my house option and hopefully catch the scum that did this in the process."

"No problem at all, Adam, I'll get straight on to it," Shane replied.

"I appreciate that" Adam nodded. "But it's not just about finding out who did this," he explained, "It's also about proving that I can't be threatened or bullied into submission." Adam's voice rose with a newfound resolve, "It's about showing everyone that I am tougher than any challenge thrown at me. A philosophy that rings true for me and the squad as a whole in this relegation battle."

As the meeting ended, Adam left the briefing room and returned to his office and desk. He felt a surge of adrenaline pulse through him, and his heart pounded with a fierce and fiery urgency he had not known before. He felt ready, ready to face whatever the next play would be. This was his crucible, and he would forge his path with courage and unwavering resolve.

Shortly after, Scott joined Adam in his office. "I'll ensure security is tightened around the training ground, your car, the stadium, etc," Scott promised solemnly.

Adam smiled gratefully and replied, "Thanks, boss. I appreciate it." Scott nodded thoughtfully and said no more before leaving the room.

After his dramas consumed the first hour of the day, Adam made his way onto the training pitch. The soft grass underfoot, the caress of the fresh morning air, the distant cheers of his team warming up, these familiar sensations brought a measure of settling calm to the storm that had been looming over his morning. Adam stood for a moment, breathing deeply, allowing himself to be grounded by the energy of his beloved sport. As he approached the squad, the players halted their drills and turned to face him. The news had spread through the ranks, bringing with them an edgy silence.

Adam stood tall before his team, feeling their anxious gazes on him. "Boys," he began, his eyes meeting each of theirs in turn, "I won't lie. We've got a tough fight ahead." A murmur swept through the team. Adam held up his hand for silence before continuing. "But remember this, it is not just my battle," Adam gestured to them collectively, "It is our battle as a collective, and we are more than any threat or challenge that comes our way."

One by one, nods of approval spread through the players like wildfire. With renewed vigour, the players threw themselves back into their training session. Every pass was sharper, every sprint carried an extra burst of speed, and every shot was fired with ferocity.

Adam could feel it; they were ready. They were fighters, every one of them. Everyone was united in their resolve; relegation would not be their destiny. As they trained, Sarah walked onto the pitch carrying water bottles for the team. She looked at Adam and nodded approvingly, a quiet admiration evident in her eyes. Her resilience and unwavering support were like a pillar of strength for him. By day's end, Adam knew they had achieved more than physical training. They had fortified their spirit, bond, and, more importantly, their determination to battle whatever came their way. Unity was strength.

As Adam arrived home that evening, worried as he walked through the door that further threats would greet him, his mind could not help but be consumed by thoughts of the previous days' threat accompanied by the bullet, which had explicitly been hand-delivered.

The silence slammed into Adam like a physical blow. The air inside the house hung heavy, thick with an unseen menace. Once familiar, every shadow was stretched and contorted into monstrous shapes, each creak of the floorboards a whispered threat. His heart hammered a frantic tattoo against his ribs, its rhythm a counterpoint to the suffocating quiet.

A phantom scent, the acrid tang of forgotten, burnt coffee, clung to the air, a faint echo of normalcy shattered by his hurried departure that morning. Each hesitant step resonated through the house, a sonic boom in the vacuum of silence. The weathered floorboards groaned under his weight, their protests a chorus of dread.

As Adam moved like a ghost through the skeletal rooms, hands brushing cobwebbed corners, he felt a cold sweat on his palms. The worn paint beneath his fingertips was a tangible reminder of the life that once filled this space, a life now shadowed by fear. The tick-tock of the antique clock, a family heirloom passed down through generations, echoed with a maddening insistence, each tick a hammer blow against his already frayed nerves.

Finally, after a circuit of the house to check for potential danger, Adam stumbled back into the living room. Collapsing onto the threadbare couch, he let out a ragged breath. Relief warred with a gnawing unease. Adam's mind, a runaway train, careened through a labyrinth of what-ifs, each one more horrifying than the last. Fear, a cold serpent, coiled in his gut, but he steeled himself. Adam went to bed that night with a fighter's resolve simmering within him. He was ready to fight for Swanford's survival, safety, and, ultimately, his life.

Later that night, Adam found himself asleep, experiencing a nightmare. The nightmare was a flashback to a time at school many years ago when he was verbally and physically bullied, recalled no doubt by his current situation of an angry fan attempting to bully him into resigning and leaving the club.

In his first year at senior school, Adam was subjected to a whole school year full of verbal and physical bullying. Aside from that, Adam found it hard to settle into his new school and be accepted. Friendships were hard, if not impossible, to find. As a result, Adam found himself alone at home each evening when others might have been playing out after school. This was when his love and obsession with video games, especially Ultimate Manager, began.

An icy wind clawed at Adam's exposed skin in his nightmare, starkly contrasting the feverish sweat clinging to his body. The crowd roar wasn't cheers. It was a cacophony of hate, each jeer a shard of ice lodged in his chest. Adam was trapped in the dugout, a lone gladiator in a hostile stadium. Across the green battlefield, his team crumbled, the scoreboard a flashing taunt of impending relegation. Then, through the blurring despair, a face emerged from the faceless throng.

Shaun, the lad who had bullied him at school, a name etched in humiliation, materialised in the stands, a cruel grin splitting his face. Adam's breath caught in his throat, a primal fear clawing its way up from the depths. The tears Shaun had once elicited, hot and stinging, threatened to spill again. A guttural groan escaped Adam's lips as the phantom pain of a thousand taunts echoed in his ears.

Then, the final, crushing blow. A goal conceded, relegation confirmed. The world dissolved into a red haze as the crowd's hatred crescendoed. A booming voice cut through the din, punctuated by the thunder of approaching footsteps. Shaun was more prominent and meaner, his short black hair a halo around a face contorted with malice.

"There you are, loser," Shaun spat, the words dripping with venom, "Just like old times, eh? Always the disappointment!" Shaun then brandished a hockey stick, the same one that he had terrorised Adam with at school all those years ago.

Adam's fight-or-flight response ignited. He wanted to run, scream, fight back, anything to escape the suffocating dread. But Shaun was already upon him, a whirlwind of fury. The sickening crack of the hockey stick against bone echoed through the stadium, each blow a hammer to Adam's sanity. Blood welled up, staining the pristine grass of the sideline Adam stood on. Adam's legs buckled beneath him, a symphony of searing pain replacing the roar of the crowd. As he crumpled to the ground, a whimper escaping his cracked lips, Shaun loomed over him.

"Still crying like a little baby," Shaun snarled, a cold satisfaction in his eyes. He spat, a glistening glob of contempt landing on Adam's cheek. Then, with a last cruel laugh, Shaun turned and vanished into the crowd.

But the nightmare wasn't over. A dark figure emerged from the shadows, a menacing silhouette clad in a Swanford jersey. In his hand, a glint of cold steel reflected the stadium floodlights. A gun. The figure pointed it directly at Adam's face, finger tightening on the trigger.

A primal scream ripped from Adam's throat, a sound that shattered the nightmare and sent him jolting upright in his bed. Gasping for air, Adam found himself in the echoing darkness of his room, the sheets tangled around him. The panic attack clawed at him, a chilling echo of the terror he'd just experienced. But through the pounding of his heart, one thought remained: tomorrow, he wouldn't be a loser in a nightmare. He'd face whatever life threw at him, the memory of Shaun a twisted reminder of the strength he possessed.

Adam sat there for what felt like an age, forcing himself to draw deep breaths, feeling the cool night air filling his lungs. Finally regaining control, Adam pushed himself out of bed and stumbled towards the kitchen. He flicked on the light switch and squinted at the sudden brightness before moving to fill a glass of water from the tap. As he gulped down the cool liquid, the remnants of his nightmare started to recede to the back of his mind.

Shortly after, Adam stood before a mirror on a wall in his hallway. His pallid reflection stared back at him, eyes wide with lingering fear. He looked weak and defeated, just like he had in that nightmare, just like he had following that incident with Shaun back in his school days. However, Adam was no longer a schoolboy at the mercy of bullies, nor would he be at the mercy of an angry fan. He was a grown man now, a fighter. He was a man who had faced numerous challenges throughout his life up until now and emerged victorious each time. The survival instinct that had kept him alive so far kicked into gear. His gaze hardened as he clenched his jaw. The memory of Shaun's malicious grin was replaced by grit. If he could face down Shaun all those years ago, he could undoubtedly face this new threat head-on.

Adam returned to his bedroom, his resolve solidifying like steel forged in fire. Tomorrow would be another day. One filled with challenges and dangers, no doubt, but Adam didn't intend to back down. He wouldn't let the fear of the past or the uncertainty of the future control him any longer.

15

Thursday 18th April

The morning sun started to break through the darkness outside in the early morning hours as Adam lay back on his bed, staring at the ceiling, willing sleep to claim him once again. Despite the anxiety and adrenaline coursing through his veins, sleep came surprisingly quickly.

It was with a newfound strength that Adam woke up at half past seven. As the golden morning light peeked through his window, Adam felt a resurgence of energy set over him. He rose from his bed, shaking off the remnants of fear and defeat that had cloaked him overnight. He walked into the bathroom, splashed cold water on his face and looked straight into the mirror again. His reflection seemed different than before. His eyes were no longer wide with lingering fear but narrowed with calm and serenity.

After a hearty breakfast, Adam slipped into his training gear and left the house for the training ground. The day saw the players go through their drills with the coaches as Adam watched on. The lads trained well and with focus, improving minute by minute. There were subtle but noticeable improvements in the team's performance.

The conclusion of Thursday's training brought with it Adam's mandatory pre-game press conference with the media before Saturday's upcoming fixture against fellow relegation strugglers Cliffe. After last weekend's result, Cliffe found themselves four points below Swanford and seven points behind Wry, who currently lay in the safety spot. Anything but a win against Swanford, and they would find themselves the first of the three teams to be relegated in this three-way battle. For Swanford, a win would not only be a step toward survival, with them sitting a point behind Wry and therefore safety, but also a chance of redemption for the performance at Newborough.

Adam, flanked by Shea and Sarah, entered the media room filled with anxious anticipation. Adam's confident stride masked his nerves as he took his place at the table facing the media, his eyes scanning the room full of reporters. Cameras clicked, and flashes illuminated the severe expressions of the gathered media's faces, casting stark shadows around the room. Sarah opened the press conference by greeting the room.

"Afternoon all, Adam is here today, joined by our new player-coach for the final three games, Shea McNamara. This afternoon, they will be taking questions about Saturday's upcoming fixture against Cliffe. Thank you," she remarked. Adam nodded respectfully as Sarah finished her introduction.

As Sarah finished the introductions, Shea interjected, "Aw Jesus, here we go again. I forgot how intimidating these things are," he remarked with a smirk, "It's good to see so many of you again. You're after asking some tough questions, I'm sure." "Oh feck, Riley, Riley James, is that you fella?" he asked, pointing his finger toward Riley.

"Hey Shea, how are you?" Riley replied.

"Like a dog with two, my fella, like a dog with two," Shea replied, laughing. "Ladies and gentlemen, let me tell you about this man here," Shea continued, "So there I was," Shea chuckled, running a hand through his hair, "Fresh off the win, feeling like I could walk on water. The press conference was packed, microphones shoved in my face like a swarm of hungry bees. I usually scan the room before answering to see who's asking what. But this time, there he was, ya man, right smack in the front row. Looking a fine figure of a man in a pristine suit, tie tighter than a drum, notepad clutched like a religious text. Looked like he'd wandered in from a boardroom meeting by mistake," Shea paused, milking the anticipation, "Turns out, he was there to cover the gardening column. Turns out, he got lost on his way to the flower show."

"Indeed, yes, many moons ago now that Shea. It was my first month in the job, in fact" Riley replied, laughing slightly.

After a moment of laughter in the room, a flurry of hands shot up, reporters eager to fire their questions. Through the cacophony of voices, Adam focused on a reporter at the back of the room before inviting him to ask his question with the point of a finger in his direction.

"Super Sports TV here, Adam, how do you feel about your chances this weekend? Cliffe need a win. Anything but a win, and they will be relegated. Will that make this a tough opponent to face, given that they will throw everything but the kitchen sink at you?" the reporter asked.

Adam met the reporter's gaze evenly and leaned forward slightly, placing his forearms on the table. "Our focus is on our team and preparing them as best we can for what lies ahead. We can not hide behind the results of others. Simply put, we have to do our job and win our games, and whatever will be will be," he replied, his tone steady and measured, "Cliffe have nothing to lose and are a strong side and have a solid following, which will act as a crucial twelfth man for them. We must respect them and their capabilities, but we are not afraid to face them" Adam leaned back in his chair, signalling an end to his answer.

The next question came for Shea, from a writer for the national newspaper UK News. "Shea, what is your role here? Did it come as a surprise to be asked to come out of retirement? What is the key to winning Saturday's game?"

Shea lowered his gaze, seemingly considering his response, before lifting his eyes to meet the reporter's curious gaze before his firm voice filled the room, "A surprise, yes, but very much a pleasant one," he confessed, a hint of a smile gracing his lips, "Even more so an honour. My role is what it has always been, to serve the team in any capacity I can," he paused for a moment, gleaning over the faces of the reporters in the room, some of them nodding at his answer. "As for the key to winning Saturday's game," Shea continued, "Resilience and discipline. It's about not letting setbacks shake our resolve and keeping our eyes on the prize, even amidst pressure."

The next question came for Adam. "Good afternoon, Adam. Swanford Daily here. Can you tell us what the latest is regarding the Michael Knight situation, especially given his appearance on Super Sports TV at the weekend with his less-than-complimentary comments?" the journalist probed.

A furious Adam looked on before replying, "This matter is an internal one that we are dealing with as a club, and I won't be making any further comment upon it today."

The next question came from Tommy Campbell, the head of the Swanford Fan's Association. "Hi Adam, Scott Brewer seems to have gone into hiding. No one has heard from him at all at this difficult time. We're wondering if you have heard from him?" he asked.

"Hi, Tommy. Nice to meet you," Adam replied, "I can tell you that Mr Brewer has been busy with a few things in his personal life. However,

Scott and I regularly communicate with each other. Scott phoned me on the morning of the Newborough game to wish me and the team well. After the game, Scott rang me again to inform me I had his full support and backing. I also briefly met with Scott in my office here yesterday."

"Ok, thank you," Tommy replied.

The final question came from Riley James of Sports Radio, Adam's foe until now. "Hi, Adam, Riley James of Sports Radio." Adam sighed and nodded in acknowledgement, knowing fore-well who he was. "I just wanted to get your thoughts on Swanford's performance on Sunday against Newborough. Does it not reaffirm the belief that you're not the right person to pull this club out of its relegation struggles? As good as the first half was, the second half was a complete disaster and showed a tactical naivety from you that the club can't afford to have at this stage amid a relegation battle. Furthermore, your conduct in the post-match TV interview, in as much as storming off in a huff, was unprofessional and not that befitting of a professional top-flight football manager. What do you say in response?" Riley asked, a challenging smile playing on his lips.

Adam's eyes hardened at Riley's words, his jaw tensing subtly. The room grew silent, reporters waiting for his response. Adam leaned forward once more, his eyes never leaving Riley's. "Your words seem to indicate a preconceived notion of me and my role as a manager. What's more, they serve to attempt to undermine me and cause disruption within the team, Mr. James," Adam began, his tone maintaining its steady rhythm but carrying an undercurrent of desire, "Your assessment of Sunday's game only highlights your lack of understanding of not only the team and its approach but also the severity of this situation we find ourselves in," Adam's voice rang out, calm and composed. "We need points, and we need them fast, so unapologetically, we will attack every match with the urgency needed to score goals and survive. Sometimes it will go well, sometimes not so well. That's football. Every match and every season has its ups and downs. It's about how we bounce back from those moments that will define us as a team. As for my conduct, I am passionate about this club and will defend it and my team fiercely when I feel they are being wronged. Everyone involved with the club was hurting after that second half and defeat, and I am no exception. What did you expect of me? To be all sunshine and light? No, sir, not me. I wear my heart on my sleeve, and that showed. I apologise wholeheartedly if I caused upset, but I stand by what I said and my conduct," he paused momentarily, "I admit that my passion may have been misconstrued as unprofessionalism."

Adam paused again, all eyes on him in the tense silence. "As for the belief that I'm not the right person to pull this club out of its struggles," he said, his eyes sweeping across the room, "That belief isn't something that concerns me because what matters most is what the players believe," Adam finally glanced back at Riley, a flicker of defiance in his eyes. "I've every reason to believe that they believe in me, but that is irrelevant anyway. What matters is that they believe in themselves." Adam again leaned back in his chair and crossed his arms over his chest. The room erupted into murmurs as reporters frantically scribbled down notes.

Sarah quickly stepped in to wrap up the press conference and promised to answer any further questions via email. As Adam, Shea, and Sarah exited the media room, they did so confidently. Despite the challenging circumstances surrounding them, an aura of hopefulness had seeped into their hearts. This was bigger than them. This was about the club surviving and proving they had the grit to overcome their struggles.

It was a sunny afternoon in Swanford, so Adam visited the local park on his way home. This would allow him to sit on his favourite bench and reflect on the past few days. As Adam sat on the bench staring out at the park's sizeable green expanse, lost in his thoughts and fears, he noticed two young boys playing football.

The young lads could have been no older than eight or nine and ran around with the ball with endless energy. They were using their jumpers as goalposts and were mainly trying to replicate skill moves and goals scored by their footballing heroes. As they scored many goals each, they would celebrate, again often replicating their footballing heroes, as if it was the first goal they'd ever scored and a World Cup-winning one.

As Adam watched on, a smile came across his face. Seeing the young lads enjoying football with joyful innocence was infectious. It dawned on Adam that boys that age, as he had many years ago, have pure joy in having a kick around. Nothing exists outside that moment, and dreams of being a big superstar of the game, like their heroes, seem achievable. They enjoy the magic of the game with the ball at their feet.

Adam had a eureka moment. Despite the troubles looming over his players in this relegation battle, he should get them to enjoy their football as they did as kids. Forget about the worries of relegation and enjoy having the ball at their feet and playing the game they love without concern for anything else. Adam thought that if he could do that, they would play with joy and happiness, without pressure, and hopefully produce good results.

16

Friday 19th April

Friday morning arrived again at the training ground, and ahead of it was a final day of preparation for tomorrow's showdown against Cliffe. Sunrise painted the training ground in orange and pink hues, the dawn chill still clinging in the air. Adam greeted the players whilst they had their breakfast in the canteen.

"Before we go out onto the pitch, I want to meet with you all in the briefing room for half an hour, please," he explained. Shortly after, at nine am, the players joined Adam in the briefing room, curious about his desire to meet with them.

"Morning lads," Adam began, "On my way home last night, I stopped at a local park for some me time. Whilst there, I observed two young boys having a kick about. They enjoyed the joy of the ball at their feet, replicating their heroes' skills and goals, and nothing else mattered outside that moment. They were determined to be the superstar footballers they looked up to one day. It got me thinking that we need to go back to that innocent joy and enjoy our football. If we do that, the results will look after themselves," he explained.

"I want to go round the room now, lads, and get an answer from each of you to a couple of questions. The first question is this, who was your footballing hero as a young boy? The second question is, what was one goal you watched as a child that amazed you? You watched repeatedly and even tried to replicate when having a kick about," Adam asked, pointing at the first of his players for an answer.

Each player gave their answers individually, conjuring up joy and nostalgia within them and the room. It reminded them why they became footballers and their passion as youngsters to become the next big football superstar. Shortly after the group discussion, Adam closed the meeting by saying, "This morning, when we get out on the pitch, we are going to play a game of one of, I'm sure, many of your favourite childhood kick-around games, Wembley. For those of you unfamiliar with it, here are the basics. Barlow will be in goal, and the rest of you will play through rounds of the game. The aim is to score at all costs, every man for himself. Everyone must score a goal to go through to the next round, and the last player left who hasn't scored in each round is eliminated. Once you score, you leave the game and wait for the next round to begin. This continues until we finally have a round of just two players, at which point it is a golden goal situation, with the first to score becoming the winner of the game. Any questions?" he asked.

Kofi replied, "No, got it, boss, love it."

As the players made their way out onto the grass, they were excited yet fiercely competitive for the game of Wembley. Round after round, the players hustled against each other for the opportunity to take a shot at goal and hopefully score the goal to secure their place in the next round. One by one, round by round, the goals flooded in, and players were knocked out of the game until, eventually, somewhat predictably, the final round came down to two strikers, Neil Cole and Hart. The final round played out for several minutes, as Barlow delayed the winning moment by making great save after great save. Eventually, Hart showed all his ability and experience by bagging the winner with a perfectly curled twenty-five-yard shot straight into the top left-hand corner of the goal, top bins.

Following the fun start to the day, training began. There was an urgency to the players' movements that hadn't been there before. Every pass was precise, every tackle firm, and each player pushed themselves beyond their usual limits. Sweat mixed with desire as they collectively fought for the cohesion of the tactics and technique ahead of tomorrow's potential season-defining match. Their every manoeuvre bore a renewed commitment and focus that resonated with Adam's words from the press conference.

Throughout the day, each drill was a testament to their resolve and unity as a team. Their shared understanding carried them through complex plays and demanding physical challenges. By noon, the players' bodies screamed for rest, but their spirits remained unbroken. Adam's voice cut through their fatigue like a beacon, guiding them towards their goal of survival before he declared a much-needed lunch break.

After lunch, Adam once again put his attacking moves and shooting drill into place, aiming to get the side to score plenty of goals to breed confidence into them. Adam declared, "Right, lads, the team bonding day is still on the table for your day off on Sunday, should things go our way tomorrow. It's the same setup drill-wise as last Saturday, but let's make things interesting, double or quits. I'll set you a target for the number of goals this time. Meet it, and I'll double the kitty. Fail to meet it, and you all pay your way out of your own pocket. The target is eighteen. Let's go," he encouraged the players, clapping his hands.

The players enthusiastically embraced the challenge, their competitive natures again sparked by Adam's words. They quickly fell into formation, moving swiftly across the pitch as they worked through the set drill. The air filled with the thuds of striking footballs, grunts of exertion, and cheers of triumph each time the ball found its way into the back of the net.

It was a gruelling afternoon. Energy levels dipped, but the players' determination held fast. Their minds focused on the goal, both metaphorical and literal. As the session ended, the tally of successful goals grew. Shouts of encouragement from teammates echoed around the training ground, urging each other onward in a camaraderie that bound them together.

The count had reached seventeen when coach Shea blew his whistle, signalling their final attempt. All eyes turned to Neil Cole, who stood poised at one end of the pitch. With sweat-laden hair sticking to his forehead and a desire in his eyes, Neil approached the ball. His boots hit the ground in rhythmic thuds as he charged forward, and then, with a swift kick, he sent the ball hurtling towards goal. A collective breath was held as the ball sailed precariously toward the crossbar until it finally dipped under, landing cleanly into the net. A loud cheer erupted from every player before they ran to Neil and jumped onto his back in a pile-up. They had done it. With eighteen goals scored, the team would have their bonding day on Sunday, tomorrow's result permitting. They would do so with a handsome kitty for activity, food and drink.

The celebrations were cut short by Adam's shouting through their jubilation. "Great teamwork, lads," he praised them with a satisfied smile, "But remember, this is only a part of our preparation for tomorrow's battle against Cliffe." The players listened attentively, still breathing heavily from their exertions. "Tomorrow is the real challenge," Adam explained, "We have trained hard, put in the effort, and now we face our adversary. Remember this moment of victory. Remember the feeling of achieving the goal you set for yourself. Let it fuel you on that pitch tomorrow."

The players nodded solemnly, understanding the gravity of Adam's words. Wiping sweat from their brows, they dispersed to cool down as Adam remarked, "Right lads, see you in the briefing room in an hour for a team briefing session ahead of tomorrow's game," before he walked off the training pitch.

An hour later, Adam was joined by the players in the briefing room for the final task of the day, a briefing ahead of tomorrow's match. The room buzzed with serious energy. Each player's face was drawn and solemn, and their eyes were locked on Adam. Adam stood before his team, a map of the pitch laid out on the big screen before them, indicating key positions and tactics.

"The first half of the game," Adam began, "Is going to be about playing our game, our tactics, and taking the lead at the earliest opportunity to take away the momentum that Cliffe will aim to start with." As Adam spoke, murmurs rippled through the room, "They need a win to survive and will go for that from the kick-off. We have to throw a spanner into that plan with an early goal. We've analysed their plays and their tactics. They will battle, be tight in defence, and aim to hit us on the break" Adam pointed to the markers on the map, tracing a defensive formation and offensive manoeuvres.

The players leaned in closer, their attention piqued as Adam continued, "We have found," his tone lightened as he continued to discuss strategies, "They have been struggling to perform at their peak for the full ninety minutes. They can't keep up their performance and resolve for the game's duration. Their defence starts to fracture around the sixty or seventy-minute mark," Adam informed the squad. The mood shifted, hope started to form, and adrenaline coursed through the player's veins. "That is when we strike and put the game to bed, confine them to relegation, and move a huge step toward safety ourselves," Adam declared with a determined grin tugging at his lips.

Adam added, "You will have seen me making the point in my press conference yesterday, but I will reiterate it now. We can not hide behind the results of other teams. We have to do our job, our work, and everything else we can not control or use as an excuse. Throughout the season, a league table does not lie, and you are in the table where you deserve to be in terms of your results over the last nine months. If we get our results from here on in and still go down, then so be it. What the fans or I won't accept is us not getting the results we need and then blaming other results elsewhere as an excuse for relegation," Adam stated.

"Finally," Adam said, "We have a new signing, and you all know what that means. It's initiation song time. Shea, get up here," he said, smiling.

A buoyed up Shea made his way to the front of the room "Ok, lads, earplugs time, although I reckon I've the voice of a fine Irish angel," he declared to a room full of laughter before proceeding to vocally murder a classic rock ballad song.

"Brilliant Shea, well in," Adam smirked, "Now then, lads, that's all for today. Go shower, change and get yourselves off home. Be sure to get a good night's rest ahead of a huge day tomorrow. I'll see you guys at the ground at half past one sharp tomorrow afternoon," Adam said.

As the players filed out of the room, each touched the club badge above the door, a silent promise of commitment and unity towards tomorrow's monumental game. That night, Swanford slept under an umbrella of anticipation and resolve. The town held its breath collectively, anticipating tomorrow's showdown with Cliffe. But inside, every member of Swanford's squad who had trained that day rested a determined heart, ready to fight till the end.

17

Cliffe Home Game

Saturday morning dawned, greeting Adam with its grey and wet April charm. Adam was awoken at ten am by his radio alarm clock. His ears focused in as Riley James's familiar vocal tones burst over the airwaves.

"Morning Swanford fans," Riley said, "First home game today for rookie under-fire manager Adam Wells and a must-win affair if the club are to survive relegation, especially after last Sunday's car crash of a defeat at Newborough."

Riley continued, "Swans fans, are you worried? Do we think a defeat and perhaps a heavy one would see Adam given the boot already?" he asked before declaring, "for the next hour, I'm taking your calls on this. Get in touch and have your say."

Adam's heart thudded in his chest at Riley's words. The bitter sting of last Sunday's defeat crept up on him, but he shook it off as he rose from his bed, a steely determination replacing the fleeting despair.

"We've prepared ourselves. We're a different team than we were last Sunday," he muttered, staring at his reflection in the mirror as he got ready to leave the house.

Adam wore his best three-piece suit: a crisp white shirt, official Swanford tie, and freshly shined black shoes. At quarter to twelve, Adam left his house and got into his car, ready to head to the stadium. The drive would only be short, but Adam wanted to be at the ground for midday.

As Adam began his drive, he had a thought that led him to call Mr Broad, the club secretary.

"Morning, Adam here, how are you?" he greeted Mr Broad.

"Not too bad, cheers, Adam. What can I do for you?" Mr Broad asked.

"How are the ticket sales for today looking?" Adam asked.

"Last time I looked, we had sold just short of forty-five thousand," Mr Broad replied.

After a moment's pause for thought, Adam replied, "Ok," knowing the ground at capacity could hold sixty thousand, "We need a pumped-up, sold-out ground today. Is there anything we can do with the final tickets? Perhaps we can offer a last-minute deal to fill the place out?" he asked.

Mr Broad went silent for a few moments before he answered. "I'm willing to say, taking the accounts and budget into consideration, as well as projected match day spend, that we could do a last-minute offer of adults for ten pounds and kids for a quid. Although this represents a dent in the income, as the tickets are usually thirty and ten pounds, respectfully, the likelihood is that those losses would be compensated by spending in the club shop and through catering, i.e. match day spend. How does that sound to you, Adam? Shall I brief the media department to advertise it and the ticket office to lower the prices?" Mr Broad asked.

A buoyed-up, excited Adam replied, "That is superb, fantastic even. Thank you. Yes, please brief everyone. See you in a bit."

Adam hung up the phone and pondered whether to make the next phone call he had in mind. In an instant, Adam decided he would make the call, one to Sports Radio and, more specifically, Riley James. After speaking to the show's producer to detail who he was and why he was calling, Adam was put on hold to wait for Riley to pick up his call live on air. A few moments later, Riley answered the call.

"Next up, we have, this can't be right, can it? Adam Wells, the Swanford manager, Adam, is that you?" he asked.

"Good morning, Riley. How are we? Listening in earlier, I heard you cheerful as ever," Adam said.

"What can I say, Adam," Riley replied, "For us fans, this is no laughing matter, mate," Riley explained. He continued, "Why are you calling in, Adam? Shouldn't you be focusing on the match right about now?" he asked.

"Yes, thank you for pointing that out," Adam said with a smirk on his face, "I am calling to appeal to all Swanford fans, despite opinions of me, let's all unite for the sake of the players who have trained so hard and well this week in preparation for today. Let's all get behind the team and drive them to safety. With that in mind, all remaining tickets for today are now priced at ten pounds for adults and kids for a quid. Let's get the place sold out and rocking this afternoon. We need our twelfth man, you fans," Adam explained.

"Oh wow," Riley replied, "Prices haven't been that low in a long time. Swanford fans, you heard the man. These tickets will go fast, so act quick and get the place rocking for the boys this afternoon."

"Thank you, Riley. See you all there, you Swans" Adam ended the call before hanging up.

Adam turned off the radio, a sense of calm washing over him as he steered onto the motorway. The stadium was only thirty minutes from his home, but today, it felt like a mammoth trek. After a few minutes, given that he only needed to drive one junction, Adam could see the stadium looming large before him as he pulled off the motorway. Its imposing form stood stark against the grey, rain-full April sky. It was a monolith of concrete and steel, an altar where battles were won and lost, Swanford's battlefield.

A sense of anticipation swelled within Adam as he pulled into the stadium's car park. The moment he turned off the engine, the magnitude of what lay ahead engulfed him. His heartbeat in his ears drowned out the dull thud of rain against the car roof. Today's game wasn't just about points or a change in league standings; it was about survival.

Adam shook himself mentally before climbing out of the car and facing the imposing architectural behemoth. As if in response to his arrival, the stadium seemed to awaken, its walls echoing with the ghosts of games past and the cheers of fans long gone. For Adam, each footstep towards the entrance was a step into history, into a battle that would decide if they were to survive or succumb to relegation. He could almost feel the anticipation thrumming through the concrete beneath his feet. Then, he caught sight of something that made his heart swell in his chest: queues of people lining up at the ticket office, streaming in from every direction under fading umbrellas and torn ponchos. Even under grey skies and relentless rain, there was an infectious energy.

Adam walked briskly past club officials and grounds staff, exchanging brief nods and forceful handshakes as he entered the ground and approached the dressing rooms. At one o'clock, the players began arriving at the stadium, greeting lines of waiting fans requesting autographs and selfies before making their way into the ground and down to the dressing room where Adam awaited their arrival. As the players entered the dressing room one by one, it slowly began to fill. The players' chattering voices filled the sterile, tiled room. As they settled and sat ready to change into their warm-up gear, Adam took a moment to look at each face, tracing the contours of determination and worry. Adam saw in them a reflection of his own hopes and fears.

"Good morning, boss," greeted a familiar voice, snapping Adam from his thoughts. It was their vice, but the current acting captain, Kofi Adams. The unwavering optimism in his eyes made Adam smile in response.

"Morning, Kofi," Adam responded, shaking the captain's hand, "Are we ready?" Adam asked.

Kofi's smile widened. "We're always ready, boss," he replied.

As Adam walked into the centre of the dressing room, it was abuzz with activity. The volume in the room lowered instantly, with all eyes on him. Adam could feel the excitement and anxiety of the players in equal measure. "Boys," Adam began, radiating confidence, "Today is more than just a game. We are not just fighting for a win. We are fighting for survival." Adam let those words sink in for a moment before continuing, "We are not alone in this battle," he said, recalling the sight of fans lining up outside under the relentless rain, "Our fans believe in us, even though it's easier not to. They are standing out there right now because they trust us to give our best today," his eyes swept across the room as he carried on, completely commanding the players' attentions, "So let's repay their faith in us," Adam asserted, clenching his fists at his side to emphasise his point. "Let's show everyone why we belong here and deserve to stay in this league," he declared.

The players' rallying cheers echoed through the stadium's corridors and beyond. Adam felt a rush of adrenaline. He was ready, and his team was prepared.

As the players prepared to step onto the pitch for their warm-up, Adam gathered the team to announce his starting lineup. The room filled with anticipation as Adam pinned a printed copy of the team sheet onto the wall for the lads to read and learn their roles in today's battle.

"Right, lads, team sheet time," Adam declared with a glint in his eye, "In goal, Barlow. Across the back, from left to right, Donovan, Kofi, Lambert, and Turner. On the wings, Fletcher is on the left, and Davids is on the right. Ethan will take on the defensive midfielder role with Price and Young in front of him. And up front, we have Hart," Adam detailed. "As you may have noticed, this is an unchanged side from last week's game. I have faith in every one of you to redeem yourselves after that disappointing performance and result," Adam stated.

Finally, Adam revealed who would be on the substitutes' bench. Shea McNamara, Neil Cole, and Louis Sims were among the options, ready to make an impact if needed. The team nodded in understanding and approval as they prepared to take to the pitch. Once again, they were ready to leave everything out on that pitch and prove themselves as a solid, united team.

As the players made their way onto the pitch to warm up, the roars of their fans greeted them. It was a wave of noise filled with hope and belief, proof they were not alone. Adam surveyed the crowd as his players warmed up. He saw old faces and new ones, all braving the rain and cold for their team. The loud chants had a rhythm all of their own, a relentless drumming that reverberated through the stands and pulsed against his skin. Adam nodded at the fans, acknowledging their support and showing solidarity.

As the warm-up drew to a close, Adam called the team into a huddle. "This is our pitch," Adam rallied, "This is our home, our fight. Look around at those stands behind you, remember who you're fighting for today." The players' faces were taut with concentration, muscles primed for action. Adam could see the fight burning in their eyes. Sweat trickled down their foreheads as they did one final sprint exercise before heading back to the dressing room to ready themselves for kick-off. As they made their way off the pitch and down the tunnel, Adam looked to the sky and said a silent prayer to his Granddad, who he hoped might be listening. Let them find their best today. Let them fight like never before. Let them win this game, Adam asked.

Adam's Granddad was more than just a figure in his life; he was his hero. From when Adam was young, his Granddad had been a constant presence, offering emotional support and wise advice through his tumultuous teenage years. His grandfather's strength and wisdom inspired Adam to become the strong and resilient man he was today. When Adam was seventeen, his Granddad passed away, leaving a void in his heart that would never be filled. Every day since then, memories of his Granddad flooded his mind, a reminder of the incredible bond they shared.

Adam focused on the present moment as he walked down the tunnel toward the dressing room. Before leaving the light of day and entering the tunnel, Adam noticed the stands were full of fans. The supporters huddled under a sea of umbrellas and plastic ponchos, passionately following their Swanford, braving the dreary sky to support their team. Their faces were hopeful as they chanted in unison, drowning out the constant patter of rain on concrete, "Swans, Swans, Swans."

Inside the dressing room, a sense of purpose permeated the air. The players were focused, their faces set with a resolve that Adam knew came from something more than training. Kofi Adams stepped forward, his voice steady, "We're not just playing for ourselves today. We're playing for every single person out there who believes in us. Let's get this done," Kofi declared.

After a moment of acknowledgement and nodding from the players, Shea interjected, "Kofi's right," he said, "We have trained well for this and have worked hard all week. We can send these down today and move massively toward safety ourselves. We will have a full house of fans cheering us on, so let's do it for them."

The team responded in unison with a resounding cheer. Adam watched on and decided that Kofi and Shea's words were all the team talk the players needed before sending them into battle. On cue, the referee's bell sounded, meaning it was time for the teams to meet each other and the match officials in the tunnel, ready to make their way out onto the pitch.

The atmosphere in the tunnel was tense, anxiety hanging like a fog in the tight space. The cold concrete walls of the tunnel felt like ice against the player's shoulders. The chill seeped through the team jackets they wore, reaching the bone and sending shivers straight to their souls. The scent of wet grass and soil lingered in the air, mingling with the sharp tang of sweat and, faintly, the metallic sting of fear. The low murmur of the crowd permeated the walls, sounding like an approaching summer storm. Suddenly, a whistle pierced the quiet anticipation. The officials looked at each other with stern faces, then motioned for the teams to advance. Voices echoed around them, growing louder as they neared the mouth of the tunnel. The roaring sea of spectators flooded their ears, only amplified by hope. Each player's adrenaline surged to overwhelming levels as they approached the middle of the pitch. A quick look was shared among them; no words were necessary; it was time to fight. The players lined up in positions before briefly locking eyes with their rivals, each look filled with a steely resolve.

With a powerful kick to the ball, the game burst into action, igniting a fire within the crowd as they erupted into a symphony of gasps and cheers, their voices blending in a chorus of excitement and adrenaline. They were on the edge of their seats with every pass and move on the pitch, feeling the intensity of the player's passion and skill. The Swanford keeper, Barlow, stood like an impenetrable fortress, easily deflecting each attack from their opponents. With every save, the crowd's applause shook the very foundations of the stadium, echoing through the air like a sonic boom.

As expected, Cliffe were unrelenting and ferocious, driven by desperation to avoid relegation. They charged forward angrily, throwing everything they had at Swanford's defence. Swanford, much to Cliffe's frustration, remained calm and focused, sticking to their planned tactics and formations. They expertly handled the onslaught of Cliffe's attacks before finding openings and making precise passes to advance into the attacking third and attack Cliffe.

Then on the thirty-minute mark, a flawless pass from midfield set up Hart for a stunning shot from just outside the area. The ball soared towards the net like a missile while Adam watched in slow motion, his heart pounding. All of a sudden, the shot hit its target. A collective breath was held within the stadium before exploding into euphoria as the ball hit the back of the net. The crowd's roar was deafening as they celebrated this crucial goal with passion and enthusiasm. The exhilarating energy filled every corner of the stadium, pulsing through veins and making the stadium feel truly alive. 1-0.

Adam's heart swelled with pride and satisfaction as the first half ended. The team had not just played well; they had dominated. But he knew this game was far from over. Each player's face was streaked with sweat and optimism as they made their way off the pitch and into the dressing room at halftime.

The players huddled together in the dressing room, gasping for air and guzzling water as they desperately tried to replenish their exhausted bodies. Adam's booming voice reverberated off the walls, brimming with unwavering confidence as he motivated his team for the second half.

"Listen up, lads. We've been in this exact position before at halftime. We cannot afford to make the same mistake again. We must push harder, stay sharper, and make every second count. This is only the halfway point. We must finish this game with everything we have and get those three crucial points."

Adam looked toward Lambert, who was being substituted off. "Lambert, you're coming off, Shea, you're on. Lead these boys over the line and get these three crucial points in the bag," Adam urged.

As the players emerged from the sanctuary of the dressing room and onto the pitch, they were greeted by a torrential downpour which began to drench them. The once pristine green pitch had transformed into a slippery and muddy battlefield, adding an unpredictable element to the already intense game.

Both teams battled fiercely against each other and Mother Nature's wrath. The atmosphere within the Cliffe camp was charged with electricity, heightened by furious shouts from their coaches pacing up and down the touchline like caged animals; it was do-or-die time for them.

Adam's heart raced on the seventy-minute mark as he watched Shea artfully weave through the opposing defence and launch a daring pass to Ethan Fox. In one swift motion, Ethan sent the ball soaring past the keeper's grasp and into the back of the net. It was a magnificent goal that evoked emotion among the Swanford players, coaches, and fans, who celebrated with pure euphoria, singing and dancing in the unrelenting rain. 2-0.

With two goals secured, Swanford continued to show no mercy in charging forward. Cliffe, however, refused to back down, launching fierce attacks despite being two goals down. Each attack they made was met with an unyielding wall of Swanford defenders who fought with every breath to protect their lead.

As the seconds ticked away, Adam could feel victory within his side's grasp. Then, in a deafening moment, the shrill sound of the final whistle cut through the air, drowning out all other noise. The stadium erupted into a symphony of cheers and screams as a wave of celebration washed over everyone present. In contrast, the defeated Cliffe players lay on the ground in despair, their dreams dashed and tears streaming down their faces. They were relegated.

In the centre of the pitch, the victorious Swanford team gathered in a tight huddle, embracing each other with pure joy and relief. They had triumphed for themselves and all the loyal fans who braved the miserable weather to support them today. Looking up at the dark clouds now breaking apart to reveal glimpses of a deep blue sky and sunshine, Adam couldn't help but imagine his late Granddad's proud face beaming down at him. He could almost hear his voice shouting words of pride and encouragement from above.

As Adam made his way onto the pitch to congratulate his players, Shea rushed towards him with open arms and lifted him off his feet in a crushing bear hug. "We did it! We did it!" he exclaimed triumphantly. Emotions streamed down Adam's face as he released a victorious roar fuelled with relief. This was just the beginning.

As the celebrations started to wane and the players began to leave the pitch and go to the dressing room, Adam stood there momentarily, taking in the chaos around him. The players were still buzzing with energy, reliving critical moments from the match as they trudged towards the dressing room. Adam felt an overwhelming sense of pride in his team. They had fought like warriors out on that pitch, never giving up even when their opponents threw everything they had at them. Adam took a deep breath for a moment, alone with his thoughts. He savoured the sharp, refreshing scent of rain and the earthly aroma of the muddy ground beneath his feet. Despite being drenched from head to toe, he felt invigorated and alive. No amount of water or mud could dampen his spirits after what they had achieved today.

Retracing his steps back into the dressing room, Adam took one last look at the empty pitch. The echo of the cheers and shouts still lingered in the air, but now it was replaced by a serene silence. It was like standing in an ancient cathedral after a grand service had ended, a feeling of reverence and triumph.

The changing room was filled with exhausted players, their adrenaline still pumping as they congratulated each other. Their eyes gleamed, excited and relieved, their chests heaving with each laboured breath. They were already dissecting the match as Adam watched on. They hadn't won because of talent or luck but because they fought together as a united team. This camaraderie was what had propelled them to victory.

Adam's commanding voice broke through their chatter, bringing the room to attention. His words rang out like a battle cry, "Listen up, lads," as each player turned towards him, he could see a newfound respect in their eyes, "That was outstanding, well done," he praised them. "It wasn't easy out there today. They threw everything at us in the first half, but we stayed strong and found a goal to take the lead. The second half was brutal weather-wise, but we stayed focused and found another goal to crush them. This is the new standard for our last two games."

Adam paused, scanning the room before fixing his gaze on Ethan, "And a special shout-out to Ethan for scoring his first-ever goal for the club. Well done, lad." The players' claps and cheers erupted as they congratulated Ethan on his achievement, and Adam shook Ethan's hand with a smile.

"That's all for now, lads. Oh, and the press wants a quick player interview, and I think that should be Kofi today," Adam concluded, "The rest of you, go get a shower and get yourselves off home. Tomorrow is our team bonding day, and I will send out the details in the group message feed later on."

The room burst into another loud cheer before the players entered the shower area. As they headed to freshen up, they patted each other on the back and congratulated one another on a job well done. Adam left the changing room with a weighty sense of exhaustion and triumph.

Next up for Adam was his post-match press conference. The hallway leading to the press room was deserted, apart from the faint echo of his footsteps as they crossed the cold concrete floor. The fluorescent lights hummed above him, casting an eerie glow on the walls. As he made his way through the silent corridors, he stopped at a forgotten water cooler to take a sip and collect his thoughts. Finally, he reached the press room, a frenzy of reporters swarming around like agitated bees. Cameras flashed incessantly, blinding him momentarily. Phones were thrust towards him eagerly, ready to capture his every word.

A reporter from Sports Radio fired off the first question, asking about today's win and the team's chances of avoiding relegation. "Firstly, my thoughts and condolences go out to Cliffe, who have been relegated following today's result," Adam replied stoically, "But we cannot let it distract us. We must stay focused on each game, and I remain confident that our results will be enough come the end of the season." Adam took a deep breath before continuing, "As for today's match, I couldn't be prouder of this team. They trained relentlessly all week, which paid off against a tough opponent in front of a packed stadium. We endured literal and figurative storms, stayed stubborn and persistent and ultimately secured the victory," a smile spreading across his face as he finished speaking.

Next up was the Swanford Daily reporter, who congratulated Adam on the win and asked for his message to the loyal fans who braved treacherous weather to support the team today. "Let me just say what many fans are thinking right now, get in!" Adam declared passionately. "Our supporters were phenomenal today. Many cancelled their plans at the last minute to come out and cheer us on. We are eternally grateful because they were our driving force in securing this win. Let's do it again next Sunday for the season's final game against Wry. For those that were here today, keep an eye on our media feeds in the next day or two. I'll see what I can do about ticket prices to ensure a sold-out crowd for that game, too. Thank you all once again." Adam's gratitude was evident in his voice.

The final question came from a stern UK News reporter asking about rising star Ethan Fox and his potential as a player. "I saw something special in Ethan from the moment I watched him play in an under-twenty-three game," Adam explained, "He has immense talent that will only continue to blossom with age and training. Mark my words, he will go far in this game. Remember the name."

The once bustling room fell silent as the press conference concluded, leaving behind only the low murmur of whispered conversations and the soft shuffle of feet as Adam and the journalists left the room. Adam's day, however, was far from over. After rushing out to his car in the pouring rain to retrieve his training gear to change out of his drenched suit and shirt, he returned to the stadium with a newfound sense of comfort. Next, Adam headed to his makeshift office in the boardroom to analyse the game they had just won.

As soon as he entered the board room, Scott excitedly greeted him. "Yes, bruv, that was quite something," Scott said with a wide grin, "Have you seen the Wry result?" he asked eagerly.

"No," replied Adam with curiosity, "Why?"

Scott's smile grew wider as he explained, "Mate, they could only draw. We've closed the gap to just one point behind them and safety."

Adam's face was filled with a delighted smile. "That's superb. Maybe we can pull this off," Adam declared.

Scott stood up and gave Adam a firm handshake and hug before exclaiming, "I told you, we're warriors. Let's go." With that, Scott left the board room with a petite blonde woman on his arm, saying to her, "Let's go, precious. London, here we come," kissing her on the forehead as they disappeared down the hallway and out of sight.

Once Scott had departed, Adam sank into an executive chair at the head of the table and exhaled deeply. The weight of the afternoon's pressures lifted off his shoulders now that things seemed to be going their way. Deciding to bask in their success for a moment longer, Adam turned on the TV on the wall before him and tuned in to Sports Radio. Riley James's familiar voice filled the room.

"Well, well, well. Against all odds and my better judgement, what an afternoon for Swanford," Riley said with awe in his voice, "I have to say, that was a fiercely competitive performance from Adam Well's team, securing three crucial points that never seemed in doubt throughout the entire ninety minutes. The result also meant relegation for a hapless Cliffe. And then, to top it off, Wry could only manage a draw, which puts the Swans just one point behind them and, therefore, safety. All I can say is, wow. I might have to dust off that five hundred pounds yet," he joked with a hearty laugh. Adam couldn't help but smile confidently at the praise of his team's hard work. But as the evening wore on, Adam focused on his next task, organising a well-deserved team bonding day with a budget of six thousand pounds.

Adam sat at the boardroom table, deep in thought and planning tomorrow's team bonding day, when a knock on the door, followed by Mike storming in, broke his concentration. "Fancy a coaches de-brief over a curry?" Mike asked with a wide grin.

Adam smiled back and replied, "Sure."

Just then, Shea appeared in the doorway. "That's good because we've just ordered what can only be described as a small banquet of Indian food, and it should be in reception in ten minutes," Shea excitedly announced.

As they waited with bated breath and discussed the Wry result, determined smiles played on their faces as Shea eagerly offered out drinks. "Whiskey lads?" Shea asked as Adam hesitated, his mind torn between wanting to fit in with the group and his own personal morals. Adam could almost taste the smooth whiskey on his tongue, but he knew it was a slippery slope he had vowed never to return to.

"I'll take a coke, please, Shea," he replied, trying not to let the slight disappointment on Shea and Mike's faces affect him.

Adam's past demons were calling out to him, tempting him to break his sobriety, but he stood firm in his resolve. A nod of approval from Shea, followed by an understanding smile, indicated that he respected Adam's choice as he handed him an iced glass of coke. "Thank you," Adam said, "I haven't drunk for ten years now."

Despite being ten years sober, Adam still struggled with the temptation to drink. The stress and pressure of his new job only intensified this internal battle. As he watched Shea pour two generous glasses of whisky before pouring his coke, he couldn't help but think of how one drink could make it all go away. But then he remembered that one drink, in his experience, seldom stops at one drink. He had worked hard and with dedication to get to where he was now with his recovery, and the thought of throwing it all away for a fleeting moment of relief made him shudder. He resolved to stick to his soft drink and push through the challenges ahead with a clear mind, the best version of himself.

The playground taunts and difficult teenage years echoed in the hollowness of Adam's skull, relics of a relentless torment that had gouged canyons into his soul. Scars deeper, far more profound, than any that marred his pale flesh. He'd fled, a desperate soul seeking refuge in the shadows of older friends, their rebellion a twisted promise of solace. But the solace turned to ash on his tongue, a bitter reminder of his folly. Two faces, burned into his memory with the searing heat of a branding iron, haunted his every waking moment, lifeless reflections of the path he'd narrowly avoided.

Drugs and alcohol, siren songs promising oblivion, became his new tormentors. A desperate attempt to numb the pain, they instead orchestrated a living hell. Adam's twenties were a nightmarish blur, a self-inflicted purgatory fueled by a gnawing desperation. His mind, once a vibrant canvas, became a battleground, ravaged by the relentless assault. Self-harm became a twisted plea for a different kind of pain, a desperate attempt to find purchase in the ever-shifting sands of his sanity. Suicide attempts, a warped cry for help in the face of an all-consuming darkness.

Then, a flicker. On the precipice of his thirties, staring down the abyss of his own mortality, Adam saw his reflection. A stranger stared back, hollow eyes reflecting a life slowly being bled dry. The taste of dirt in his mouth, a grim communion wafer reminding him of the life he was surrendering.

Recovery wasn't a clean break. It wasn't a hospital stay or a support group meeting. It was a brutal war fought on the jagged terrain of his own being. Each sunset, a hard-won victory against the demons whispering promises of oblivion. Every day clean, a battle fought tooth and nail, a desperate scramble up a treacherous cliff face, the wind howling with the voices of his past. The substances were gone, but the fight raged on. The memories, the urges, they lingered like phantoms, whispering promises of a seductive darkness. Yet, with each shaky breath, Adam refused to surrender. He chose life, a defiant roar against the storm raging within.

As the trio sank into plush leather armchairs, their ears were enveloped in the familiar sound of an old rock song drifting from a radio station on the television. The room was heavy with the musky scent of well-worn football gear and aged whisky, creating a cosy atmosphere. The conversation flowed effortlessly between discussions of team strategies and reminiscing about favourite moments from the afternoon's game.

Suddenly, the receptionist's voice cut through the light-hearted haze, announcing their food had arrived. A flurry of activity ensued as several large bags were brought in, releasing a delicious cloud of cumin, turmeric and cardamom. Adam's mouth watered as he eyed a tray of tikka masala and piles of fluffy naan bread. As the trio dug into their assortment of curries, beef vindaloo, spicy rogan josh, creamy korma, and tangy tikka masala, the room was filled with joy. Sweat dripped from Mike's forehead as he braved through a naan, dripping generously with the vindaloo, while Shea delicately picked at his pilau rice, making a point to avoid the green chillies. Adam found himself lost in a symphony of spice and aroma. He could feel the heat spreading across his tongue and down his throat, igniting a sensation that temporarily made him forget about his churning internal turmoil of moments before. He found peace in dissecting every flavour, the sweetness from the caramelised onions, the sour tanginess of tomatoes, and the fiery heat from the chilli, much like dissecting a football game. As they finished their feast and wiped their lips clean, they revisited today's game in more detail. Each goal was analysed, each pass was commended, and each slip-up was scrutinised. Adam listened to Mike and Shea talk excitedly about tomorrow's team bonding day plans, harnessing the power of the victory over Cliffe to enhance team spirit. He couldn't help but admire their passion.

"So, guys," Adam asked, "Any ideas on what we are going to lay on for tomorrow's team bonding day?" he mused.

Shea's eyes sparkled with excitement as he devoured a mouthful of korma. "What about a paintball match?" he suggested, his voice filled with adrenaline-fuelled enthusiasm.

Mike's brow furrowed in thought as he grabbed another piece of naan and replied through a mouthful, "No, too risky. We can't afford any injuries," but then he brightened up, "How about go-karting?" he suggested.

Shea's grin widened as he nodded enthusiastically, "That's it! Brilliant idea," he declared.

Adam observed them with a small smile, feeling the anticipation building between them. The ideas flowed wildly now, each more daring and intense than the last: a massive inflatable obstacle course, a heart-pumping zip line challenge, and a fierce cooking competition. As they brainstormed, Adam realised that this wasn't just a bonding session but also a chance to toughen up the team for their remaining two matches physically. The competitive fire burned within him, eager to see what challenges they could conquer as a team.

It was Adam, as manager, who suggested the ultimate plan. "Let's gather the lads here in the morning and then take them for a go-karting tournament at a privately hired venue. The winner will receive a trophy and unlimited bragging rights. After that, we'll head to Swanford's top Italian restaurant, Ginos, which we'll have exclusively for ourselves. We'll feast on endless pizzas and sides, with a maximum of three drinks each to keep us in line for training the following morning. Any leftover funds from the budget can go towards our end-of-season dinner bar tab."

A moment of intense silence passed before Mike and Shea exchanged glances and nodded in agreement. "I love it," Mike declared, "It's perfect."

Adam smiled smugly, knowing he had hit the jackpot. "Alright then," he said confidently, "Shea, can you handle booking the go-karting venue and Ginos, as well as arranging the food and trophy? We need this to be flawless."

Shea nodded eagerly, mentally mapping out his tasks, "Consider it done, boss."

"Mike," Adam asked, "Can you please relay the message to the players to meet here at noon tomorrow?"

"Sure, I will do it straight away," Mike replied.

As the meeting ended, Adam's eyes swept over the remnants of their curry feast, empty pots and greasy naans before locking focus with Shea and Mike. With a fierce determination in his voice, he lifted his glass of coke, signalling for them to do the same. "To us," he proclaimed, his voice quivering with emotion, "To keeping Swanford up." The words were charged with purpose as the three clinked their glasses together and downed their drinks.

18

Team Bonding Day

Adam arrived at the club early the next morning, eager to start the team bonding day at half past eleven. As he sat outside reception, his eyes were drawn to the luxurious stretch limousines parked before him. The sleek black exterior and tinted windows exuded an air of extravagance. One by one, the players began to arrive in their luxury cars, adding to the already impressive lineup in the car park. Each player stepped out of their vehicle, dressed in designer clothes, radiating confidence and excitement for the day ahead.

As Adam watched them gather, it was clear that this would be a memorable day. After all the players had arrived, they curiously eyed the limousines before Adam revealed their first stop, a go-karting venue where something special had been arranged. The players exchanged looks of excitement and laughter as they piled into their designated limousines, ready for the adventure ahead.

The luxurious vehicles were parked in a row, glistening in the warm sun like jewels waiting to be discovered. As the players buckled up, the roar of the engines filled the air with a tangible current of excitement. It was a powerful symphony that synchronised with everyone's racing heartbeats. Despite their size, the vehicles moved with surprising grace as they approached the go-karting venue. Inside, there was a constant hum of conversation punctuated by laughter as the players let loose and bonded over this unconventional outing away from the pitch. In the rearview mirror, Adam watched them with a slight smile, grateful to see his team relax and bond as comrades in arms rather than fierce competitors.

As the sun peaked in the sky, the team arrived at their destination, a sprawling go-karting circuit on the edge of town, hidden away from curious eyes. As they piled out of the limousines, their gaze swept over the vast expanse before them, trying to decipher what challenges awaited them.

Adam cleared his throat, commanding attention. "Today, lads, we will have a full squad knockout competition. We have this place all to ourselves, and in a moment, Mike and I will randomly draw out the first races to see who will face off against each other. The winner of each race will proceed to the next stage until, eventually, we are left with two finalists. The ultimate victor will not only receive this striking trophy," he gestured towards a large silver cup adorned with a metal go-kart being held up by Mike, "But also bragging rights among you all."

A wave of excitement and competitiveness washed over the players as Adam continued, "Each race leading up to the semi-finals will consist of three laps. The semi-finals will be five laps, and the final will be ten laps. Without further ado, let's get on with the draw," his words met with a chorus of cheers.

Adam and Mike stepped forward, their hands trembling as they reached for the large glass bowl filled with slips of paper. The team's eyes were fixed on them, breaths held in suspense as they waited for their names to be drawn out. With a flick of his wrist, Adam began to shuffle the slips, each bearing the name of a player, each slip containing the fate of the opening races. As Adam pulled out each slip, the tension grew thicker, names announced in pairs like a ticking time bomb waiting to explode. When he drew Hart against Cole, the cheers erupted into a deafening roar, two titans, new and old, ready to clash in a battle for glory.

"Remember Wembley," Cole said, pointing toward Hart, "Ding, ding round two, old timer," he joked.

Against the blazing sun, the go-karting circuit loomed like a fiery inferno, its asphalt tracks radiating heat that seared through the air. The stench of burnt rubber and hot oil permeated every breath, mixing with the adrenaline-fuelled scent of fresh tarmac. Like gladiators ready to spill blood, the contestants were finally given the signal to storm onto the track and inspect their deadly machines. The races commenced with engines revving and tyres screeching as the players strapped themselves into their karts, preparing for a high-speed battle.

Round after round, each heat was a fierce struggle for victory. Jubilant winners basked in their triumphs while defeated competitors swallowed their pride and cheered on their teammates. The atmosphere pulsed with electric energy as onlookers roared in support, swept up in the intense competition unfolding before them.

The sun began to lower, casting an eerie glow over the racetrack as the competition progressed and the final race approached. The air was thick with tension and the sound of roaring engines. This was the ultimate test of speed and skill to determine who was the best.

The final came, with its competitors being Neil Cole and Kofi Adams.

With every muscle tensed and ready, Neil and Kofi revved their engines, their eyes fixed on the track ahead like predators eyeing their prey. Then, with a sharp downward movement from Adam's arm, they were off. The karts screeched against the track as they accelerated, leaving behind trails of smoke and tyre marks. The crowd of watching players fell into a hush, wholly engrossed in the intense battle unfolding before them. Lap after lap, Neil and Kofi pushed themselves to their limits, navigating sharp turns and blazing down straights at breakneck speeds. Adam could see the fierce determination in both of their faces as they battled for first place. As they zoomed past the spectators' stand, Adam couldn't help but be caught up in the excitement of it all.

It all came down to the last lap. Both racers were neck and neck, each refusing to give up even an inch. As they approached the final corner before the home stretch, Neil made a bold move to overtake Kofi, but Kofi wasn't about to let him pass that easily. With expert precision, he blocked Neil's path and maintained his lead. Adam watched the two fight for victory in those last few seconds; he could see Kofi's unwavering resolve through his helmet visor. At the same time, Neil's face was contorted with fierce concentration. Then, in a burst of speed and adrenaline, Kofi crossed the finish line first, claiming the title of champion. The squad erupted into a frenzy of cheers and applause, their voices ringing out in thunderous praise for both racers. Kofi threw his hands up in triumph, a wide grin spreading across his face as he revelled in his hard-earned victory.

As the two go-karts screeched to a halt at the finish line, Kofi was lifted out of his kart and greeted by a roaring crowd of ecstatic teammates. Meanwhile, Neil trudged off his kart with defeat etched on his face, slowly approaching Kofi. Neil begrudgingly shook Kofi's hand before muttering, "Fair play mate, congrats."

Mike presented Kofi with the exquisite trophy, which he hoisted high above his head in triumph. The entire squad erupted into a loud chant of "Kofi, Kofi, Kofi." Their voices reverberated through the air for what seemed like an eternity, solidifying Kofi's victory as one of epic proportions. Adam's voice cut through the noise as the victorious cheers faded into the background.

"I know you're probably famished and thirsty after that intense afternoon. Hurry up and load into the limos, we're heading to Ginos," Adam declared as the players erupted into another round of raucous cheers and quickly piled into their designated vehicles, leaving the go-karting track behind.

The team's limos rolled to a stop in front of Ginos, the low light from the windows casting a warm glow on their shiny bodywork. The inviting aroma of sizzling pizza wafted out to greet the team, making their mouths water and stomachs rumble. As they stepped onto the cracked pavement, their hearts still racing from their adrenaline-fuelled afternoon, they were led into the restaurant by Kofi, who was pridefully holding his trophy high above his head, his face beaming with a wide grin.

Upon entering the restaurant, the smell of fresh dough, tangy tomato sauce, and melted cheese filled the air, creating a welcoming atmosphere for the team. Upon arrival, the maitre d' showed them three long tables set up exclusively for their group, adorned with white tablecloths and glittering silverware. The walls echoed with the team's boisterous laughter and animated chatter, filling the space with excitement and camaraderie. As the players took their seats at the tables, servers scurried around, bringing in bottles of wine, beer pitchers, and soft drinks trays. Before anyone could reach for a drink, Adam raised his hand to silence them.

"Lads," he exclaimed, "Tonight, all the pizzas and sides you can eat are coming out of your kitty. We also have beers, wines, and soft drinks available, all paid for. However, I must ask that we limit ourselves to three drinks only, as we have training tomorrow morning and an important game on Wednesday to prepare for."

Adam's words were met with nods of understanding from the team. As Adam finished speaking, the servers began to bring out baskets of hot garlic bread, filling the room with a mouth-watering aroma that elicited approving noises from everyone's hungry stomachs. As they waited for the pizzas to arrive, Kofi couldn't shake off the images of the final race that played on a loop in his mind. He glanced over at Neil, who was deep in conversation with Barlow on the other side of the table. Despite losing the race, Neil's attitude exuded positivity and sportsmanship, putting camaraderie above competition. Kofi raised his glass with a small smile towards him in admiration and support. The sound of sizzling pizzas being placed on the table interrupted his reverie.

Plates piled high with thin-crust pizzas continuously emerged from the kitchen, their surfaces glistening with melted cheese and piled high with an array of toppings. The atmosphere in Ginos transformed into a buzzing energy as everyone eagerly dug into their food. Adam surveyed his team, all grinning widely and filled with merriment as laughter resounded. This team was united in spirit, relaxed and confident as they prepared for the battle. As the night dragged on, the voices grew louder and more intense, a chaotic symphony drowning out the distant soft rock music playing from the restaurant's speakers.

As the night drew to a close, and it was hometime, the players shuffled out of the restaurant to make their way into the night after a memorable and enjoyable day. The limos had long been abandoned, and taxis were now the mode of transportation for the players.

19

Monday 22nd April

As the early Monday morning rays of sunshine peaked over the horizon, Adam's car pulled into the training ground car park. As he walked to his office, the scent of freshly cut grass and damp earth filled his nostrils. With a flick of his wrist, he flipped on the lights and settled into his leather chair behind his desk. He glanced at the clock on the wall; it was quarter past eight, time for the start of another busy day. Adam took a moment to sip a coffee, awaiting the arrival of Mike and Shea, his trusted coaching team, for their daily pre-training briefing.

The distant sound of footsteps echoed down the long, empty hallway approaching Adam's office, causing Adam to sit abruptly in his chair. Then, with a hearty laugh that could only belong to Mike, the door swung open, and the two coaches burst into the room. Unlike Mike's towering frame, Shea's nimble figure seemed to fly through the doorway. But despite their physical differences, their passion and enthusiasm for the game were equally infectious.

"Morning, boss," Shea greeted with a wide grin. His gaze immediately fell on the various strategies and notes scattered across Adam's desk. Shea picked up one of the papers, his brows furrowing in concentration as he examined it.

Meanwhile, Mike collapsed onto one of the chairs opposite Adam's desk. "Adam, mate, you're earlier than us today," Mike remarked jokingly, his voice filling the relatively small office.

Adam leaned back in his seat, a smug smile on his lips, "I like to be prepared," he replied confidently as he watched Shea critically analyse his proposed training plans.

A deafening silence descended upon the room, each coach consumed by their racing thoughts as they took desperate gulps of bitter coffee they had hastily snatched on their way to the meeting. Blinding rays of sunlight pierced through the blinds, casting sinister shadows across the floor like bars in a prison cell. Beyond the walls, the distant sound of whistles and raucous laughter echoed from the training ground canteen, starkly contrasting the office's atmosphere of deep contemplation. The coaches felt the pressure of the gruelling challenge that awaited them over the next six days, the season's final two games, to survive or not to survive. Arguably the most challenging six days of their young coaching careers.

Adam's abrupt question broke the silence, "South Swanshea away on Wednesday night, thoughts?" he asked.

Mike's gaze flickered from Shea to Adam as he responded grimly, "Tricky. In truth, we probably couldn't ask for a worse fixture in our position, but…"

Before Mike could finish his sentence, Shea interjected with urgency, "After this weekend's results, they only need one more win to secure European football next season, and this is their last home game at the ever-intimidating Cave Stadium, which will be packed to the rafters with a carnival atmosphere ready to cheer them on."

"Exactly," Mike added, "and to make matters worse, they are unbeaten in seven, and we haven't beaten them in twelve attempts now."

After digesting this information, Adam replied, "Let's be the party poopers then! Can we do it? Will we be able to?" he asked.

Mike hesitated before responding with a dose of reality, "I hate to say it, Adam, but I'm not sure we can. They look too strong for us and most of the division right now."

Adam, refusing to accept defeat, replied, "Oh, balls to that! It's just their eleven footballers on Wednesday night versus our eleven footballers. There has to be a way. We can't afford to roll over and be beaten before a ball is even kicked!"

Mike and Shea exchanged sceptical glances before Adam continued, "Shea, your assignment for today is an hour of light training followed by scouting South Swanshea's last two games for weak points and intel. Got it?" Shea nodded in agreement.

Turning his attention to Mike, Adam gave his instructions for training, "Mike, diamond passing formations with successful completions. Tight defence, goals and A-grade shooting. Can you relay that to your team of coaches and get to work, please?" Mike acknowledged Adam with a quick nod before asking if there was anything else.

"That's all. Thanks, guys. Let's get to work. I'll see you both back here at four o'clock to discuss your findings and how we'll approach the game Wednesday evening," Adam said, nodding towards Shea and Mike.

As the meeting ended, the two coaches left as swiftly as they had arrived, their minds racing with strategies and plans. Adam watched them go, then leaned back in his chair, allowing himself a moment's reprieve. His gaze drifted to the framed photographs lining his office walls, moments of victory and celebration from yesteryear, each a testament to the blood, sweat and tears shed on their journey to glory. But now, facing their most formidable opponent yet, those moments seemed like distant memories. As he sifted through the pile of notes and stats strewn across his desk, he could feel the weight of the coming week pressing down on him. The aroma of stale coffee lingered as Adam's fingers traced over his haphazard notes and diagrams, his mind trying to decipher a possible path to victory and safety.

With a deep breath, Adam grabbed his training jacket and stepped out into the crisp morning air. His heavy boots crunching against gravel provided a soundtrack to his walk, intermingling with the earthly scent of freshly cut grass as he walked across the training ground towards the team.

"Morning, lads," Adam began, addressing the players before training started, with a fire in his eyes, "We have a tough match against South Swanshea this Wednesday evening. They may seem like giants to you now," he continued, locking eyes with each player, "But every giant has its weak spot." A sense of belief rippled through the team at his words, "In this game, it's not about the names of their players or their physical strength. It's about belief and fight," Adam declared, his voice growing louder and more passionate. The players exchanged glances and nods, fuelled by Adam's David and Goliath analogy.

"Over the coming hours me, Mike and Shea will analyse every move they make, every tactic they employ," Adam stated firmly, gesturing to himself and the other coaches, "With that knowledge, we will devise a masterplan to route our way to victory. Our opponents may be bigger or faster, but remember, brain always conquers brawn."

The team nodded in agreement, a newfound spark igniting in their eyes. "Train hard, keep the right mindset, and trust in us coaches," Adam concluded with unwavering confidence, "I know we can pull this off."

Just then, Adam was interrupted by the vibrating ring of his phone. He glanced at the screen; it was a withheld number. "I best take this, lads," he said, "As you were, blood, sweat, and tears, please, nothing less will do," he said before pressing answer on his phone and strolling away from the group.

The players exchanged glances as Adam's voice trailed off into the distance before bursting into action. The football pitch became a bloody battlefield, and each drill was a crucial battle towards the upcoming war. The air was filled with the stench of sweat and fear, punctuated by shouts of encouragement and grunts of exertion.

Meanwhile, Adam retreated towards his office, his heart racing as he pressed the phone to his ear. His expression was grave as he listened intently to the voice on the other end.

"Adam," the voice began, urgency pulsing through every word, "This is Shane Finn, head of police. We met the other day about the bullet in the post," he explained.

"Yes, I remember," Adam replied, trying to steady his racing thoughts, "How are you?" he asked.

"All good, thanks, Adam," Shane said before dropping a bombshell, "I'm calling because we have an update on the case. We made an arrest last night."

Adam's heart dropped into his stomach as he processed the news, "Oh, ok. Well, that's a good thing, right?" he managed to choke out.

"Well, yes and no, really," Shane replied, "At this stage, we wouldn't usually disclose the suspect's identity since we only have suspicion upon which to question them. Certainly not enough evidence to get a charge against them from the CPS, the crown prosecution service. However, I felt it necessary to bring it to your attention as it involves a member of the club."

Adam's heart was being ripped apart as he faced the harsh reality that this could be someone from within their ranks, somebody very close to home. Gathering himself momentarily, he forced a weak reply, "Oh, right, ok." Before he could speak further, Mr. Finn continued with even more alarming information.

"It was Michael Knight," Shane announced heavily, "After examining the ongoing conflict between the two of you and his history of violent behaviour, we have reason to believe that he may have been behind the threat, whether directly or indirectly. I'm sorry."

The gravity of the situation hit Adam like a ton of bricks, and he stammered out a response, "Ok, thank you for letting me know. I appreciate it."

Shane's voice turned sombre as he replied, "No worries. I just thought you should be aware so you can handle it within the club. Meanwhile, we will proceed with our investigation and actions."

The call ended, leaving Adam grappling with the terrifying realisation that the enemy could lay closer to home than imagined and that this verbal disagreement with Michael might be something altogether more sinister.

Michael Knight was a notorious figure in the game, feared both on and off the pitch. His past was riddled with dark secrets and infamous incidents. He was a ruthless enforcer on the pitch, known for his bone-crunching tackles and fiery confrontations. He thrived on provoking opponents and taunting opposition fans, earning him one of the most abysmal disciplinary records in the sport. He had served numerous lengthy FA suspensions, including a twelve-month ban for deliberately shattering an opponent's leg in three places, causing irreversible damage and ultimately ending the player's career.

Michael's life off the pitch was also a chaotic and tumultuous rollercoaster, filled with reckless decisions and destructive behaviour. At the height of his career, representing his country regularly and revered by fans, one fateful night out turned into a brutal brawl in a nightclub. In a fit of anger, Michael unleashed a flurry of blows on an innocent man, shattering his eye socket and jaw, an assault so vicious that it landed Michael a fifteen-month prison sentence. Prison was no refuge for this football star. His fame made him a target for violence, and he refused to back down from any fight, leading to repeated extensions of his sentence due to his unruly behaviour.

After two long years behind bars, Michael was finally released. His return to the game would be challenging. He spent a gruelling season with a local semi-pro club to regain his strength and stamina, determined to make a comeback.

With his ruthlessly driven agent, Mr Jenkyn-Jones, by his side, Michael embarked on a desperate crusade to find a new football club and earn a professional contract. Despite facing countless rejections and doubts about his abilities, Michael refused to relinquish his dream of playing at the highest level of English football again.

After enduring multiple humiliating trial periods at different clubs, Mark Booth took a chance on the now twenty-five-year-old Michael, offering him a contract at Swanford despite his three-year absence from the professional game. The decision was met with harsh criticism and intense scrutiny, but Mark saw potential in Michael that others couldn't. He knew it was a gamble that could blow up in their faces, but he was confident he could tame the beast, unleash the raw talent within Michael and make him a star once again. Mark truly believed that Swanford could still get Michael's best years ahead.

In recent years, Michael's life off the field had taken a drastic turn for the better, aside from an incident of speeding on a motorway, which nearly resulted in him having his license revoked before, ultimately, it was, for eighteen months following a driving under the influence charge. These charges were now in the past as Michael found love and family. Five years ago, Michael met a loving woman named Gemma, who helped him find inner peace and settle down. After a year of dating and becoming inseparable, they married. Michael became a devoted father for the first time a year later, going on to have another child a year after that.

After being rehabilitated in prison, Michael emerged as a model citizen, aside from the driving incidents, determined to make up for his past mistakes. His transformation was remarkable, catching the attention of his team captain at the time, David Llewyn. Despite some scepticism, David saw potential in Michael and handed him his captain's armband when he retired two years ago. This was a decision fully endorsed by Mark as the team's manager. The role suited Michael perfectly, and he excelled at it, quickly earning the respect and admiration of his teammates. His behaviour had improved tremendously on the pitch, setting an example for the entire team. Michael's newfound dedication and leadership drove the team to success on and off the pitch.

Adam's heart raced as he read the text messages on his phone that he'd received a few days earlier from Michael's agent, scolding him, unhappy with how his client was being treated. Adam was all too aware of the seemingly irreconcilable tension between him and Michael but never could have imagined this. His hand trembled as the device slipped from his grasp and clattered to the ground. A wave of dread had washed over him, but a small part of him couldn't help but wonder if there was any truth to these accusations. How well did he really know Michael? Adam's mind warred with conflicting emotions as he tried to process the implications of the phone call he had just taken.

Adam inhaled deeply, attempting to calm his racing heart. He needed absolute clarity of mind now more than ever. The stakes were too high for any distractions, especially with the crucial game on Wednesday just on the horizon. It was only a matter of time before the story could be leaked to the press or an enraged Michael confronted him again. Gazing out his office window, he saw the lively training pitch below, where his players trained tirelessly. Brimming with passion and hope, the sight of their flushed faces suddenly took on a whole new significance. Doubt crept into Adam's thoughts as he observed them. Who could he truly trust? Were there others involved in this scandal? As club captain, Michael undoubtedly had his allies within the team. The seemingly innocent camaraderie among his players now seemed tainted with potential hidden motives.

As the chaos in his mind settled, Adam took a moment to collect himself and take a sip of now-cold coffee. It dawned on Adam that he needed to make a conference call with Scott and Sarah to discuss the next steps. He reached for the phone, dialling Scott's number first. The line rang twice before Scott's energetic voice answered. "Easy, bruv, you good?" Scott asked.

Despite his inner turmoil, Adam kept his voice steady as he explained the situation to Scott. After putting Scott on hold, Adam dialled Sarah's number. The call connected after a few rings, and Sarah's clear voice echoed through the speaker, greeting Adam as if she was fully expecting his call. "Sarah, please, can you join Scott and me on a conference call?" he asked.

"Sure, no worries," Sarah replied.

Once Adam had Scott and Sarah on a three-way conference call, his voice shook as he recounted every chilling detail of his conversation with Shane Finn. Absorbing the gravity of the situation, Scott replied, "This is serious," his voice low and tense, "We need to discuss this fully. I'll be at the club at one o'clock for a meeting with accounts. I'll push that meeting back so we can meet at one. Can you both make it for the meeting?" he asked.

Adam and Sarah agreed in unison before Scott replied, "Good, see you there." Before ending the call, Scott quickly added, "Sarah, can you call Mr. Finn? We need him or one of his team to be in attendance also."

Sarah instantly agreed, "Sure, I'll get onto it now."

After ending the call, Adam took another deep breath, combatting the knot of worry tied tightly in his stomach. He looked once more at his team through the office window. They were still training hard, unaware of the storm brewing off the pitch. A wave of protectiveness surged through him. They were his boys, he thought. They were fighters and deserved nothing less than a safe environment where they could focus solely on doing what they loved.

With a newfound resolve, Adam paced his office, formulating an action plan. He'd take this storm head-on and not let it derail their collective focus from the imminent big game. The club's safety was his responsibility, and he wasn't about to let this incident shatter their resolve. Stepping out of his office, Adam walked towards the training pitch. His boys were scattered across the green, their wind-tousled hair glistening under the sunlight. For the next couple of hours, Adam let go of the weight of his dire situation and immersed himself fully in the training session. He joined in with the lads, feeling a sense of unity and camaraderie amid their shared struggles. In that moment, they were not just a group of individual players but a team fighting for the future of their club, troops in the trenches at war together.

As the morning session drew to a close and the players began to make their way off the pitch for a lunch break, Adam motioned for Mike and Shea to walk behind the pack. He had something important he wanted to discuss with them. Without missing a beat, the pair fell back, their conversation stalling as curiosity flared in their eyes. Adam took a deep breath before looking at them. "Shea, Mike," he began, his tone serious, "There's something we need to discuss." Adam's voice was urgent and laced with a tinge of fear as he began to explain the latest developments with his death threat case. Mike and Shea could see the gravity of his words etched on his face, and they exchanged a worried glance before focusing their attention back on him.

Without hesitation, Adam explained what he had learned from Shane Finn about Michael's potential schemes. The information hit them like a freight train, causing Mike's brow to furrow angrily and Shea's eyes to harden. A heavy silence followed as they tried to process the enormity of the situation. Finally, after a few moments, Shea broke the silence with a sharp, "Oh feck, are you ok?" he asked.

Meanwhile, Mike's tense jaw trembled as he asked, "Who else knows?"

"Just Scott and Sarah," Adam replied evenly before assertively stating, "And it stays that way. We can't let this tear apart our team right before Wednesday's game. We need to handle this quietly." Shea and Mike nodded in agreement. Adam was grateful for their unwavering support; he knew he had made the right choice in picking them as his closest allies. Their loyalty and practicality were precisely what this situation required. "Anyway," Adam continued, his tone now brisk and businesslike, "I have to head up to the ground for a meeting with Scott, Sarah and Mr. Finn to figure out how we will handle this. Please make sure this afternoon's training session goes as planned, and I'll update you when I return for our meeting, which will now be pushed back to five o'clock." Mike and Shea both nodded solemnly, understanding the weight of this situation.

Shortly after, Adam got into his car, departed the training ground, and headed to the stadium. While driving on the familiar small route of internal campus roads, Adam's mind was a whirlwind of thoughts before arriving at the stadium a few minutes later. Adam parked his car and went to the boardroom overlooking the empty stadium. Anxiety knotted in his stomach, but he pushed it down. This was not a time for nerves.

Inside the board room, Adam was greeted by Mr Finn, Scott and Sarah, who were already waiting for him; each sat around the large wooden table, their faces etched with varying degrees of concern. Upon seeing Adam, Mr. Finn stood up, offering a firm handshake, to which Adam responded in kind. Mr Finn then sat back down at one end of the table whilst Scott sat across from Sarah on the side of the table. Adam proceeded to sit in the other seat at the head of the table, facing Mr Finn.

Sarah exuded a calm and collected presence as she scanned through a mound of paperwork and asked, "Adam, are you sure it's not just best to take this threat seriously and walk away? Somethings are just more important than football, and I'm sure everyone would understand your decision," she remarked.

Adam instantly replied without hesitation, "These bullies won't beat me. I'm seeing this through," his tone adamant and stubborn. Adam then opened the meeting, "Mr Finn, I know you explained the situation on the phone, but can you please explain the latest developments to me again in front of Sarah and Scott?" he asked.

"Yes, sure," Mr Finn replied, "Last night at exactly eight pm, we arrested Mr Michael Knight contrary to the offences against the person act of 1861, in relation to the death threat and bullet you received to your home address, Adam. We held Michael under caution for questioning, upon which, with lack of sufficient evidence for the crown prosecution service to press a charge at this time, we let Mr Knight go pending further investigation. Upon executing a warrant to search his home address, we found no evidence, vis-a-vis other bullets or a gun, with which to incriminate him," Mr Finn explained.

After absorbing and understanding the information, Sarah replied, "Ok, thank you," she continued, "So how would you suggest we proceed?"

"Well," said Mr Finn, "This is a somewhat difficult and unusual situation you find yourselves in. Usually, we would ask that victims and potential suspects be kept well apart. However, Mr Knight is one of the club's players who requires daily training. If this were a normal workplace, the employer might suspend the suspect while investigating the matter."

Scott's face, consumed in thought, turned to Adam, "Ad, do you feel safe? Do you think it could have been him?" he asked.

"I'd like to think not," Adam replied, "It's one thing to have a verbal conflict like Michael and I have, but this is a different level and somewhat extreme in context. I do not know what to think."

Turning to Sarah, Adam asked, "Sarah, what are your thoughts?"

"It seems like a closed case to me, to be honest. Michael has a dogged history, after all. However, we risk more trouble if we suspend Michael, given that this is his job, and being unable to train would have a major impact on him. Also, this country is meant to exercise an attitude of innocent until proven guilty, something that, by the sounds of it, we are a long way from being the case," she said.

An hour into the meeting, the four of them were well into dissecting every angle and every possible consequence that could arise from

Michael's accused actions and their potential reactions to them. Mr Finn's deep voice cut through the silence as he proposed an action plan. Scott and Sarah shared their thoughts, contributing valuable insights to the discussion.

Another hour passed in the blink of an eye before Scott declared, "Ok, I think we've covered all options. That said, there is only one victim here, and only he can decide how safe he feels and how he wants to proceed as manager of this football club. Adam, what are you saying?" he asked.

After a few moments, Adam replied, "Considering everything and the lack of evidence so far, I don't wish to suspend Michael at this time. I would ask that he be instructed to steer clear of me and continue to train with the under-twenty-three squad. I find this whole situation saddening. Coming into the role, I had envisaged Michael being a key part of my plans, a star player leading this club to safety, and therefore, from my point of view, I wish this whole situation with him wasn't so," he explained.

As the clock neared four pm, Adam ended the meeting, promising to keep everyone updated on any further developments. Mr Finn also made a promise to leave no stone unturned in catching the individual responsible for the death threat. Despite the seriousness of the situation, there was a shared sense of unity among them, and they were all determined to protect their club from those who wished it harm. The four agreed on an immediate course of action: a discreet investigation into Michael's actions by the police while maintaining utmost confidentiality within the team.

Driving back to the training ground, Adam mulled over everything that had happened during the day. The drive was a silent, short one, but his thoughts were anything but. Images of the meeting, Michael Knight's mugshot, and the bullet were all muddled in his mind, mingling with strategy plans and player profiles for the upcoming game.

As Adam's car rolled into the now deserted car park of the training ground, the glow of the floodlights illuminating the pitch was a comforting sight. Adam's mind turned to the forthcoming meeting and how he and his coaches would plan to get the better of South Swanshea in just forty-eight hours time, in what felt like a sink-or-swim situation of a match. The training ground was empty, the usual hum and bustle of players, coaches, and staff replaced by a disturbing silence. Adam stepped out of the car and took a deep breath, the cold air filling his lungs. He stood there for a moment, staring at the training ground building. This was his safe space, where his mind focused entirely on the game he loved, untouched by external worries. Passing through the entrance to the training complex, he walked towards his office. He could see Mike and Shea waiting for him through the glass panel in the door.

Shea looked up as Adam entered the office and nodded, his face serious but composed, "We've got a mountain to climb, boss," he said.

Adam smiled wryly at Shea's words, understatement of the century, he thought to himself, before replying, "The mountain is steep," he admitted, "But not insurmountable."

Adam decided to get straight down to business. "Shea, lay it on us. What did you find out?" he asked.

Shea sighed, then opened his laptop, his fingers dancing on the keyboard in a well-practised routine.

"Well, boss," Shea started, his voice betraying a hint of optimism that struggled to make itself heard amidst the seriousness of the situation, "Their defence is good, they play tight," Shea began, "They've had the lowest number of goals against them in the league this season, and they know how to protect their goal. Fear not though, I think I've discovered a hole." Shea continued, "In their game at the weekend, their star defender Jamie Cross was stretchered off with a painful-looking injury. I've made some calls, and it sounds like he suffered a broken ankle, so his season is over. I've looked at their backup players to come in for him, and they only have inexperienced kids. Therefore, this is now a weak spot for them," he declared.

After a pause of silence, Mike chimed in; his eyes locked onto the screen as he pointed out a midfielder, letting a ball slip through his legs. "Their midfield is another major weak spot, and their wingers are slow on transitions," Mike explained.

"Yes, I noticed that," Adam mused, squinting at the footage. His mind was racing, analysing patterns, finding loopholes and weak points. Looking at Mike and Shea again, he felt hope shining amidst the looming pressure. It was no small task ahead; beating South Swanshea required more than mere tactics. It needed something more profound. "We're going to need every bit of courage and determination we've got," Adam said slowly, his voice thick with resolution, "More than that, we're going to need to believe we can do it," he paused, looking between his two key allies, "Because we can."

The room fell silent for a moment before Mike broke it with a firm nod, "We can and we will," his tone filled with conviction, lifting Adam's spirits.

Adam nodded passionately at Mike and Shea before declaring, "We write our own destiny."

Adam wrapped up the meeting by asking, "So you're both clear on how we need to train tomorrow?"

Mike, nodding at him, replied, "Yes, of course."

"Perfect," Adam replied, "Get yourselves off then. Have a good evening, and I'll see you in the morning."

Mike and Shea rose from their seats, and Shea couldn't help but glance back at the laptop screen one last time before leaving. His analytical mind replayed the footage endlessly. On the other hand, Mike was already halfway out the door, his thoughts filled with formations and strategy. As Adam watched them leave, he couldn't help but feel that the task ahead was gigantic and almost arduous, but he felt fortified by their conviction as coaches and players. He knew they had what it would take to rise to the occasion. They were not just professionals; they were warriors.

As the room's quietness sank in and the door clicked shut behind Mike, Adam sat in his chair, deep in thought. He flicked through some more video clips hesitantly. His eyes were alert, scanning for patterns and potential tactics they could use against South Swanshea. He started devising a plan based on what he knew of South Swanshea's gameplay and their present situation regarding Cross's injury. Involuntarily, a smile tugged at the corner of his mouth as an idea began to form. It was audacious yet simple, a series of quick manoeuvres focusing on their opponent's weak midfield and slow wingers. Adam's mind raced with schemes and permutations as he refined his idea. Hours later, exhaustingly satisfied, Adam finally shut down the laptop and leaned back in his chair. He took a moment to relax before leaving his office to head home, to possible danger, for the night.

A sudden knock at the office door shattered the stillness. Adam's heart raced as he shouted, "Come in!" thinking that it would be the security guard coming to force him out of the building as it was eight pm. Instead, a massive figure loomed into the room, standing at six feet with broad shoulders and a thick beard covering his face. It was Michael Knight, and the air around him crackled with unease as he slowly approached Adam. Fear and anxiety washed over Adam as he waited for Knight's purpose in being here and stood in his office, following the events of the past twenty-four hours. Each step Michael took toward sitting opposite Adam was infused with tension, like a ticking time bomb waiting to go off.

Adam's hand trembled as he reached for his phone, fear gripping him like a vice. Before he could even unlock his phone to call for help, Michael's voice cut through the silence like a razor blade, "Don't do it," Michael pleaded desperately, his eyes darting to the phone in Adam's hand, "I'm not here to hurt you. I swear, you're not in danger," he reassured Adam with wild urgency. "I just need to talk to you, please? For the sake of our club?" Michael's thick Geordie accent sent chills down Adam's spine.

Slowly, Adam stepped back and lowered his hand, gesturing for Michael to sit at his desk. Adam felt an intense alert as he waited for Michael to speak.

Michael's eyes glimmered with a dangerous intensity in the dimly lit room, his hands trembling with anticipation as he sat. Adam couldn't tear his gaze away, suddenly consumed with curiosity and a gnawing sense of panic. Adam leaned forward, fingers clenching onto his desk, desperately trying to steady his nerves as his mind raced with fearful speculations. Adam's cold stare pierced through Michael as he began to speak. "Ok, Michael, I'm listening," he said.

Michael hesitated, his eyes wandering to the dark corner of the room to the right of Adam's desk. Finally, he spoke, desperation evident in his voice. "It wasn't me," he pleaded.

Adam remained unmoved, his expression unchanged. "That's exactly what a guilty man would say," he replied, disappointment and anger simmering beneath the surface.

With a look of defeat, Michael stared back at Adam before pleading, "I swear on my children's lives, it wasn't me." Both men locked eyes, each daring the other to make a move. Michael's voice trembled as he continued, his words dripping with desperation, "I'm putting everything on the line for you here," he said, his hands shaking, "Just give me this one chance to explain, please," he asked.

Adam's jaw clenched as he braced himself for what was to come next, "Fine," Adam replied through gritted teeth, "Explain it to me."

Michael put his hands on his lap, hidden from Adam's view, as he leaned back in his chair. His voice shook as he spoke, apologising for his past behaviour and regretting the conflict he had caused. "I was grieving," Michael explained, his eyes filled with sorrow, "Mark Booth was like a father to me. I owe everything that I am today to him for taking a chance on me, and I lashed out in my pain and anger at his dismissal. It wasn't your fault, and I shouldn't have taken it out on you. For that, I'm sorry."

Adam nodded sympathetically as Michael continued, his voice cracking with emotion, "I don't blame you for taking the job. Anyone would want to be part of this great club. It's not your fault Scott appointed you, and it's up to the players and myself to respect his decision and be professional for the fans and the club." Michael paused, taking a deep breath before confessing, "I didn't send that bullet. I'm just as angry as you are about it, and I hope whoever did send it gets caught and punished."

Tears welled up in his eyes as Michael shared, "When I was a youth, my twin brother Rob was shot dead," he revealed, tears now streaming down his face, "We were playing football around the neighbourhood when a fight broke out after a mistimed tackle. The other boy stormed off, only to return with a gun an hour later. He shot my brother at point-blank range, and Rob died in my arms before an ambulance could arrive."

Adam's shock quickly turned into sympathy as this tough man broke down before him. Without hesitation, he rose from his chair and wrapped an arm around Michael in a comforting embrace. Michael shook with suppressed sobs as he poured his heart out to Adam, "He was a part of me, you know?" Michael choked out, his voice raw with emotion, "Only sixteen years old, with his whole life ahead of him. And I, I couldn't save him," he cried.

The weight of guilt consumed Michael, threatening to suffocate him. An eerie silence filled the room before Adam spoke, his voice laced with genuine sympathy, "It wasn't your fault. He'd be proud of you, you know."

Michael scoffed bitterly, "Proud of me? For going to prison and destroying that kid's career? He almost never walked again because of me, that player," Michael said.

Adam shook his head firmly, "No, not for that, maybe, but certainly for everything you've done since then. You turned your life around and became an inspiration to others, a leader, a captain, a husband, and a father. He would be so proud of you for all that," Adam said.

Michael's tears flowed freely now, but a glimmer cleansed them of hope and gratitude. "Thank you," he whispered hoarsely to Adam. Michael realised how much he needed this fresh start, this chance to make things right. With newfound composure, he reached out a hand towards Adam, "I'm sorry for everything, boss. I never meant to cause trouble or unrest. As for the bullet, if I ever hear of someone doing something like that again, they better pray they don't cross paths with me."

Adam nodded understandingly and took Michael's hand firmly, "In that case, then, I propose we make a fresh start, skipper," he declared warmly, "Welcome back."

The two men genuinely smiled before Adam joked, "Shall we hug it out?"

Michael rolled his eyes but couldn't stop himself from laughing. "Behave you tart," he joked.

As the two settled back into their chairs, Michael's voice was filled with admiration, "I have to say, I am thoroughly impressed. The boys can't stop raving about you and how much they love playing under your leadership. They finally get to attack and enjoy their training sessions and games. I want to be a part of that."

As Michael leaned in closer, his eyes gleaming excitedly, he said, "I watched the Newborough game, as you know. Your tactics were flawless in the first half. We should have had a second or third goal, but sometimes luck isn't on our side. And then there was the Cliffe game, my god, it was incredible. I don't know how you managed to pull out such a performance from the team after our lacklustre season so far. Well done."

Adam couldn't help but smile at Michael's praise, feeling pride and satisfaction in his chest, "Thank you, Michael. That means a lot coming from you."

Finally, Michael asked, "So what now, gaffer?"

A moment passed before Adam responded, "The lads need their captain, Michael. Can you promise me there won't be any more trouble? Are you on board with us in our fight to keep the Swans up?"

Michael's answer was immediate and resounding, "A hundred and ten percent, I'm in, boss."

With a slight nod from Adam, the deal was sealed. Michael would return to first-team training the next day. Before he could leave, Adam made one last request, "I still want you to issue a public apology to the club and the fans. Can you do that for me?"

Without hesitation, Michael agreed and promised to do it right away. As for the hefty fine looming over his head, Adam surprised him by offering a reduction to just one week, a weight lifted off Michael's shoulders. Grateful and relieved, he thanked Adam before leaving, ready to make things right with his team and the fans.

As soon as Michael's figure had disappeared from the office, Adam was left alone in stunned silence. He couldn't believe what he had just witnessed. It was like a dream that he desperately wanted to hold onto. Did the infamous Michael Knight show emotion and apologise? On top of that, revealing one of his most traumatic experiences, which he rarely spoke about. The room was still as if the walls were trying to process what had just occurred. Adam couldn't shake off the feeling of disbelief, yet somewhere deep down, he knew this significant moment would change everything.

The worn leather creaked under his weight as Adam leaned back in his chair. He stared blankly at the closed office door, Michael's unexpected vulnerability lingering in the otherwise empty room. Adam could smell the faint musk of Michael's cologne and the sharp scent of raw fear. A sight and scent unfathomable just a few hours ago.

The image of Michael, a usually bombastic, ego-driven sports superstar, unravelling like a weak child was startling and painfully human. In that unexpected moment, Adam saw a side of Michael that he had never known existed. Adam was swamped with sympathy, an emotion he rarely associated with Michael Knight. Revealing such sensitive information was only done when one was desperate, at breaking point, or both.

20

Another Day, Another Drama

Tuesday morning brought with it more drama. As Adam woke to the familiar sound of Sports Radio, his attention was drawn to the latest breaking news announced by its presenter. Adam's initial thoughts were that perhaps the story about Michael's arrest had been leaked, but much to his surprise, this was a different matter altogether.

"Good morning, Swanford fans," the presenter remarked, "This morning, new information has come to light, suggesting that the club's future might not be certain, not just on the pitch but now off it as well." As Adam listened intently for more information, he wondered what the presenter could be on about.

The presenter continued, "We have received an anonymous leak from within the club that suggests that Swanford are in danger of going bankrupt and possibly into liquidation amidst serious financial issues." Adam was in shock; this was the first he had heard of any of this, and he questioned whether it could be true and why Scott hadn't mentioned any of it to him as the club's manager.

After eating some toast to digest the news and downing his coffee, Adam left the house to go to the training ground. En route, Adam decided to make a couple of phone calls. The first call was to Shane Finn, the head of police. The dial tone grated on Adam's nerves as he waited for Shane to pick up. Relief washed over him when a gruff voice filled the line. "Shane," Adam said, urgency coiling in his gut, "Threat update."

Silence stretched on the other end before a guarded "Go on" came from Shane.

"Look," Adam said, "I met with Knight last night. There's no way he's behind it. I'm positive."

A sceptical scoff travelled down the line, "Hundred percent sure?" Shane asked.

"Absolutely," Adam replied.

"Fine," Shane sighed, the tension crackling between them, "Knight's off the hook. But that leaves a rather gaping hole in this little investigation of ours, wouldn't you say?"

"A hole that stinks of the club," Adam said, the pieces clicking into place in his mind, "Delivered by hand, remember? My address wouldn't exactly be public knowledge unless," his voice trailed off, the unspoken accusation hanging heavy.

A tense silence followed. Finally, Shane stated, "We're on it, Adam. You'll be the first to know anything."

Next, Adam decided to phone Scott. After a couple of rings, Scott picked up the call. "Morning, boss," Adam opened the call with, "I've just been listening to the radio. What's all this about financial issues?" he asked.

"Adam," Scott replied, "I don't know what to say to you right now." There was silence, then a strained sigh, "Adam, trust me, if I find the weasel leaking all this information, their desk will be clearer than a referee's conscience." After another moment of silence, Scott spoke further, his voice uncertain. "Look, Adam, a phone call isn't the right place for this discussion. I'll meet you in your office at eleven o'clock. Is that ok with you?" he asked.

"Sure, see you there," Adam replied before ending the call.

Once at the training ground, Adam sat in the canteen amongst the players having breakfast. The talk of the canteen was speculation about the morning's news and concern that this could lead to them not being paid moving forward. Before the players made their way onto the training pitches, Adam addressed them amid the speculation.

"Lads," Adam began, "We've all heard the news and rumours. For now, let me say two things. Firstly, our job is the footballing side of affairs, and that alone must be our sole focus. The business side of the club is of no concern to us. Secondly, I know as much as you guys. I'm meeting with Scott this morning, and should there be any more information you need to know off the back of it, I will tell you in due course. Thank you. Now let's go get to work," he said, leading the lads onto the training pitch.

Another surprise was yet to come for the squad. They were unaware of the showdown meeting between Adam and Michael the previous evening. Therefore, there was an atmospheric hush of anticipation as Michael Knight walked onto the first-team training pitch. Adam watched as Michael's athletically built figure, always imposing on the pitch, stepped onto the lush green expanse.

The players began their stretches alongside pre-training chatter, but their eyes kept straying to Michael. Whether they sensed the change in him or were simply wary of the explosive superstar's mood, Adam couldn't tell. As Michael joined his teammates, displaying an uncharacteristic restraint, Adam could see heads turning and whispers exchanged. As he watched, Michael displayed a calmness unlike anything the team or he had seen before. Adam blinked in surprise. Michael was displaying a composure that didn't just radiate from within him but also seemed to settle across the pitch like a calming mist. Was it possible? Could Michael have already started implementing a calm over the squad on such a profound level?

From where Adam stood, he watched Michael conversing earnestly with his teammates, gesturing animatedly yet respectfully. His voice wasn't audible, but his body language spoke volumes. Michael was not just participating but leading a mature discussion about tactics. Adam sighed with relief as he observed the scene unfold before him. This was progress. The challenge ahead of them seemed slightly less daunting now. Although wrought with potential pitfalls, the road to redemption seemed brighter with hope. This wasn't just about winning anymore. It was about healing and rebuilding, not just for Michael but for the entire team. It was time to transform this group of talented individuals into a cohesive unit that played well together and supported one another through their struggles.

Adam watched on as the training session unfolded, everything going according to plan until one sudden and crippling incident. He saw Hart, the team's star striker, sprinting towards an attacking pass when, out of nowhere, he fell to the ground with a scream that reverberated throughout the training complex. It was as if Hart had been shot in the back of his leg, bringing him down in a burst of agony. Writhing in pain, the team physios rushed to his aid, their urgent movements signalling that this was not a mere stumble. As they carried Hart back to the training ground building, Adam could see the pain on his face, knowing that this injury would end today's training and possibly even his season. Adam couldn't shake off the sickening feeling in his gut that this incident could affect the team's chances of safety, as he could not see where else crucial goals might come from.

Adam's eyes snapped open as the reminder alarm on his watch rang out. It was ten am, time to leave the open pitch and head back indoors for his latest pre-match press conference. Adam barked orders at the team, their adrenaline pumping as they prepared for tomorrow's intense game.

"Alright, lads, I'm off to do my pre-match press conference. But before I go, let's focus on tomorrow. You'll report here in the morning for training at the usual time. We'll have a light session before a team meeting, and then you'll be dismissed to go home and prepare for the match. Don't forget, we meet at Manchester Cargo Airport at three pm sharp for our flight to the south coast." With a final nod of determination, Adam strode off the pitch and towards the training ground building, ready to face the waiting media.

As usual, Adam expected to meet Sarah before attending the press conference. Sarah, however, was nowhere to be seen. Adam rang her phone several times, but his calls went unanswered. Adam thought that perhaps attending the press conferences with him wasn't a usual occurrence, and she had only done so initially to offer guidance. This time, Adam would have to face the press alone. He strode confidently into the intimidatingly sterile briefing room where the media had gathered. With tense shoulders and a determined gaze, he prepared to face the barrage of questions about his team's upcoming match against South Swanshea tomorrow and the day's breaking news about the club's financial issues. The smell of stale coffee and anticipation filled the air. Microphones stood prepped and ready, and phones were set out on his table to record his voice. The press were poised like hungry vultures awaiting a meal of words.

Adam took his seat at his desk, a large banner bearing the team's emblem in front of it, cleared his throat, and began. The lights were blindingly bright as camera flashes danced and flickered over him. The sweat trickling down his neck felt cold.

"Good afternoon, you charming lot," Adam remarked in a light-hearted tone, "Let's do this, first question, please."

A journalist's sharp voice cut through the silence, asking, "Hi Adam, Super Sports TV here. Firstly, what can you tell us about today's news of financial woes at the club? Secondly, how do you plan to overcome the unbeaten in-seven South Swanshea tomorrow, a team that has been your achilles heel for the last twelve meetings with them? They are desperate for a win to secure their spot in European football next season, whilst your team is fighting for survival, and a defeat could condemn you to relegation. What is your plan going into this one?"

Adam's voice dripped with sarcasm as he responded, "Well, thanks for stating the obvious. As if I haven't been losing sleep over it every night." Adam's smirk turned into a snarl as he continued, "Firstly, I will not answer any questions about today's news this afternoon, please. As and when there is anything to say, I'm sure the club will relay any information via the usual outlets. As for South Swanshea, let's not forget, they're a damn good team, and they'll be fighting tooth and nail to secure that European spot. It's all good and well to respect them and their abilities, but sentiment means nothing on the pitch. We need a win, plain and simple. The past few days have been gruelling, with intense training sessions leaving the players exhausted and drained of blood, sweat, and tears. Off the pitch, thorough scouting has given us a game plan that I am confident will lead us to victory. It's like I told the players at the start of this week, ultimately, this game is nothing more than their eleven footballers against our eleven footballers. Names don't mean anything out on the pitch."

The reporter from Swanford Daily was next to speak, her voice laced with eager anticipation. "Adam, what's the latest in terms of how training has gone today? We've heard rumours that Michael Knight has returned to the first team. Any injuries we should know about?"

Adam shifted uncomfortably before responding, "Yes, Michael has rejoined the first team. I won't disclose any details as they're private, but we had a lengthy chat yesterday, and all issues have been resolved. He's now back in training and up for selection consideration. As for injuries, just as I was leaving the pitch to come here, Hart let out a blood-curdling scream and crumpled to the ground. It looked like a serious injury, but I haven't received an update yet. I'll let you know as soon as I do."

The reporter's eyes widened in excitement before she quickly composed herself, "Thank you, that's all for now," her mind buzzing with the scoop she had just gotten on Knight's return and Hart's injury.

Next, the UK News reporter, his voice laced with sarcasm, addressed Adam. "Do you really believe that your team can pull off a victory at South Swanshea? Really?"

Adam bristled at his tone and responded assertively, "I wouldn't be in this position if I didn't have faith in myself and my team. They need to see that belief to have any chance of survival," Adam spoke through gritted teeth, his eyes blazing with determination, "If I don't even believe, how can they?"

The room fell into an eerie silence as all eyes turned to Adam. His sharp gaze locked onto a taciturn figure lurking at the back, Riley James of Sports Radio.

Adam called out to him with a sly smile, his words loaded with malicious intent. "Well, if it isn't Riley James. What's up? The cat got your tongue, bud? Do you have anything to say to me at this pivotal moment?"

The atmosphere in the room thickened as Riley squirmed under Adam's intense scrutiny, beads of sweat forming on his forehead. In a shaky voice, he finally mustered a response, trying to mask his fear. "I, I was impressed with your result against Cliffe and the way you played," he stuttered, "But there are rumours that after that game on Sunday, you took the lads on a jolly up. With relegation looming over your team, do you see such actions as irresponsible?" sweat now dripping down his face as he awaited Adam's answer.

Adam's voice quivered as he spoke, "I don't understand how this information got out. We took every precaution to keep it private." Despite the club's best efforts, the details had somehow, again, leaked, and now Adam was left to defend himself and his team. Adam knew their success in the season's final two games depended on their unity and trust. So, with an assertive voice, Adam continued, "I won't bore you with the specifics. I believed we needed to come together and build morale and confidence before our crucial upcoming games. I can proudly say that our efforts were not in vain. The mood in our camp is one of unshakable confidence, and that will only propel us towards safety." The intensity in Adam's words was evident, conveying just how vital the team bonding day was to their success.

Riley's voice trembled with urgency as he fired another question at Adam, "If you don't suffer defeat and relegation tomorrow evening, the entire season and battle for survival could come down to a final, winner-takes-it-all showdown against Wry at home on Sunday. What do you make of this potential outcome?" he asked.

"Well, Riley," Adam's voice was firm, "My thoughts are solely focused on tomorrow's crucial match. That is all that matters right now."

Riley nodded quickly, knowing the gravity of the situation. "Thank you," he replied.

With that, Adam called time on the press conference and stormed out of the media room. He had no time to engage in small talk with the media. He was due in his office at eleven o'clock to meet with Scott.

At eleven o'clock on the dot, Scott walked into Adam's office, upon which Adam stood to shake his hand before the two of them sat down and got down to business. "Morning, Adam," Scott began, "Let me start by saying that the rumours are true, in the interest of honesty and transparency. The club is in a grave financial situation, to say the very least," Scott explained.

"Oh gosh," Adam replied, "So how bad is it? What does it all mean?"

"Well," Scott replied, "First and foremost, let me make it clear, we have more than enough to keep the operations going, and everyone paid in full until at least the end of the season," he assured Adam. "After that, however, as it stands, is uncertain," Scott explained.

Scott continued, "With this being a business like no other, it goes without saying that the connotations after the conclusion of the season vary, dependant mainly on our survival within this division. I wouldn't say relegation would spell the end, but it'll be fairly close to doing so, certainly in terms of the club as we know it currently," Scott explained.

"Oh my, that doesn't sound good at all," Adam replied.

"Sorry, I can't sugar-coat it, Adam, this is serious," Scott declared, "Staying up is worth an estimated one hundred million pounds minimum, as well as TV rights money, which would go a big way to helping the situation. However, if we are relegated, we will only get a small fraction of that in parachute payments and a smaller amount of TV rights revenue. On top of that, our operation costs are among the biggest in this division, and that would not be sustainable if we were relegated," Scott explained.

Scott continued, "Despite the fact we are in one of the lower positions in the league and have been consistently for the last two seasons, we have the third highest wage bill in the division, which, to be frank, is crippling the club even in this division. Under no circumstances would that be sustainable in the lower division. Looking at your team sheet from Saturday, all but three of the starting eleven are out of contract this summer and, voluntarily or otherwise, will have to leave the club to ease that wage bill. As helpful as that would be, it means that we would need to build a whole new side with the pressure of knowing that financially, anything but an instant promotion back to the top flight would be a disaster. If we stay up, perhaps we can retain a few current players if we can structure a pay cut against performance-based bonuses, which would help. The problem, however, is that the club has found itself in the lower part of the division the last few years due to lack of investment in bringing in a better calibre of player to propel it up the league. So should we survive, it is likely that any re-building of the side wouldn't be to a level that would see the team competitive enough to rise up the league table, which would lead to another season of desperately fighting against relegation," Scott added.

"So, in a nutshell," Adam replied, "We need to survive to stand even the remotest chance of surviving as a club."

"Basically," Scott replied. "Rest assured, I am working tirelessly with Mr Broad and our accounts department to try and find a way forward. It would seem that Dad knew about the financial issues for the last year or two and was meeting with accounts regularly to try and navigate a way forward. I now believe that the stress of all this is what killed him. He was seen at the club the morning of his heart attack and crash, and I have since found out that this was to attend one of these meetings with accounts," he added.

"For now, leave those meetings to me, and I'll keep you in the loop as best I can. Please try your best to bail us out of a disaster and keep us up. In terms of communications, I ask that any questions asked to you or the players about the rumours by the media be met with a 'no comment'. Can you please relay that to the team for me?" Scott asked.

"Absolutely," Adam replied.

"Thank you," Scott replied, "Please keep the finer details of all this between us for now. Do, however, assure the players that everything is ok, and they will be paid in full and on time with no issues," he asked.

"Of course," Adam said.

As the meeting ended, Adam opened his laptop and his email inbox. He had received two new emails. The first was titled 'Mandatory interdepartmental club meeting re: next season strategy plans'. The second email had the subject line 'Up The Swans Podcast, guest appearance request - speak to us fans'.

Adam opened the email about the club's interdepartmental meeting, which read: Please see below a video meeting invite link for our annual strategy meeting ahead of next season. The departments in attendance will be media, club shop and merchandise, ticket office, player recruitment, first and youth team managers and accounts. Club secretary Mr Broad will chair the meeting. Attendance is mandatory.

Adam added the meeting to his digital diary. It was scheduled for this Thursday, the twenty-fifth, at three pm.

Next, Adam opened the email about the fan's podcast, which read: Hi Adam, this is Chris from the 'Up The Swans' fans podcast. We are doing a special live episode on Friday before the final game. We would love it if you would join us for an interview. We will allow you to vet all questions before we go on air. It would mean the world to the fans to hear from you directly and would significantly improve the club-fan relationship in light of recent discontent and scrutiny.

Adam replied: Hi, thanks for your email and invite. Time permitting, I would be delighted to join you guys on air via video link, subject to your proposed questions agenda-wise. I look forward to hearing from you further regarding the meeting link and time.

As Adam drove home that evening, his mind was consumed by tomorrow's high-stakes game, the most challenging game the team had faced yet in his short tenure. The pitch-black darkness outside his car seemed to mirror the uncertainty gnawing at the pit of his stomach. The car engine purred ominously in the silence, each mile throwing him further into a pool of anxiety. The once-familiar streets seemed cold and alien, reflecting the shadows that played on his doubt-riddled mind. With every streetlight he passed under, passing moments of illumination brought flashes of memories from the past. He remembered their heavy loss in his first game, how it felt like every sinew was being torn apart, and how the team spirit disintegrated under the weight of that defeat. Then his thoughts turned to their first win in the last match, the exhilaration that coursed through him when he saw their hard work and training manifest into success.

As Adam pulled onto his driveway and got out of his car, he received a call from Daryl, the team's physio.

"Hi, Adam. Just a quick one," he continued, "We've run tests on Hart. He's done his ligaments and won't play again this season. Sorry to be the bearer of bad news. See you in the morning," Daryl said.

"No worries, thanks for letting me know," a disappointed Adam replied.

With a creak and a click, Adam unlocked the door and stepped into his house, instantly greeted by an eerie silence. The musty smell of old books and memories filled his nostrils as he gazed around his dimly lit front room. His eyes were drawn to an antique photo frame perched atop a dusty bookshelf, its golden edges glinting in the faint light. In the photo, a younger version of himself stood proudly next to his Granddad, their matching grins capturing a moment frozen in time. A surge of conflicting emotions washed over him, threatening to drown out all rational thought. On one hand, he was consumed by dread at the prospect of tomorrow's game and what it could mean for the team's fate in the league. But on the other hand, a spark of passion ignited within him, urging him to channel that fear into motivation. It was a battle between hope and despair, and he wasn't sure which side would win.

With renewed energy, Adam went over to his plush sofa and sank into its comfortable cushions. The soft hum of the TV filled the room as Adam switched it on, the glowing screen casting a warm light across the space. A familiar voice greeted him, that of an ex-football pundit emanating from the television speakers. It was the preview show for tomorrow evening's fixtures, and Adam settled in to watch with anticipation. After thoroughly analysing Wry's game against Cliffe, the pundit turned his attention to the crunch fixture between South Swanshea and Swanford, eager to debate how the game would play out.

The pundit was Steve Daniels. Steve was a legendary figure in the world of football. He commanded respect and admiration from all who knew him. His career had been remarkable, reaching the highest level of the game as a midfielder with an incomparable pass and endless stamina. But it was not just his physical abilities that set him apart. Even at a young age, Steve possessed wisdom and a maturity that surpassed his years. He was a vocal and commanding presence on the pitch, a true leader among his teammates. It was no surprise when Steve was appointed captain of Newborough, the club where he spent the best years of his career and ultimately retired. He had also proudly represented England on the international stage seventy times, most often as their esteemed captain. Retirement did not mean the end of Steve's involvement in football, seamlessly transitioning into the role as a pundit for Super Sports TV, where he was known for speaking his mind and never holding back his opinions. His sharp insights and no-nonsense approach made him a fan favourite and respected expert in the sport.

Adam's hand trembled slightly as he reached for his pack of cigarettes on the coffee table, fingers fumbling to extract one from the tightly packed rows. He couldn't help but feel a sense of anticipation as he lit the cigarette with a trembling match. It had been years since he last smoked, but in his journey to recovery from substance abuse, cigarettes had become his coping mechanism. They offered a replacement for the numbing effects of alcohol and drugs. As Adam inhaled deeply, the smoke filled his lungs, momentarily clouding his mind and senses. As he exhaled, a wave of relief washed over him. The familiar burn in his throat was almost comforting, a reminder of past vices now replaced by this one habit. With each drag, Adam relaxed more and more, the tension slowly seeping out of his body. The television screen before him seemed to blur as he drifted into calm and contentment. As he savoured the temporary release that cigarettes provided, a small part of Adam couldn't help but acknowledge the irony of using one addiction to suppress another, yet, at that moment, it was all he needed to distract himself from the looming pressure and anxiety of tomorrow's events.

"Let's dive into Swanford's trip to South Swanshea," Steve sneered, his voice dripping with disdain, "Unfortunately for Swanford fans, I can only see a heavy defeat at the hands of South Swanshea," he declared, "A victory that will seal Swanford's relegation fate, especially since Wry are sure to win their home game against Cliffe," he stated.

Now ripping through cigarettes in a frenzy, Adam watched in horror as Steve continued, "Sure, they may have pulled off a decent result against Cliffe at the weekend, but appointing Adam Wells was a death sentence for this team. In my opinion, as pitiful as Wry have been, they'll still just about manage to survive. The real issue is that Swanford desperately need a win tomorrow night, but, I highly doubt they'll stand a chance against a dominant South Swanshea team that remains unbeaten in seven matches now and are just one good home performance away from securing a spot in Europe next season. My condolences, Swanford fans, but it's time to say goodbye I'm afraid," he declared with an assassin's grin.

With a resolute look etched on his face, Adam turned away from the glowing TV screen and called out, "We'll show you. We ain't going down without a fight!" Adam stubbed out his cigarette and shuffled off to bed, feeling exhausted from the day's excursions. Adam was tired and keen to get an early night to be fully refreshed and at his best for the crucial day ahead, not just for the club but for his own future. Tomorrow would be a battle, but he was ready to face it head-on.

21

Match Day – South Swanshea Away

After a restless night of often disturbed sleep, Adam woke at six am the next morning. Today was the day. A day that could once again make or break Swanford's future.

Quick as a whip, Adam rolled out of bed and headed towards the kitchen. He watched as sunlight timidly crept over the horizon, painting the sky with shades of gold. Despite the early hour, Adam's mind was already buzzing with tactics for his team and techniques to outwit their opponents. In the stillness of dawn, he made himself a cup of coffee while going over every detail of today's game in his mind. There was no room for error.

As Adam drove toward the training ground a short time later, the car glided through the cobblestone streets of Swanford, a charming town that seemed to be held together by its loyal football team's shared passion and dreams. The early morning stillness loomed in the air, broken only by the occasional paperboy on his route or the baker beginning his day. A sense of foreboding crept over Adam as he realised their small world would face a monumental challenge today.

As Adam pulled into the training ground, it lay shrouded in the cool embrace of dawn. Adam parked in his designated spot and switched off the engine, listening to its gentle hum fade into silence. With a sigh, he exhaled a plume of smoke and absentmindedly flicked away what remained of his cigarette out of the window.

Adam strode confidently into the bustling training complex, his coat slung over one arm and his laptop tucked under the other. Adam reached his office and set his belongings down before heading to the team canteen to wait for the players' arrivals. The stillness of the usually chaotic canteen was a pleasant surprise to Adam, and he found himself oddly at peace in the muted atmosphere. He went to the fridge for a drink, his fingers trailing along the smooth surface of the drinks cans before selecting one. The satisfying pop of the tab echoed as Adam opened it in the quiet room, breaking the silence like a gunshot.

One by one, Adam's team trickled into the canteen, their faces a mix of concern and excitement mirroring his own. Adam studied each player intently as they came in, taking note of their body language, expressions and mannerisms. He saw the nervous energy radiating off them like electricity on a stormy night, filling up the room and crackling with anticipation. As Adam observed them, he couldn't help but think about their strengths and weaknesses, not just as individual athletes but as integral parts of the team. They were all crucial cogs that needed to work together seamlessly for success.

When all the lads were settled and eating their breakfasts, Adam stood up from his seat and went to the front of the room. His movements were confident and assured, masking his inner turmoil. The room fell silent as he began to speak. Adam's voice was initially raspy with emotion and the strain of chain smoking since the evening before but quickly settled into a commanding baritone that demanded attention.

"Morning lads," Adam began, projecting his voice to reach every corner of the room, "Today is a massive day for us, but we can't let that overwhelm us. We've trained hard leading up to this and should feel confident. We will navigate this day and our survival bid one step at a time. Step one, enjoy a nice hearty breakfast because you'll need it. After breakfast, Mike, Shea, and I will meet you on the pitch. Let's do this," he concluded with a smile and nod of reassurance. The room erupted into a chorus of cheers and clapping as Adam's words filled the players with fiery resolve and drive. They were ready for whatever challenges lay ahead today.

Adam, sitting back down to finish his coffee with Mike and Shea, continued observing the players closely as they breakfasted. He continued to note their body language and the tone of their conversations, trying to gauge their morale. Their easy camaraderie and occasional bursts of laughter were a good sign, but an underlying tension lingered like a thin veil of fog. Adam finished his coffee quickly, slipped out of the bustling canteen, and headed towards his office. The cold fluorescent lights flickered briefly as he entered before settling into a steady hum. The pale glow cast by the lights illuminated the tactics board lining one wall, covered with notes and scribbles in Adam's handwriting. Adam studied it intently, pinching the bridge of his nose as if trying to squeeze out any lingering doubts or uncertainties.

A short time later, Adam went onto the training pitch to meet with his players and coaches. The towering floodlights created a natural cathedral-like atmosphere as the team huddled together, resembling armoured gladiators ready to enter the arena. Adam's voice raised over the team, declaring, "Mike and Shea will lead training this morning, light stretching and cardio work through light jogging." Adam emphasised the importance of preparing their bodies and minds for battle, cautioning against overexertion before the match.

As Mike and Shea began leading the players through their training routines, Adam stepped back, observing each athlete from a distance. He watched their bodies move with fluidity and purpose, muscles flexing and releasing as they stretched and jogged around the expansive pitch. The cold morning air nipped at his skin, causing his breath to mist in front of him. Though their faces appeared stoic, Adam could sense the mounting pressure within the players, reflected in their eyes.

As his watch approached eleven am, Adam put his whistle to his lips and declared the training session over with a sharp, quick blow. "Right, lads, that's good. Warm down, and I'll see you in the briefing room for the pre-match meeting in fifteen. Cheers."

The clock on the wall ticked its way to ten-past-eleven as the team began to shuffle into the briefing room. Each player, dressed in matching team tracksuits, found their designated seat. The room filled with the low rumble of their voices as they chatted and joked, building excitement for the upcoming meeting. As Adam approached the front of the room, the chatter died down to a hush in anticipation. With a slight upward curve of his lips, Adam glanced at the clock again, noting that it was precisely quarter-past-eleven, time to get down to business.

"Right on time as always," Adam began, his voice echoing through the silence. He looked around the room, meeting each player's eyes. "I'm not going to lie, we're up against a tough team, but you've faced challenges before, bigger ones than this, and you all know how that ended. You won," Adam's voice thundered with a raw, unwavering conviction that filled the room with electric energy. Each word he spoke was like a lightning bolt, striking each player in the heart and igniting a fire within them. Adam watched as the players' bodies straightened, their heads held high with fierce determination. The once doubtful eyes now glimmered with an unshakable resolve. They were primed for victory.

Adam passionately outlined the tactical plan for the upcoming match, emphasising the crucial role of cooperation and discipline on the pitch. As he spoke, his eyes sparkled, and his hands gestured animatedly like a conductor leading an orchestra. He enthusiastically shifted the team's focus from defensive manoeuvres to offensive tactics, urging them to exploit their opponent's vulnerabilities while capitalising on their strengths.

After Adam had delivered his powerful message, Mike rose to his feet to discuss the importance of fitness and precautions. His words were amplified by Shea, who then took to the stage with a tactical overview of the opposing team. Both men echoed Adam's sentiments, skilfully balancing brutal realism and contagious optimism. Their voices filled the room like a symphony, each note perfectly complementing the other in a harmonious melody.

As Shea's words faded, Adam's muscles tensed, and he explosively rose to his feet. The room was engulfed in a sudden silence as he surveyed his team, a fire burning in his chest, "We've worked tirelessly. We've prepared for this moment. Now it's time for us to unleash our fury on the pitch and dominate like the warriors we are," he declared with ferocity.

The room exploded into thunderous applause, each clap and hoot a resounding declaration of hope and commitment. The sound reverberated through the walls and halls of the training ground. As the team began to disperse, Adam's voice cut through the noise with a commanding reminder, "Three o'clock sharp at the cargo airport lads."

A few hours later, Adam pulled into the cargo airport's car park, glancing at his watch to make sure he was on time. It was half past two, perfect. After parking his car, Adam strode confidently towards the airport entrance, eager to meet with his players. As Adam entered the bustling terminal building, he was optimistic about his team's chances on the south coast tonight.

The players began to arrive one by one, their footsteps echoing in the cavernous space. By three o'clock sharp, the whole team had gathered near the entrance, their bags packed and ready for the journey ahead. Together, they made their way towards the private plane that awaited them on the tarmac. As they approached, the gleaming steel fuselage of the aircraft stood tall and grand against the dull grey sky. The team felt pride and privilege as they realised this plane was chartered especially for their journey to South Swanshea. They boarded the plane with awe and settled for their journey towards the south coast.

The players' hearts raced in unison as the plane roared down the runway, gaining speed with each passing second. They could feel the raw power of the aircraft beneath them as if it were an extension of their bodies. With a smooth lift-off, the plane ascended into the dull grey sky, leaving behind the familiar sights of the airport. Adam looked out the window, where he watched the world below shrink and disappear from view. Turning back to his team, he saw each player lost in their thoughts, their expressions reflected in the windows of their souls. In that suspended moment, all was quiet except for the gentle sound of the engines against a backdrop of silence. The earth below passed by like fragmented pieces of a hastily stitched quilt.

As their plane soared higher and higher through the clouds and settled at a height that allowed movement within the cabin, Adam stood tall at the front of the cabin to address his team. His voice echoed confidently as he announced, "Right, lads, tonight's lineup." The team leaned in, eager to hear their positions for the upcoming match.

"In goal, we have Barlow. Across the back, from left to right, we have Donovan, Shea, Kofi, and Lambert. In midfield, Ethan again will take on the defensive role with Price and Young in front of him. On the wings, we have Fletcher and Davids. And finally, we have Neil Cole to replace Hart up front. The bench remains unchanged except for one familiar face returning, Michael Knight."

As Adam scanned his team for their reactions, he could see the disappointment etched on Michael's face. It was natural for him to expect to be starting as one of the team's key players, and in truth, Adam was tempted to start him, but he also knew that he needed to assert his authority as the manager. Showing Michael that he would be making his return from the bench was necessary for their dynamic as a team and the development of their relationship as team manager and player.

After what felt like an eternity, but was only forty-five minutes, a voice came over the speakers within the plane, announcing that it was time for the passengers to return to their seats and buckle up for their descent and arrival at Southampton airport. Once the plane landed, the players eagerly stood up from their cramped seats and stretched their legs before exiting. Alongside their aircraft sat a sleek coach, ready to transport them to South Swanshea's ground, located eighteen miles away. The players mainly remained silent, each lost in their thoughts and preparations as they waited for the coach to arrive at the ground.

The coach arrived at South Swanshea's stadium at five pm. As Adam stepped off the coach, the fresh sea air of South Swanshea blew into his nostrils, and the stadium loomed before him, a colossal steel and concrete structure. The floodlights glowed ominously against the encroaching twilight, a beacon in the growing shadows. Adam made his way into the stadium and down the corridor into the away dressing room as the players took a moment to greet their fans who had made the journey by posing for selfies and signing autographs.

The dressing room was nothing more than a hollow chamber, filled with echoes of victories and losses it had once witnessed. The dank smell of sweat and antiseptic hung heavy in the air, the lingering ghosts of past battles fought and often lost on South Swanshea's sacred turf. As quickly as he had absorbed the atmosphere, the players began to enter the room, filling it with buoyant, hopeful, motivated voices. The air was electrified, a current that wove into every corner of the room, replacing the stench of defeat with a scent of fresh optimism. One by one, the team started taking off their tracksuit jackets and putting boots on, ready for their warm-ups.

As Adam sent the players out onto the pitch with his coaches for their warm-up, he sat deep in thought in the solitude of the empty dressing room. The room around him seemed to breathe heavily, reflecting the weight of the impending match. Adam's fingers traced over sheets of paper filled with statistics and strategies drawn up meticulously for this match. His trepidation was visible as it threatened to choke his resolve, but Adam refused to be swallowed by it. His mind whirled, churning out formations and substitutions, second-guessing South Swanshea's lineup and tactics. He let his thoughts wander back to all the training sessions he had watched, remembering the fleeting moments of brilliance, the potential injuries and the lapses in concentration. All these intricacies ran around his mind, a whirlpool threatening to pull him in. After much contemplation, Adam carefully illustrated his tactics and critical plays on the flip chart in the corner of the room. Shortly after, the players returned to the dressing room with fifteen minutes until kick-off.

The players' training jerseys, which clung to their sweat-laden bodies, were quickly removed and replaced with the team's kit by the players, as the smell of fresh grass consumed the air. One by one, they glanced up toward Adam, ready for his final words before kick-off. Adam cleared his throat before addressing them.

"Alright, boys, here's the plan," he declared. A dramatic pause descended over the room, and the ticking rhythm of studs against concrete filled it like a metronome. As Adam began outlining his strategies, marker squeaking on the glossy surface of the flip chart, something sparked in each player's eyes. His words flowed like poetry, crisp and rhythmic, painting pictures of conquests to come. The dressing room was filled with newfound energy, potent with optimism and focus. The players nodded, mirroring the other's resolve as if a silent pact had been made. The game plan was set.

With ten minutes to spare, a hush fell over the dressing room again, but it was different this time. It was a calm before the storm, an understanding that soon they would be out under those bright lights with thousands watching. Their bodies hummed with heightened senses, anticipating every sprint, every turn and every kick of the ball. This was their moment, one they had worked tirelessly for. They knew what needed to be done and understood that only through unity and grit could they get victory over their opponents. With heartbeats that mirrored the tick-tocking countdown in their heads, they could only wait for that familiar bell from the referee's room, meaning that it was time to storm into battle.

With five minutes left until the bell, Michael Knight decided to break the silence, "I've no right to command your attention and respect after my recent behaviour, but please hear me out for a moment. Remember what we've trained for," he said, his voice ringing out clear and confident. He looked around the room, meeting each of his fellow teammates' eyes, "Remember, our strength lies in unity. Out there, we're not eleven individuals. We're one team. One force. It's just our eleven players versus their eleven players, level playing field. Each player equals with another." A ghost of a smile played on Michael's lips as he added, "Heaven help those who dare to stand in our way." The dressing room erupted with laughter, easing the tension slightly. Each player found comfort in Michael's words, a beacon of assurance they held onto as the minutes dwindled to seconds.

There were two minutes until the bell rang. The once deafening silence was replaced by the distant roar of the crowd beyond the concrete walls, a primal sound that sent the team's adrenaline coursing through their veins.

There was one minute until the bell rang. The players gravitated towards the door to exit into the tunnel, with an unspoken agreement to have each other's backs and fight for three crucial points tonight. The players' hands rested briefly on each other's shoulders, a signal of unity and solidarity.

Zero. The bell from the referee's room sounded loud and clear, echoing like a war cry.

This was it.

They exploded into motion with a shared deep breath, barreling into the tunnel and then out onto the pitch under the dazzling floodlights. The roar of thousands of South Swanshea fans washed over them like a tidal wave as they sprinted towards their positions, a frightening roar. The players felt like a contender in a Roman arena, with the overwhelming majority of the spectators willing the gladiator, who in this case was South Swanshea, to rip them apart limb by limb. Fuelled by desire and united by one common goal, victory, the players steeled themselves for the challenge ahead. This was their stage now, every move calculated, every pass practised hundreds of times.

Adam took his place in the dugout alongside Mike, ready to lead their team into battle. As they waited for the game to begin, Adam couldn't help but notice the ear pod headphone nestled in Mike's left ear, a constant reminder of the Wry match playing on the radio and its potential impact on their team's survival bid. Swanford's collective dreams pressed on Adam like a heavy burden resting on his shoulders. He looked across at his players one last time before the game started, taking in each hardened face. He saw traces of fear melt away in their eyes, replaced by fight and grit as they prepared to give it their all on the pitch.

Then, beneath the stadium's glowing lights, the game began. The ball came to life at the sharp blow of the referee's metallic whistle, as did the twenty-five bodies on the pitch. The first half an hour of the game was evenly matched, with both teams feeling each other out like two familiar sparring partners. The game was mainly contested in midfield. The only chances to speak of were a header from a South Swanshea corner, which looked to be going in before Barlow caught it comfortably, and an Ethan Fox venomous shot from thirty-five yards out, which sailed over the crossbar and into the South Swanshea fans behind the goal.

Then on the forty-minute mark, South Swanshea made an attacking move before baring down upon the nervous-looking Swanford defence. They found a way to pass through Shea before the ball fell to their lethal striker, Ricks, who powered the ball past Barlow into the top right-hand corner, almost taking the net off the goal frame. 1-0.

A shellshocked Swanford somehow limped their way through to the halftime whistle before dragging themselves off the pitch, looking like the world's weight was on their shoulders, and into the dressing room. As Adam and Mike followed, Adam turned to Mike and asked, "What's the Wry score?"

A defeated-looking Mike declared, "They're winning 1-0."

"Dam!" Adam bluntly replied. As it stood, Swanford would be relegated tonight.

The dressing room was a maelstrom of chaotic energy. Glistening in sweat and the stench of impending failure, the players descended into an unusual silence. Nobody dared to speak up; no one wished to wallow further in the harsh reality. But they couldn't ignore it either, even if they tried. It clung to them, like the shirts they wore sticking to their damp bodies.

"You've got one half left" Adam finally broke the silence. He looked at each player, trying to reignite the dying embers in their hearts, "And that's a lot of time. It only takes a minute to score a goal, and we've got at least forty-five of them to come," he rallied.

A few heads turned towards him, uncertain glints in their eyes. Mike stood beside Adam, his face shadowed by a thick veil of worry, but he managed to keep up an encouraging facade. Adam pushed on, "In football, fortunes change. Remember who we are. We're Swanford! We've been buried before, only to rise again, stronger. You've seen what we can do in training. Now it's time you showed them out there. Our fans have travelled two hundred-plus miles to back us today. Let's back ourselves and repay their faith in us" his words were a beacon of resilience against the cruel tide seeking to drown them.

With renewed desire burning in their hearts and minds readjusted, the players filed out of the dressing room and back into the cacophony of the crowd's jeers and cheers. Underneath the scorching glow of the stadium's lights and thousands of watchful eyes, Swanford resumed their battle positions on the pitch. Adam watched from the touchline as his players began the second half with a fiery resolve painted across their faces.

The second half began fiercely as there was a newfound urgency in how Swanford moved. They were no longer the tentative, overwhelmed team of the first half. Their passes were sharper, their attacks more decisive. They pressed higher up the pitch, suffocating South Swanshea's attacks before they could take shape. In the sixty-fifth minute, a brilliant counterattack led by Ethan Fox led to him sliding the ball through to Neil Cole. The young star used his blistering pace to leave his marker trailing in his wake before cooly slotting the ball under the goalkeeper, who had come off his line early to try and stop him. His timing was perfect, and his precision and accuracy were cool and calm. 1-1.

The away section of the ground erupted with joyous scenes of hope and jubilation. The grim reality of the situation soon brought Adam back down to earth, though. As he turned to Mike to ask how Wry were doing, they were still 1-0 up, leaving Swanford in danger of being relegated despite their equaliser.

Adam knew that to stand any chance, his team had to avoid defeat, ideally win, but if Wry conceded an equaliser, a draw would still be enough to keep Swanford in the battle. Adam decided that his side would need to defend what they had and shift to a counter-attacking model to try and win the game. Given that South Swanshea needed a win for the European spot, Adam knew they would throw everything but the kitchen sink at them. With that in mind, he would deploy an extra defender, soak up all the pressure, and then use any loose balls to launch a counterattack to try and score a winner. This would rely on South Swanshea pushing their defenders, hopefully, up into attack, thus leaving them short on numbers at the back if Swanford attacked. Adam decided to make a substitution to allow for the new tactical approach. Young, the midfielder, was to come off as Adam put on another defender. The defender of choice was also a leader who, along with Shea, could lead the team on the pitch and ensure they did not concede another goal. It was Michael Knight.

Michael, by nature, was a midfielder, not a defender. Adam addressed the issue with him as he got ready to enter the game. "Michael," Adam began, "I know you don't normally play in defence, but I feel you could put in a shift there beside Shea and see us over the line. Up for it?" Adam asked.

Michael warmed up, stripped down to his kit, primed and ready to enter play, and replied, "Of course, gaffer. I'm a team player and will play anywhere and do anything to keep this team up," as he smiled at Adam and shook his hand.

After some final words of encouragement, Michael entered the fray to a massive cheer from the away end. The game had shifted, the air now vibrating with an undercurrent of fierce resolve and quiet hope for Swanford. Michael Knight was faultless in defence, making impenetrable blocks and displaying unwavering leadership. His mere presence bolstered Swanford's resolve, steeling them against South Swanshea's relentless attack surges.

With each passing minute, the pressing panic within Swanford intensified, an overwhelming urge to survive at all costs. Like two gladiators locked in a deadly struggle, the two teams traded blows with ferocious energy. The searing heat of the stadium lights beat down on the players' faces, blinding them with their intensity. The deafening roars of the crowd merged into a chaotic cacophony, both empowering and terrifying. Under Michael and Shea's leadership, Swanford's backline transformed into an impenetrable fortress, repelling South Swanshea's relentless attacks with stoic endurance. Every tackle was a battle cry, every clearance a desperate gasp for air. But as the clock ticked towards the final minutes, Wry remained ahead by one goal. And then it was over; the referee's whistle blew, signalling the end of a gruelling ninety minutes. 1-1.

Adam's Swanford had fought with everything they had, leaving it all on the pitch. Many of the team slumped to the ground, exhausted and battered. Before making his way onto the pitch to praise his players and thank the away fans for their dedication in making the long journey to support them, Adam turned to Mike and asked, "What's the latest?"

A disappointed Mike looked at Adam and replied, "Still 1-0, it's in added on time."

Adam shook his head as he walked toward his players on the pitch. Many of them were slumped on the ground inconsolable, given that they couldn't find a winning goal. Adam picked them back up and marched them to the away section to thank their fans for making the long journey and their unwavering support. Adam's heart sank as he looked at the sea of disappointed Swanford fans, their faces twisted in despair. But suddenly, like a wave crashing onto the shore, their expressions changed to ones of joy and jubilation.

Confused, Adam wondered how they could be ecstatic with a draw and Wry winning, meaning they had been relegated. Before he could process it all, he heard a voice screaming his name and getting closer by the second. As the noise grew louder, he felt a monstrous weight jump onto his back and crush him in a hug. It was Mike, screaming into his ear that Cliffe had equalised at Wry in the ninety-seventh-minute to level the scores. The draw kept Swanford in the relegation fight. The away fans erupted into loud cheers and screams, and Adam realised they still had a chance. They were still in this fight.

Sunday's match against Wry would now be a do-or-die winner-takes-it-all battle, with Swanford having the advantage as the home team. The stakes were higher than ever before, and the tension in the air was electric as everyone anticipated the ultimate showdown.

After an extended period of celebration with the fans, which included selfies, signing autographs, and the players giving selected fans their match-worn shirts, Adam and his players trudged off the pitch, their breath visible in the crisp spring air. They made their way up the tunnel, its concrete walls damp and cold. As they approached the away dressing room, their footsteps echoed off the walls, mingling with their raucous laughter and cheers. Adam shouted over the din to usher his team into the dressing room for his post-match team talk.

As the heavy metal door clicked shut behind them, a silence descended upon the room. Adam closed his eyes and inhaled deeply, taking in the familiar scents of sweat and stale air mixed with a lingering hint of grass from the player's boots. His eyes swept over his team of warriors, some of whom hadn't given their shirts away and were still wearing their mud-covered jerseys and bearing the marks of a hard-fought battle. Every muscle in their bodies screamed from exhaustion, yet their eyes shone with passion and fight. Their unwavering spirit and unbreakable bond as a team spoke volumes louder than any roar from the cheering crowd outside.

Adam's prideful voice cut through the quiet like a cold winter wind, bringing all the players to attention. Obediently, they draped themselves over the benches, their brightly coloured boots leaving muddy imprints on the scrupulously clean tiles. "Firstly," Adam began, "Well done on that result. Many wrote us off before kick-off, even more so when they took the lead. But you stayed strong, stuck to the tactics and plan we had worked on, and found the equaliser. They then threw everything at us, but we remained resilient and fought hard for the point. I am proud of every one of you tonight." As Adam finished speaking, he looked directly at Neil Cole and pointed at him, "And finally," he said with a smile, "Can I get a massive round of applause for Neil on his first senior goal?"

The room erupted into delirious applause as Neil blushed and grinned from ear to ear. The sound of clapping hands filled the air with cheers and congratulations for their teammate's achievement, a moment of pure joy and camaraderie bonding them even more strongly as a team.

After a pause, Adam ended the team talk by declaring, "As we all know, Wry could only draw, which means that Sunday's home game against them is a winner-takes-it-all, high-stakes affair in our bid for survival," Adam continued, "The day after a game would usually be a day off. However, I want to see you all at the training ground tomorrow at one pm. We won't be training, but we do need to do a post-match briefing and a pre-match briefing for Sunday, as well as another task I have in mind for you. We will provide a buffet lunch. You will be finished by three o'clock," he explained. "Remember this about Sunday. It's not just about what we do on that day. It's about who we are and where we want to be," the intensity in his tone grew as he spoke, a fire burning within him to ensure his message was understood, "We haven't come this far to simply fade away."

Adam's words rippled through the room like a pebble thrown into still water, sending energy waves crashing against the walls. His voice was solid and unwavering, devoid of coddling or false promises. As the players rose from the benches, their bodies aching but their spirits lifted, Adam greeted them with a fierce grin and a firm pat on the back. They returned his smile, feeling their confidence strengthen until it was unyielding. As Adam left the room to head to his post-match press conference, the players began to strip out of their kits and make their way for a well-earned shower.

Adam stormed into the chaotic media room, the deafening roar of voices and flashing cameras assaulting his senses. He pushed through the crowd of reporters to reach the front desk, a determined glint in his eyes. With a tight-lipped smile, he began his address.

"Evening all. Before we begin, by show of hands, how many of you expected us to get slaughtered tonight?" Adam asked. He scanned the room as every single hand shot up in response. "And how many of you thought that even more strongly once they took the lead?" Adam asked. All hands remained raised, "So, let me get this straight," Adam said, his voice rising with each word, "You all wrote us off before a ball was even kicked tonight. But yet here we are, defying your expectations," he paused for effect before continuing, his tone becoming more forceful. "You wrote us off when I was appointed as manager. But guess what? We're still fighting. Still in the game, and with a chance of survival," Adam said, slamming his hand down on the table to punctuate his words, "Sure, it may be because Wry dropped points, but we are not giving up. So don't even think about writing us off just yet," Adam stated.

The press conference began as the crowd of journalists gasped at Adam's statement. "Hello, Super Sports TV here. Can you share your thoughts on tonight's game and Neil Cole's first senior goal, a crucial one at that?" the journalist asked.

After a momentary pause to gather his thoughts, Adam replied confidently, "Neil is a remarkable young man with an unbreakable desire to succeed in the game, and I have no doubt he will. As for tonight's game, I thought we were exceptional. We stuck to our plan, played fluid and inspiring football, and fought relentlessly to come back and secure the point. Our resilience was truly admirable." Adam's words were met with nods of approval from the journalists, impressed by his team's performance.

The next question was from a young female representing UK News. "Hi, Adam," she began, her voice laced with a hint of challenge, "Some fans may be wondering what you were thinking when you decided to substitute a midfielder for an additional defender after scoring. It seems like you were playing for a draw and lacked ambition. Can you explain your reasoning?" she asked.

Adam's response was immediate and passionate as he slammed his hand down on the desk again, "Not at all," he retorted firmly, "We knew that South Swanshea would come at us with everything they had, desperate for a win to keep their European hopes alive. That's why we needed an experienced player like Michael to help solidify our defence. I felt he would, and indeed, he did make a significant impact for us." Adam continued, "Let me make it clear, our goal was always to win the game. But we also had to be strategic and calculated in how we did so. We planned to counterattack whenever South Swanshea made a mistake or lost possession during their aggressive attacks. Unfortunately, they were flawless and didn't give us that opportunity. But that was our plan from the beginning, to go for all three points while still being smart about it so as not to lose the game," Adam explained.

"Next?" Adam asked. A hush fell over the room as Super Swanshea magazine's representative stood and addressed him.

"Hi, Adam. Simon from Super Swanshea magazine here, thank you for speaking with us. We would love your thoughts on South Swanshea's performance tonight," the reporter inquired.

Adam nodded, his face a mask of composure, "Firstly, let me offer my commiserations on the result. I know you all hoped for the win." Adam paused to gather his thoughts before continuing, "Tonight only confirmed what I already knew, South Swanshea are a truly fantastic side and have been all season. The European spot, which I'm sure you will secure on Sunday, is fully deserved, and I wish you all the best of luck with that next season."

The journalist nodded, scribbling down notes as Adam spoke. "Thank you. We appreciate your kind words, and good luck for Sunday," Simon replied with a genuine smile, unable to hide his admiration for Adam's kind words.

Next up was the Swanford Daily newspaper. "Evening, Adam. What are your thoughts now looking ahead to Sunday. The season's final game will be a home game and a winner-takes-all showdown with Wry."

Adam took a moment to consider his answer before replying, "What a finale it is going to be for the mutual," Adam remarked, "Not so much for us and Wry. We both have it all on the line, the stakes are high, and it will be a day and a match full of tension and nerves. That said, we will be fully prepared and ready for battle, and I'm positive the home advantage will be the marginal gain we need to ensure our safety in this division."

As the questions continued, Adam kept a confident front despite the negative and positive questions. The next question came from The Weekly Whistle podcast, "Adam, there's been rumours about your job as manager being uncertain regardless of the outcome on Sunday. How do you respond to that?"

Adam briefly paused before responding, "Rumours are just that, rumours. I'm focused on the task in hand, which is working hard with this fantastic team to ensure our survival in the league. Let's save speculations for after the final game and the seasons done."

Next, it was time for an inquiry from Pitch Side Press. "Hi Adam, Wry's head coach, Paul Lacey, has just suggested in his post-match interview that his team has more to lose than yours going into Sunday's match, as they've consistently been a top-ranking club and find themselves in the safety spot one point above you. Do you have a response for him?" the journalist asked.

"Well," Adam stated, "Our team has something to lose every time we step on the pitch, our pride and our standing. But let's be clear here, we're fighting for our place in this division. Yes, Wry have had a solid run in the league over the past few years, but so have we. We're not planning on making their job easy come Sunday."

The final question came from Sports Radio, "Adam," the young journalist began with hesitation in her eyes, "Some people say that this upcoming match against Wry represents more than just football. It symbolises hope and perseverance against all odds for the locals, who've seen many ups and downs with the club over the years. How much does that weigh on your shoulders going into the final game?" she asked.

Adam didn't hesitate; his response was immediate and heartfelt, "It weighs very heavily indeed. We know what this club means to our fans and what it represents in our community. But I'll tell you what, pressure makes diamonds, and we plan on shining bright come Sunday."

With his final response, Adam rose from the cushioned armchair, his muscles tense and a resolve in his eyes that could not be ignored.

Amidst the clamour of clicking cameras and eager reporters, he thanked the gathered media for their attendance before striding out of the room.

Adam approached the team coach, his steps heavy with exhaustion after the intense evening. The players and coaching team were already gathered on board, their faces etched with weariness and a sense of satisfaction for their hard-fought point. As the coach rumbled towards the local airport, the players sat silently, each lost in their thoughts as they listened to music through their headphones. The engine's noise and the occasional jolt from potholes on the road created a lulling rhythm, allowing them to relax and reflect on their performance tonight.

With a sharp turn, the coach arrived at the airport, and the team eagerly filed out, eager to swap the cramped coach for an aeroplane's slightly more spacious interior.

The plane's interior was bathed in a soft, warm glow as the flight attendants dimmed the lights, signalling for the players to relax and rest as they took off into the night sky. Adam sat comfortably in his seat, pulling out his phone to watch highlights of the Cliffe vs Wry match. As he watched, a small notebook emerged from his bag, its pages blank and waiting to be filled with his thoughts. His mind was still whirling from the game and the post-match interview, replaying key moments and analysing plays from his team's performance. Throughout the flight, Adam meticulously jotted down notes, identifying weaknesses in Wry's game. These scribbles would be the backbone of the final two training days, shaping their game plan for Sunday's highly anticipated match.

As the aeroplane touched down in Manchester, the team filed out into the night's cool air. Each player carried within him the knowledge that Sunday's match had far-reaching implications beyond mere points on a league table. It was a fight for their place in this division, a testament to their tenacity in an unforgiving sport. Most importantly, it would be a beacon of hope for their fans, who had stood unwavering by their side through it all.

After walking into the car park to his vehicle, Adam got into his car, sinking into the plush leather seat and taking in the familiar scent of his air freshener. With a flick of a switch, Sports Radio crackled to life, filling the small space with the voice of the host's show. His gruff tone held a deep knowledge and love for football, having once been a professional player. Tonight's show was all about the evening's fixtures, with callers sharing their thoughts and concerns on the upcoming showdown between Swanford and Wry.

Each caller's voice trembled with worry, their words laced with fear and uncertainty. But underneath it all, there was a strong sense of belief. Adam listened intently, absorbing their words and letting them fuel his determination. As he pulled out of the car park, he couldn't help but feel a surge of excitement for what lay ahead in the game on Sunday. As Adam drove toward home, the streetlights glinted off his windshield like stars in the night sky. One caller to the show stood out above others to Adam. Her name was Molly. Molly's voice shook with raw emotion as she introduced herself to the radio show host. She was a die-hard fan of Swanford, having supported them since she was just a young girl. Molly's journey home from South Swanshea was long and fraught with anxiety, but her love for the club drove her forward.

"I've been listening to your show for years," she said, "And I always love it. Tonight, I'm so proud of our boys for fighting back against all odds. When we went a goal down and Wry were winning, I feared the worst. But then we equalised, and that glimmer of hope kept me going until the end." Molly's voice cracked as she spoke of her late grandfather, a lifelong Swanford supporter who passed away at Christmas.

"I know he had a hand in that last-minute equaliser at Cliffe. I know he'll be watching over us on Sunday too." Her words carried an unwavering belief in her team and their management. "We've come through tough times before, and we always come out stronger. These lads have it in them. I believe in them, and I believe in Adam, Mike, and Shea, our management team," she declared.

Adam found himself nodding along with Molly's words, feeling a swell of pride and gratitude in his chest. They were not just fans, he realised, but an integral part of the club's heart and soul. Their unwavering support was like a steady drumbeat, driving the team forward.

As Adam pulled into his driveway, he took one final moment to sit in the stillness of his car. The sound of the engine cooling down and the distant sounds of the night were comforting after a long day at work. Adam closed his eyes and pictured Sunday's match in his mind, imagining the stadium filled with thousands of passionate fans. Molly's words echoed in his head, instilling a sense of duty in Adam. The weight on his shoulders felt lighter, knowing that they were not alone in this fight. Adam stepped out of his car, taking a deep breath as he gazed at the glittering stars above him. The quiet darkness provided a momentary respite from the world's chaos before he turned and entered his home with a grateful heart.

22

Thursday 25th April

Adam arrived at the training ground with optimism and purpose, ready for another long, eventful day. His first port of call was his office, where, after grabbing a coffee from his machine, Adam took some time to plan his agenda for the upcoming meeting with the players to discuss last night's game and Sunday's big showdown, winner-takes-it-all affair with Wry.

As one o'clock drew nearer, Adam entered the briefing room, where his players greeted him. Their energy and excitement from the previous evening's events still radiated from them, filling the room with a buzz. The atmosphere was one of excitement as they eagerly awaited their manager's feedback from last night's game and instructions for the days ahead and Sunday's game. Despite the long journey home and the late night the previous evening, the spirits were high.

Adam made his way to the front of the room, cueing an immediate silence as every eye turned towards him. "Last night was a good series of events for us," Adam began, his voice steady and commanding attention effortlessly, "You fought back when you were down, and you showed what it means to be part of this team. The equaliser was a testament to your perseverance and your belief. You stayed strong, and you worked tirelessly. Well done," he gestured towards the screen behind him, where highlights from last night's match were playing.

"We can't rest on our laurels, though," Adam continued, "We must take that momentum into Sunday's game. We need to channel that same grit and desire. We have a tough opponent ahead of us in Wry who are also fighting for survival. It's us versus them, one safety spot left, winner takes it all." At the mention of Wry, there were a few sharp intakes of breath around the room.

"I believe in each one of you, just as our fans do," Adam stated, his eyes scanning the room, meeting each player's eyes in turn, "I want us to work on our strengths but also improve on our weaknesses. We will spend these next two days training hard and strengthening our fight and resolve." Adam paused momentarily before adding, "There's pressure for sure, but remember, pressure makes diamonds." The room met Adam's words with nods of affirmation and a few optimistic smiles.

Adam turned his attention to analysing the previous evening's game, "Alright, lads," he began, his voice firm but laced with empathy, "We all know the feeling right now. A point gained, but the chance for two more lost." A ripple of agreement went through the room, "But," Adam continued, his voice rising, "Let's not dwell on what could have been. We focus on what we did well."

Adam gestured towards the whiteboard, where a tactical breakdown of the match awaited. "Defensively, we were solid. Kofi, that block in the first half? Top draw, saved our bacon there." Kofi, the veteran centre-back, a faint bruise blooming on his cheekbone, offered a curt nod, a hint of a smile on his lips.

"And Davids," Adam continued, turning to the young winger, "Your pace down the flank caused them all sorts of problems. You created a real threat out there." Davids, usually quiet, puffed out his chest a little, a surge of pride evident in his eyes.

Adam continued acknowledging the positives, but now the more challenging part came. "Right, areas for improvement," he tapped the laptop to move on to the following video clip, highlighting a missed pass in midfield that led to South Swanshea's goal, "There," he explained, "a misplaced pass can be costly. We need sharper, cleaner connections in the middle of the park on Sunday."

Heads nodded in agreement. Adam continued, dissecting missed opportunities, tactical oversights, and moments of individual brilliance overshadowed by collective lapses. He wasn't harsh, but he was honest. This was a team on the precipice, and every detail mattered.

"Sunday," Adam said, his voice filled with quiet intensity, "It's winner-takes-all against Wry. We all know what's at stake. Relegation. The very future of this club." He paused, letting his words sink in, "But here's the thing, lads. We've fought our way back from the brink. We have the talent, the heart and the fight. We just need to channel it all, every ounce of it, onto that pitch on Sunday." A slow smile spread across Adam's face, "We can do this. We will do this. Together. At the end of the day, it's not about the name on the back of the shirt; it's about the crest on the front. It's about this club, this town, this family."

A collective fire ignited in the players' eyes. Where once shrouded in disappointment, there was a renewed sense of purpose. The draw against South Swanshea was a missed chance, but this battle was far from lost. Swanford were still in the fight. On Sunday, they wouldn't just be playing for points but for their pride, future, and Swanford. And they were ready to fight.

As the meeting ended and the players got up from their seats and started moving towards the exit, Adam said in parting, "I need six volunteers to stay behind, please. The rest of you enjoy the buffet lunch, and I'll see you at training in the morning."

Adams volunteers gathered once the rest of the team had left. He had Shea, Michael Knight, Neil Cole, Barlow, Ethan Fox and Turner at his disposal. "Ok, lads, thanks for volunteering," Adam began to explain, "I want you to go and see the media department, who are waiting for you in the canteen. I want you to record a rally call video to be put out across the club's media, urging the fans to sell out Sunday's game and be the twelfth man for us. We need them to get behind our cause in our hour of need."

"Sure, that'll be great. Let's do it," Michael declared, leading the other five men off to the canteen.

Following the meeting, Adam made his way to his office. For the next hour or so, he sat at his desk, meticulously planning Sunday's game and devising plans to exploit Wry's weaknesses, which he had noted down during his flight back home. Adam also worked on plans to strengthen his side's vulnerabilities that Wry could exploit. Throughout the long hours, he returned to Molly's words from the radio call-in, letting them propel him forward. "I believe in our boys. I believe in the management team of Adam, Mike, and Shea" The echo of her words filled his mind.

Adam was disturbed from his focus by his phone's alarm at five minutes to three, a reminder to log onto the club meeting at three o'clock. Adam logged on and was greeted by a panel of members of the retail, media, accounts, ticket office and commercial teams, as well as the meeting host and chair, Mr Broad. Mr Broad, muting all the microphones, opened the meeting.

"Good afternoon, everyone. Thanks for attending. I appreciate that we are all very busy before Sunday's huge game. Today's meeting aims to get ahead of the curve and plan for next season. Each of you, department-wise, will be given the chance to speak and explain anything that needs to be planned or actioned. Following the meeting I will then take the minutes to a board meeting chaired by Mr Brewer, who will have the final say on all action points and suggestions. For now, let's get started with retail, please," Mr Broad said, unmuting the head of retail's microphone.

"Good afternoon all," Mr Stone, head of retail, began. "The main thing we need to nail at this point is next season's kit so that we can order them for summer sales ahead of next season. We have three weeks to get the design for all three kits to the manufacturer. What I need to know is, firstly, from the commercial team, who will be the front-of-shirt sponsor for next season? Secondly, as first team manager, I need to know from Adam if you have any ideas on kit designs?"

The first to answer was Mr Andre, head of commercial. "Ok, sure. We are currently in a three-way negotiation about who will be next season's front-of-shirt sponsor. We have set a deadline of the end of next week to have it all wrapped up. I will email you the details as soon as everything is sorted. Is that ok?" he asked.

"Sure, thank you," Mr Stone replied.

Adam unmuted his microphone next to address Mr Stone. "Hi, so I must say all this is a bit mind-boggling. I don't even know if I will be here next season. Regardless of whether or not I'm here to see it through, I think it would be nice to involve the fans, our main customers for the kits, in their design. With that in mind, I would suggest that we run a competition. We ask fans of all ages to design home and away kits. Once we have all the entries, we set up a panel, including the players, to whittle the designs down to a shortlist of ten designs for each kit, after which we run a public vote to decide the final designs. As for the third kit, retro is all the trend, so with that in mind, what is one of our most iconic away or third strips from recent history?" Adam asked.

"Iconic kit," Mr Stone thought out loud, searching for an answer, "It's probably got to be the black and gold away kit from the ninety-five to ninety-six season, which had a funky, now iconic design. It was the kit we wore on the day we won the title for the second division with a romping seven-nil win at Shredford."

"That's that decided, then," Adam replied, "A copy of that will be next season's third kit," he declared.

"Perfect, thank you, Adam. I'll get onto all that straight away," Mr Stone replied.

"And we will get the competition advertised," Kevin, assistant head of media, interjected.

Next to speak was Mr Edinburgh, head of accounts. "Hi all," he began, "My main concern today is in hearing intentions for next season's ticket prices and also intentions in terms of recruitment and required transfer and wage budget in the summer so that I can start to try and balance the books," he said.

"Thank you," replied Mr Broad.

Next to speak was Chad, head of the ticket office. "Hi all," Chad said, "We need to discuss next season's season tickets. We will adhere to the usual renewal scheme, including an early bird window and a general sale date. However, we need to discuss a price point. What are your thoughts as manager Adam and Mr Edinburgh of the accounts department, please?"

Immediately, Adam answered, "My initial thoughts are that we should facilitate a price freeze," he explained, "I know that this is the last thing we want, given the club's financial issues. Indeed, staying in this division, if we can pull it off, would give us the opportunity, as many other clubs have, to increase prices to help with the financial issues. However, I feel that the price freeze would be best as it would retain the support we may need to survive again in this division next season or would reflect value for money in the lower division should we be relegated. If we are relegated, we can not afford to lower our prices. Why should we do this? No club lowers their prices when the supporters buy at the price set, but if we drop to a lower league, we can't justify raising the prices either," Adam explained.

"Reluctantly, against my better will to improve the financial issues surrounding the club, I agree with you, Adam," interjected Mr Edinburgh.

"Ok, great, that's that settled then," replied Mr Broad.

Finally, it was the turn of the player recruitment department to provide input. "Hi all," Mr Craig, the club's technical director, said, "I am head of the player recruitment department. We will be working hard from as soon as the last ball of this season is kicked until the first ball of next season is kicked to put together our squad for next season. As the current first team manager, Adam, we need your guidance on several issues. Firstly, there are a lot of players whose contracts are up at the end of the season, and we can not afford to offer many of them renewals on their current terms, especially if we are relegated. We need to know which of those players would be an asset to us next season so that we can attempt to retain them on improved terms to suit the club. Secondly, we need to know what areas of the team would need new players once players have left the club, either through release or sales. We also need to know what sort of player the side needs, such as experienced, young, fast, technical, etc. Thirdly, we need to know if there are any specific targets you want us to attempt to sign," he explained.

"You'll forgive me if I can't get my head around that at this moment. I don't even know what league we'll be in or if I'll be here next season," Adam replied, "However, I feel the wise thing to do at the moment is look at team selections in the last few months and exclude all the players out of contract. From there, the positions we need new players in should be clear. Then, lean upon the scouting department to draw up two lists, one based on who we can realistically attract to the club should we stay in this division and then a list of players we can recruit if we are relegated. Once the season is finished and we know my position, or not as the case may be, we can work through the lists once we know which league we will be in. As for the type of player, if it were my side next year, I'd want to lose a lot of the old guard, which would ease the wage bill significantly. We can then rebuild with fast, hungry young players committed to developing into top players and, therefore, will develop the club into a top side. Players with a point to prove who will improve game by game, in a side with a point to prove and desire to improve game by game," Adam explained.

"Ok, perfect, I'll get onto it right away," Mr Craig replied.

Mr Broad wrapped up the meeting, thanking all for attending again. Adam shut down his laptop, completing his day at the training ground and work.

23

Friday 26th April

As the sun rose over the training ground on Friday morning, Adam and his team were already gathered, their minds focused on the upcoming battle in just two days. Mike and Shea, the trusted leaders of the team, took charge of the training session, guiding and pushing each player to reach their full potential. The atmosphere was tense yet optimistic as they prepared for Sunday's crucial game against Wry. The players trained tirelessly, their muscles straining and sweat beading on their foreheads as they worked on their fitness levels and tactical game plans. It was clear that every move made and strategy discussed had one aim: victory on the battlefield on Sunday. The usually boisterous training ground was now severe and serene, each movement executed with precision and focus. Every pass, every sprint, every header carried the weight of their team's success, as if they were already on the pitch with Wry, battling for victory.

Mike's intense focus was locked onto the attacking drills, determined to push his players to their limits and prepare them to exploit Wry's notoriously weak defence. His passionate voice echoed across the pitch, a combination of gruffness and encouragement reverberating in the players' ears. "That's it, good pass," he bellowed, urging his players to repeat successful moves, "Eyes up, always anticipate the next move," he commanded, driving them to be constantly aware and alert.

Meanwhile, Shea devoted himself to the defenders, working alongside them with a fierce desire to make them unbreakable. While Wry may have a weaker defence, their offensive tactics were like a powerful storm, relentlessly striking and moving forward. Shea drilled the players in precise blocking techniques, emphasising the crucial need for communication between the goalkeeper and his defenders. Shea scanned over every team member as he stressed, "Do not underestimate them. Wry are fast and unpredictable. They will exploit any gap we leave open."

Adam observed from the sidelines, pleased with the progress made during training as the day slowly dwindled on.

As Adam drove away from the training ground just after three o'clock, his mind raced with thoughts, and his heart ached with pressure. Adam knew he needed guidance, and there was only one person he could turn to: his late Granddad. The streets of Swanford were bustling and chaotic, but Adam navigated through them with a sense of purpose. He weaved his way through winding roads before turning down a familiar lane that led to the cemetery where his Granddad had been laid to rest. As Adam parked his car, he took a moment to prepare himself for what lay ahead.

Here, amidst the chaotic symphony of the city, a hushed reverence settled over Adam. The air was heavy and thick with the scent of damp earth and the cloying sweetness of lilies. It felt as if the entire world held its breath, paying a silent tribute to those who had passed on.

Adam's steps were deliberate, crunching softly on the gravel path. Each one was a heartbeat in the profound stillness, a slow, steady rhythm that mirrored the solemn thud of his heart. Flanked on either side by rolling green hummocks, the path was a vibrant tapestry of wildflowers in bloom. Poppies, ablaze in fiery red, brushed his ankles as he walked. Delicate white daisies swayed gently in the breeze, each one a silent prayer whispering on the wind. Interspersed amongst the flowers, weathered granite plaques stood sentinel, each etched with a name, a date, and a story waiting to be unearthed.

A sudden shift in the air sent a shiver down Adam's spine. It was more than just the cool caress of a passing breeze. It felt like a spectral presence, a whisper brushing against his cheek. A presence he couldn't quite define, but one that sent a jolt of recognition through him. It was like a hand reaching out from the veil, a connection bridging the gap between the living and the dead. Could it be his Granddad? Was his spirit lingering here, waiting to guide him towards the answers he desperately sought?

With a renewed sense of purpose, Adam quickened his pace. Each step brought him closer to his Granddad's final resting place, a simple granite bench nestled in the tranquil outer perimeter of the remembrance garden. As he drew nearer, a wave of peace washed over him, a calming sensation that settled in his bones like cool water on a parched throat. In the quiet communion with his past, Adam felt a flicker of hope ignite within him. Perhaps, here, amidst the whispers of the wind and the memories of the departed, he would finally find the solace he craved.

The remembrance garden, a haven of serenity amidst the city's relentless change, remained stubbornly the same. Here, under a canopy of ancient oaks draped in emerald moss, time seemed to hold its breath. Yet, for Adam, the world had become a kaleidoscope of blurred colours, the vibrant tapestry of blooming roses and lilies a hazy watercolour through the veil of his tears. He sank onto the bench, the same one where he'd last spoken to his grandfather, and the weight of grief settled on him like a suffocating cloak. The gentle sighing of the wind through the leaves mocked his choked sobs, and the scent of damp earth and blooming honeysuckle, once a familiar comfort, now felt heavy and cloying. Each blossom, a testament to life's enduring cycle, only amplified the stark finality of his loss. With a ragged breath, Adam fought to compose himself, a tidal wave of memories threatening to drown him. Here, in this sanctuary of memories, the dam holding back his grief threatened to crumble.

As Adam's gaze drifted across the rolling green expanse of the remembrance garden, memories flooded his mind, vivid snapshots of his beloved Granddad, Bill. Bill was a man built like a redwood yet gentle as a summer breeze, his eyes twinkling with an unshakeable positivity that defied even the harshest storms.

One particular cherished memory unfolded before him: countless afternoons and evenings spent huddled with his Granddad over the television, the flickering light dancing across their faces as they dissected game highlights. The smell of Bill's pipe tobacco mingled with the murmur of excited commentary, their lively debates about tactics, players, and the beautiful game.

A sigh escaped Adam's lips, the wind rustling the leaves in a mournful reply. As if summoning his Granddad's spirit, Adam began to speak, his voice a mere whisper against the vastness of the sky. "Granddad," he rasped, the word heavy with vulnerability and a desperate yearning for guidance, "I need you now more than ever."

His eyes, reflecting the storm brewing within, darted about the garden. He delved into the details of the upcoming clash with Wry, the formidable giants that loomed on the horizon. He spoke of their strengths, an avalanche of tactical prowess and clinical finishing. Yet, he didn't shy away from their vulnerabilities, a chink in the armour waiting to be exploited. He described the crippling weight of expectation, the deafening roar of the crowd, and the relentless scrutiny of the media, all pressing down on him like an iron fist.

But most importantly, Adam confessed his deepest fears with a rawness he hadn't expected. Was he leading his team astray? Was he letting them down? His voice, a torrent of emotions threatening to break the dam of his composure, rose and fell with the rhythm of a breaking wave. Words tumbled out like a confession, a downpour that wouldn't cease until he was finally drained, his body slumped against the damp, worn bench, the silence as heavy as the grief he carried in his heart.

A voice, faint yet resonant, echoed in the garden's stillness. It wasn't the wind nor a trick of memory. It was Bill, his Granddad, a titan of a man with a heart as soft as his worn baseball cap. "Focus, Adam," the voice rumbled, each word a boulder anchoring him. "Train hard, believe in your team. But even if," the voice hitched, a rare tremor in its certainty, "Even if it falls apart, remember, it's just a game. Not life or death. There's a bigger picture, a reason for the twists and turns. You'll be ok, win or lose."

The world seemed to slow its frantic pace, the vibrant blooms blurring at the edges as Adam clung to his Granddad's words. A wave of solace washed over him, a balm on the raw wound of self-doubt. It wasn't a promise of victory but a more profound truth: his resilience, his ability to weather any storm. In that quiet moment of connection, Adam found the strength he needed for the game and whatever life threw his way.

Adam confidently rose to his feet and left the cemetery, his face etched with serenity. Tomorrow marked the final day of training, and he was prepared to face it head-on. As Adam walked back toward his car, his footsteps echoed against the cold marble gravestones, a reminder of the weight of his mission and what was at stake.

As Adam arrived home, he fixed himself some dinner before using the video link emailed to him to log onto the fan's podcast, 'Up the Swans', for his guest appearance. It was seven pm, and the podcast was about to begin. Chris Palmer hosted the podcast with co-hosts Alex Rice and Roger Webster. "Welcome today, listeners. This is Chris, your host. Of course, I'm joined by my regular co-hosts, Alex and Roger. Lads, how are we feeling about the result at South Swanshea first and then ahead of Sunday's winner-takes-it-all final game against Wry?" Chris began the podcast while Adam watched.

"Well," Alex began, "I thought we were fantastic at South Swanshea. We showed passion and fight, and that's all we can ask for as fans. We certainly had lady luck shining upon us with that equaliser at Wry. I'd be lying if I said I wasn't nervous before Sunday. However, I've seen enough in the last two games to make me think that we will fight with heart and courage and maybe, just maybe, pull this off."

"Absolutely," Roger added, "I echo what Alex said, and I believe we will do it and survive," he said.

"Thanks, guys. Although I am so nervous too, to be fair," Chris replied.

"Ok, listeners," Chris said, "At this time, I would like to bring in our special guest, Adam Wells. Adam was a surprising shock appointment as our manager going into the seasons final four games, given that his only experience is on the video game Ultimate Manager. The appointment was met with anger and scepticism, a fact only affirmed by a nightmare of a second half at Newborough in his opening game, which led to a 6-1 defeat. Since then, we have beaten Cliffe at home and got a valuable point on the road at South Swanshea to keep us in the fight going into the final day and a winner-takes-it-all showdown against Wry, all be it with a little bit of luck other results wise. Adam, welcome, and thank you so much for taking time out of what I'm sure is a hectic schedule ahead of Sunday to talk to us," Chris said.

"My absolute pleasure, guys," Adam replied.

"Adam," Chris began, "First and foremost, what is the mood in the camp like ahead of Sunday? How are preparations going?" he asked.

"Well, Chris," Adam replied, "The mood is one of optimism. The defeat at Newborough feels like a lifetime ago now, and our last two results have been positive, with us being unbeaten in both of them. We know we can match and hopefully beat Wry on Sunday. We back ourselves and have the fight and heart to battle in this relegation war for you wonderful supporters, our twelfth man. Win, lose or draw Sunday, it won't be for lack of effort. We won't be leaving anything out there, rest assured."

"Adam," Alex began, "Do you worry that the rumoured off-the-pitch financial issues could affect the players, creating a negative attitude on the pitch?" he asked.

"Not at all," Adam replied, "On their passports, the players have two simple words, professional footballer. This is what they shall be at this time. Their wages are paid to them to be a footballer for this football club and produce on the pitch as part of that job role, and that is what they shall do," Adam stated.

"Thank you," replied Alex.

"Hi Adam, Roger here," Roger said, "It seems you have been doing a lot of work around team bonding and breeding confidence into the players, with a rumoured team bonding day. What else have you been doing to help, and what role do camaraderie and confidence play in this relegation battle? Some critics have debated that there is no time for fun and games. How do you reply to that?" he asked.

"Hi Roger, great question," Adam replied, "When I arrived, it was off the back of a poor run of form and results, something which has been the case for the whole season in reality. Confidence and spirit were at an all-time low. I knew that we had to get that back. A confident team is a happy team that produces the best results, simple as that. I needed to get smiles back on faces and belief instilled again. We are in a relegation battle, and a cohesive team with camaraderie is key. We need our guys arm in arm in the trenches fighting for each other, the supporters and the club."

"Brilliant, thank you," Roger replied.

Next to probe Adam was Alex again, "Adam, some critics have questioned your choice to bring in the three youngsters Ethan, Neil and Louis. They feel that experience is needed at this time, not young lads who are still learning. What do you say to this?" he asked.

"In a word, nonsense," Adam replied, "Age is no barrier to skill. If anything, these lads' desire and passion far outweigh the experience factor. I spotted something in these lads, so I initially promoted them to first-team training. I wasn't sure if they were good enough for the first team in this key relegation battle, but they forcefully changed my mind with how they conducted themselves, trained and ran rings around the so-called experienced first-team players. They're in the side on merit," Adam explained.

Next to speak was Chris again, "Adam, how do you anticipate the game against Wry on Sunday going?" he asked.

"Well," Adam began, "We are both, Wry and us, fighting for our future in the league. We have to beat them to survive, whereas they can afford to take just a point. I anticipate it being a close affair, and I think whoever wins will only do so by the odd goal. I believe that can be us, and I'm sure the afternoon will be a to-and-throw rollercoaster of emotions and permutations. It won't be one for the faint-hearted, but the players and I believe we can be the ones with victorious smiles come the final whistle," he explained.

Roger asked, "Adam, do you have a final message for the fans?"

"Yes, I do," Adam replied, "We need you now more than ever. If you haven't already got a ticket and are able to, please do. We need a sold-out, rocking ground on Sunday to be our twelfth man and get us over the line. Together and united, we can do this," he declared.

"Brilliant," Chris replied, "Adam, thank you so much for joining us today and good luck for Sunday. You heard the man, you Swans fans, let's get Sunday sold out and rocking for the lads."

24

Saturday 27th April

The following day, Adam joined the players on the training pitch. "Good morning, lads," Adam greeted them, looking around at each player, confidently meeting their looks, "Today is the final day of training. We face Wry tomorrow, a formidable opponent who will throw everything at us. We are a strong team, united in spirit and strengthened by our relentless training and teamwork."

Electric energy was in the air, fuelled by the upcoming game and the bond between teammates. As training commenced, the players pushed themselves to their limits, sweat pouring down their faces as they honed their skills and strategised for victory. As the gruelling training session ended, Adam gathered up his players.

"Ok, lads, this is it," Adam began, "Tomorrow is the big day. Please go shower and change, then after my press conference, I want to see each of you one-on-one in my office before you head home. I know kick-off isn't until four o'clock tomorrow, but I want to see you all at the ground at nine am sharp. There are no excuses and no exceptions to that. After our one-to-ones, get yourselves off home. Have a sensible dinner and breakfast and a great evening with your families, but above all else, get an early night and be well-rested for tomorrow."

The time had come for Adam to face the press again for his pre-game conference. Again, he strode alone, without Sarah, whom he hadn't seen or heard from for a few days, into the press room. Despite facing the press alone again, Adam appeared confident as a wave of calmness washed over him. The bustling briefing room was filled with reporters from every major news channel, their cameras trained expectantly on the podium where he sat.

"Good afternoon, all," Adam greeted the gathered media, "I'm sure you're all keen to hear about my approach to and thoughts on tomorrow's final battle with Wry."

A torrent of inquiries flooded the air, swirling around with hungry intensity. The press prodded and poked, trying to extract any information they could about the team's readiness for their upcoming match against Wry.

Adam stayed calm, confident, and composed, answering each question with a steady gaze and concise responses. His words instilled a newfound sense of admiration for his leadership among the crowd of reporters. Adam spoke eloquently of the team's rigorous preparations, leaving every detail addressed in their pursuit of perfection. Above all, he emphasised their unbreakable bond and unwavering fight and spirit.

"But at its core," Adam concluded, looking at the journalists, "What truly sets us apart is our belief. Belief in ourselves as individuals and as a cohesive unit. I'm fully aware that under the old regime in the reverse fixture a few months ago, we lost 3-0, but that was then, and this is now."

A soft murmur of agreement rippled through the press room, accompanied by the scratching sound of pens scribbling furiously on notepads. Adam's chest swelled with satisfaction. He had bared his soul to the reporters, answering their questions honestly and sincerely. The nerves and uncertainties about tomorrow's game still lingered, but an overwhelming sense of optimism overshadowed them. As Adam made his way out of the press room, the echoes of reporters' comments filled the air around him. Words like inspiring, confident, and focused floated on the excited buzz of conversation, bringing a smile to Adam's lips as he headed back to his office.

After the press conference, Adam sat down with each player for a one-on-one meeting. He gave each player his undivided attention, offering encouragement and advice tailored to their strengths and weaknesses. The players listened intently, hanging on every word as they prepared for the upcoming match. Each one promised to take his advice on board and give their all on the pitch. Each player was confident and ready to face tomorrow's challenges as they left their meetings individually.

As the last of the players left his office, Adam finally allowed himself a moment to breathe. He stood in his spacious office, admiring the view from the floor-to-ceiling windows. Tomorrow was a pivotal day for the club that could determine their fate for years to come. The room's stillness was broken only by the distant sound of players leaving the training facility. Win or lose tomorrow, Adam knew they had given it their all, and that was something to be proud of.

As the clock struck half-past-three, signalling the end of another long day at the training ground, Adam's mind was buzzing with an idea. He knew that Riley James, the popular host on Sports Radio, was set to take to the airwaves at nine pm for a three-hour call-in show ahead of tomorrow's crucial fixtures. One match was on everyone's lips: the relegation showdown between Swanford and Wry.

Adam made a spontaneous decision; he wanted to join Riley in the studio and speak directly to the Swanford fans. With driven steps, he made his way to his car and typed in the address of the station's central London location into his trusty sat nav. The screen lit up with an estimated journey time of four and a half hours for the two-hundred-and-twenty-mile trek. Adam didn't hesitate. He knew this was an opportunity he couldn't pass up. The sun was beginning to dip as he merged onto the motorway.

As Adam drove through sprawling countryside and bustling cities, his excitement grew for what lay ahead. He couldn't wait to make it to the station and address the passionate Swanford fans to lift their spirits before tomorrow's crucial match. This journey may be long, but it was worth every mile for this chance to make a difference. The trip was long and arduous, but Adam was determined to see it through. He believed in connecting with his fans directly, in sharing with them firsthand about the team's progress, their hard work and sacrifices. The radio show provided the perfect platform for him to do so. As he drove, each mile brought an increasing sense of anticipation. The soft hum of the motor and the occasional chime from his navigation system were the only sounds breaking the stillness of silence within the car. Adam's mind buzzed with thoughts of tomorrow's showdown with Wry, tactics to execute, plays to call, and words of encouragement to deliver to his team. Whilst en route, Adam attempted several times to phone Sarah to brief her on his intentions to appear on the radio, but each call was unanswered.

At precisely ten past nine, Adam's car rolled to a stop in the deserted car park of the radio station. He took a deep breath and stepped out into the cool night air, crossing the car park and entering the building. Adam proceeded to introduce himself to the receptionist and explained his unexpected appearance. After a brief phone call to the show's production suite, Adam was led down a narrow hallway towards the bright studio lights. As he entered the bustling production suite, the producer approached him with curious eyes and asked about his intentions for wanting to go on air. Adam explained his desire to address the fans directly, take their calls, and speak exclusively to Riley about tomorrow's game.

Suddenly, Riley's voice filled the room through the monitor speaker, causing Adam to look frantically through the studio window towards him. "Listeners," Riley announced, "There seems to be some excitement in our production area. It appears that Swanford Town's rookie video game manager, Adam Wells, has made an unexpected appearance in our studio. I don't know what this is all about, but we'll take a quick break while I learn more. See you on the other side, where I might have Adam Wells by my side" his words were filled with excitement as he threw to a commercial break.

Despite his larger-than-life presence, Riley stood at a very average five-foot-six. His medium-length blonde hair was shabbily tousled, and his beard was barely more than un-groomed stubble. He exuded confidence and often shared his opinion without hesitation, making him an arch-enemy of Adam's in the past few weeks. Riley had been bold in criticising Adam's credentials for the Swanford job, citing his only experience managing a football club being on a video game. The magnitude of this job was grave, defying the odds and keeping Swanford in the division, and Riley made it clear that he did not believe Adam was up to the task. Despite their rivalry, Adam admired Riley's brashness and straight-talking. With every verbal jab they had exchanged in press conferences, Adam felt the tension rise between himself and Riley. Adam anticipated this unprecedented appearance on Riley's show could be a battle of words.

As the ad break began, Riley strode out of the studio and entered the bustling production suite to welcome Adam. The two locked eyes, both brimming with animosity towards the other. But amidst the hostility, there was an undeniable sense of respect burning in Riley's steely blue eyes as they exchanged a firm handshake, each gripping with equal force a silent challenge.

Riley greeted Adam, "Welcome, Adam," he said, "You want to join me on air, do you?"

Adam kept his face neutral, but inside, his mind was racing with preparations for the inevitable barrage of questions, "Yes, if I may please," he replied.

Riley led Adam into the studio. The two men sat in their positions, one behind the desk and one in the hot seat across from it. The atmosphere was energetic and exciting, like before a grand performance or an intense competition. The producer's hand flew up swiftly, signalling to the studio that they were live again. Although practised and polished, Adam's smile failed to reach his eyes as he locked eyes with Riley. With a deep breath, Riley resumed the show, his voice projecting through the microphone and into the world beyond.

"We are here once again," Riley began, his deep, authoritative voice reverberating through the speakers, "And joining me is none other than the rookie video game manager of Swanford, Adam Wells. Adam, how are you? To what do we owe this honour?" Riley asked with a hint of curiosity in his tone.

Adam took a deep breath, a slight tremor visible in his clasped hands as he leaned back in the plush chair. He crossed his legs and settled into a calm demeanour, even though a tight knot of anxiety twisted in his gut. At last, he replied with steady confidence, "I'm well, Riley. Thank you for asking, and yes, it is a pleasure to be here," he said, "As for why I am here," Adam paused for dramatic effect before leaning forward and delivering his next line with a suave smile, "It seems like your show could use a ratings boost with the dynamic presence of Swanford's 'rookie video game manager' ," he said, signalling inverted commas with his hands for effect.

Riley and the production suite erupted into genuine laughter, breaking the tension hanging in the air just moments ago. The sound of their amusement filled the room and lifted Adam's spirits as he settled into his role as a guest on the popular talk show. A fleeting flicker of tension crossed Riley's face before he broke into an amused grin, his eyes sparkling with amusement. "Fair enough, Adam," he conceded, matching humour for humour, "Let's get down to business then. You took on quite the daunting task with Swanford teetering on the edge of relegation. What drove you to believe you could save them from their fate?" his voice was laced with genuine curiosity as he leaned forward in his seat, eager to hear Adam's answer.

Adam maintained his calm demeanour, even under Riley's intense gaze. The bright light above him seemed to shine directly into his eyes, but he refused to waver. "You know what, Riley," he began carefully, "I understand your doubts and those of others who question my abilities.

It's not every day that someone goes from managing a football team on a video game to commanding one in real life. But I am no less committed or equipped than any other manager that the club could have appointed." Adam's voice was steady and confident as he spoke, "I have honed my skills through years of playing an ultra-realistic video game, widely used within the industry to scout players and analyse teams. I believed this knowledge would translate effectively into real-life football," Adam continued, passion rising in his tone. "Football is football, whether played on a computer screen or a grassy field. The principles remain the same. Teamwork, tactics, and desire. I possess all the qualities needed to get the best out of the players and make them believe they can survive, just like any other manager."

Adam's love for the game shone through his words as he spoke, convincing even sceptics like Riley that he could lead a real-life team to victory.

"Ok, mate," Riley replied, "We've never seen a manager appointed based solely on experience from a video game. It is a bold, seen by many as a stupid, careless one by Scott Brewer. In context, my teenage boy plays shooting war and car racing games. Doing so for the many hours he does does not mean he can race a real car or fight in a war. Do you understand the scepticism, therefore?" he asked.

"Mates, is that what we are now?" Adam joked, "You could have fooled me the last couple of weeks" he smirked. "Yes, I fully understand the scepticism, and looking in from the outside, I'd have the same attitude toward the appointment if I'm honest with you. However, here we are. I was offered the job, and my only focus can, therefore, be on keeping our magnificent club up. You won't always please all the people all the time, and the haters to this left-field controversial appointment were inevitable. From my point of view, the proof will be in the pudding come the final whistle tomorrow," Adam stated.

The atmosphere was tense as both host and guest awaited the next move in this verbal chess game. Taken aback, Riley posed his next question with curiosity and apprehension: "So what compelled you to make the four-plus hour drive from Swanford to our studio here in central London for my show?"

Adam's response was calculated and cool, laced with underlying motives. "Well, among other things, I thought it was high time we cleared up this little misunderstanding between us. Wouldn't you agree?"

Riley's eyebrows shot up ever so slightly, betraying a hint of surprise on his otherwise composed face. "Misunderstanding?" he scoffed, his voice dripping with sarcasm, "You come into Swanford with your experience from your fancy video game, and suddenly, we're all expected to bow down to your superior wisdom?" he inquired.

Adam maintained his composure, refusing to take the bait Riley had expertly thrown his way, "I see you haven't changed," he replied calmly, leaning forward in his chair, "But let's get one thing straight here and now. I didn't come to Swanford seeking adulation or blind obedience. I came to do a job, to help this team reach its potential and survive."

A dismissive snort escaped Riley's lips as he leaned back in his chair, content to let Adam take centre stage, "Potential? At Swanford?" he laughed bitterly, taking a sip of coffee from the cup in front of him. "Swanford hasn't had any potential since, well, since forever really. Especially since big Don passed away and left the club to his clueless son and heir, Scott."

Adam's conviction grew brighter at these words before he replied, "Well then," his voice carrying a confident undertone, "It looks like we're about to make history at Swanford then."

"Adam, this is a live call-in show, and plenty of Swanford and Wry fans are eagerly waiting on the phone lines to speak with me. Now, with your presence, I'm sure they'll also want to talk to you. Are you ready to take some calls?" Riley asked, his voice steady and professional.

"Sure, let's do it," Adam replied coolly before adding, "But first, may I ask something?"

Riley couldn't help but feel intrigued by this confident newcomer. "Go ahead," he gestured for Adam to continue.

"After the South Swanshea match, a caller named Molly contacted the station. Her words stayed with me, and I would like to speak with her directly. So, I must request that she pick up the phone and call in this evening. Molly, if you're listening or anyone who knows her is listening, please urge her to call in. I am very eager to speak with her." Adam's words held a sense of urgency that captivated Riley's attention even more.

Following Adam's call for action, Riley signalled with his finger to the production team and stated, "Ok, let's take the first call, Smithy from Wry you're on. What did you want to say?" he asked.

The voice that echoed through the speakers was dripping with hostility, as if every word was laced with venom. "Yeah, I just wanted to say that what Swanford are doing is a travesty," the man ranted. He spoke as if he knew the truth, and everyone else was foolish for not seeing it. "You've got a mere child who's spent all his time playing video games put in charge of a professional football team. It's an insult to the hardworking men and women who have dedicated their lives to mastering this sport. The fans are going to be the ones who suffer as they go through the heartbreak of relegation after this careless move from Scott Brewer." Smithy from Wry sneered, spitting out the last word like it was poison, "Trying to play with our beloved teams like their insignificant toys is unforgivable from, in this case, a joke of a chairman who isn't taking this seriously!"

Riley tried to suppress a smirk as he prodded Smithy further, knowing how easily worked up he could get from previous occasions he'd called up. "So you're not one of Adam's fans, then?" his eyes twinkled with mischief as he took another sip of his coffee.

Smithy continued in anger, "No, absolutely not. This isn't some kind of game, Riley. This is people's livelihoods at stake here, and we've got this wannabe trying to make a mockery of it all. However," he continued, his tone dripping with malice, "It's also an absolute gift for us. We are going to make sure Swanford and Adam get exactly what's coming to them tomorrow and nail that coffin shut, sending them down for good," he declared.

Adam remained silent, listening intently to Smithy's outrage. He knew emotions were running high but couldn't let them cloud his judgment. Finally, he calmly responded to Smithy's call, "I understand your concerns, Smithy. However, allow me to remind you that in the end, all that matters is results on the pitch. And I intend on delivering those results and keeping Swanford up tomorrow."

The next call came from Mo, a loyal Swanford fan and town resident. "Mo, you're on," Riley invited.

The reverberating sound of Mo's voice filled the studio, bouncing off the walls and filling every corner with its soft, considerate tone. It was a stark contrast to Smithy's aggressive demeanour. "Hello, Adam, hello, Riley," Mo greeted them warmly, "First and foremost, I want to commend you on the positive changes you've made here in Swanford. Despite initial scepticism, many of us can see your dedication and passion for this club. We support you fully as we would any manager or player proudly wearing our badge." There was a brief pause before Mo continued, his voice taking on a more wary tone, "However, I have to admit, this is a huge gamble. Managing a football team based solely on experience from a video game? It's unheard of."

Adam took a moment before replying, "I understand your concerns, Mo, and I agree, it is a gamble," his voice trailed off as he considered his response carefully, "But isn't life itself a big gamble? We never have guarantees, only opportunities, and when one presents itself at our doorstep, we can either let fear hold us back and watch it slip away, or we can take it on with bravery," he paused for effect before adding confidently, "I choose the latter."

The next caller was Molly herself, whose sweet and timid voice had captured Adam's attention during her previous call to the station. As her soft and delicate voice filled the studio, an anticipatory silence engulfed the room. "Hello, Adam," she began shyly, her voice trembling with nerves.

Instantly recognising her tone, Adam responded warmly, "Hi Molly, I'm so glad you called in."

With Adam's friendly acknowledgement, Molly regained some of her confidence. "Adam," she started again, this time with more determination, "I just wanted to say that I believe in what you're trying to do with Swanford and that we will survive."

Her words touched Adam deeply, and he replied gratefully, "Thank you. That's very kind of you. As for why I wanted you to call in," Adam continued, getting to the reason for reaching out to Molly in particular, "I assume you'll be attending tomorrow's game?"

Molly confirmed his assumption without hesitation by excitedly saying, "Indeed I am. I've been a loyal season ticket holder for the past ten seasons in the Kevin Woods stand."

A smile spread across Adam's face as he responded enthusiastically, "Ok, good. Well, I hope tomorrow will be a little different. I would like you to report to the reception at the club tomorrow morning at half past ten, where I will personally meet you for a special task I have planned for you. As a token of my appreciation on this special day, a reward will await you. What do you say?"

Molly's excitement grew as she eagerly replied, "Yeah, that's fine, I'd love to."

Pleased with her response, Adam added one more request with a slight chuckle, "Ok, good. Can you also do me a favour, please, and bring some photos of your Granddad? Preferably ones where he's wearing club colours or at a game. Even an old kit or something of his would be good," Adam explained.

Without hesitation, Molly promised to fulfil his request and bid their conversation farewell with an enthusiastic "Of course, I will. See you in the morning."

As the show continued, a constant stream of calls flooded in. A diverse mix of diehard fans, sceptics, and nostalgics voiced their opinions and hopes for Swanford's fate. Adam listened intently, his calm and confident demeanour never faltering as he patiently responded to each caller. Amidst the chaos, one call stood out from the rest. It came from an elderly fan named George, who had been following the team since he was a young boy. His aged voice was nostalgic as he spoke of the glory days when Swanford reigned supreme in the game. "I've watched this club through its ups and downs," George reminisced, his words ringing through the studio like a haunting melody. "I remember when we were giants. We used to command such respect. I still believe in this club, in its heart. And I believe you can lead us to safety, son," he said, addressing Adam.

The studio fell silent as everyone listened intently to George's heartfelt words. Adam cleared his throat, deeply moved by George's unwavering faith in him and their beloved team. "Thank you, George," he replied slowly, pausing to collect his emotions before continuing, "Thank you for your faith in me and the team, as well as your unwavering support for Swanford over the years. I promise you that tomorrow will be a fight that we will not back down from." Adam's words reverberated not just through the studio but throughout all of Swanford. The collective breath of the residents held tight as they awaited what tomorrow would bring: a battle for redemption against all odds.

As the clock wound toward ten o'clock, Riley gracefully threw to the advert break and top-of-the-hour news bulletin. He turned to face Adam before declaring, "Well, Adam, that was enlightening," Riley chuckled lightly before extending a hand towards him. "Good luck tomorrow," Riley said sincerely, a newfound respect evident in his voice.

Adam nodded in response as they shook hands firmly, "Thank you, Riley. We will fight with everything we have and work even harder to ensure that luck won't be needed. We will pull this off, mark my words," he returned with a small but confident smile before rising from his seat and exiting the studio.

As Adam left the building to make his way to his car for the journey home, the night air felt crisp and invigorating against his skin, energising him for the challenges that tomorrow would bring. As he settled into the car's driver seat and programmed the sat nav for his return journey to Swanford, he couldn't shake an intense headache that seemed to constrict his head in a tight grip. His fingers trembled as he typed in his home address, the pulsing pain making it hard to focus. The rush of blood through his veins was deafening, each beat of his heart like a frenzied drum against his skull. His mind raced with thoughts of tomorrow's game, playing out worst-case scenarios and pitfalls that could jeopardise his reputation and the club's future. It felt like a matter of life and death, particularly with the ominous threat hanging over him from the bullet-laced letter he had received, an impending doom that hung over Adam, reminding him that any misstep could be an execution warrant for himself, if not physically, then by the press and their scathing words, as they had been eagerly waiting for his blood since the moment his appointment was announced.

Adam pulled out of the car park and began the long journey home. The bright city lights and blaring car horns blurred together in a chaotic symphony around him. But none of it registered in his mind as he was lost in thought, replaying the anxiety and racing thoughts that had consumed him throughout the day. The once soothing sound of the car's engine now felt like a loud roar, pulsating in time with his heart pounding and thumping of his headache. As he focused on navigating through the bustling streets of London, his vision momentarily blurred, causing his heart to skip a beat. He forcefully blinked, trying to clear his mind and refocus on the road ahead. The looming headache grew more intense with each passing moment like a relentless vice squeezing his temples with every twist and turn. Sharp jabs of pain shot behind his eyes like rapid-fire strobe lights, making it increasingly difficult for him to concentrate on anything else but the agonising pressure building inside his head.

Adam's mind was a battlefield filled with fear and uncertainty as he waged war against an unknown adversary who had promised him death in unyielding ink. The letter's words, dripping with venom, were etched into his consciousness, burrowing deeper into his psyche by the second. As Adam approached the outskirts of London, the bright city lights faded away, giving way to a sprawling darkness only broken by the occasional lonely lamppost or the passing headlights of rushing traffic. Adam's sat nav chimed repeatedly, jolting him back to reality as he navigated the winding streets. Finally, he reached the motorway, his car gliding smoothly along the open road. A short while into the drive, Adam made a decision. It was time to confront this headache. Adam decided to stop at Toddington Services before it got any worse and impaired his driving, especially on the motorway.

As he parked his car, Adam dragged himself out of the vehicle. His legs were like lead and ached from the tension he had been holding in. The bright lights of the service station appeared as hazy orbs in the night, his vision still blurry around the edges. Adam rubbed at his temples, wincing from the throbbing pain that seemed to dart through his skull. Stumbling into the services, he sought refuge in a bottle of water and a packet of painkillers. As he stood waiting in line to pay, every pair of eyes felt like they belonged to the phantom who had sent the threatening letter. Faces were blurred, words seemed indistinct, and anxiety gnawed at him with ferocity. Despite straining his ears and squinting his eyes, nothing made sense. Finally, with a sigh of relief, he paid for his items and retreated to the safety of his car. Downing half of the bottle of water in one gulp, he washed down two painkillers in an attempt to calm his pounding head. The silence inside his vehicle starkly contrasted with the chaos raging within his mind, taunting reminders of tomorrow's high-stakes game intertwined with the looming threat from an unknown perpetrator.

The sat nav chimed again, its robotic voice urging Adam back onto the motorway. There was still some way to go before reaching home. The hum of traffic was a distant murmur now. Adam was alone with the road stretched out ahead and his thoughts. He journeyed in silence, each mile adding weight to his worry, his mind an explosive cocktail of fear and responsibility. His hands clutched tighter at the steering wheel as if it could anchor him against this storm. Every signpost whizzing by was a reminder that he was inching closer towards home and an uncertain future.

The painkillers kicked in, softening the sharp jabs of pain into dull throbs. The road ahead was now clear. His mind, however, was anything but. As the night deepened, so did Adam's sense of unease. His thoughts remained firmly on tomorrow's game as the relentless metronome of fear and threat kept time in his mind. Adam gripped the steering wheel even tighter than before, a silent promise to himself that he wouldn't let fear win, not tonight, not ever. The weight of his racing thoughts threatened to drag Adam into a pit of exhaustion. He knew he needed help to manage them, and the familiar call of his recovery fellowship beckoned to him. As the clock struck eleven-thirty, Adam realised it was too late to find a physical meeting, but the beauty of technology meant that he could still connect with his worldwide fellowship through online meetings. No matter the hour, support and guidance were just a click away from nations all over the globe.

Adam's car rolled to a stop on the motorway's hard shoulder, and he reached for his phone, eagerly opening the fellowship app. He scrolled through the list of online meetings, his heart sinking as he realised most were already in progress or didn't fit his schedule. But then he noticed a meeting being hosted by a group in Washington, USA, which was about to begin. With relief, Adam logged onto the meeting, needing the support and connection now more than ever.

As a public figure constantly scrutinised, Adam knew he needed to maintain his anonymity. Adam displayed as AW with a blank profile picture. As he placed his phone into its holder on the dashboard and resumed driving, he waited for the meeting to begin.

As the hands of the clock reached midnight, the meeting started. The meeting host cleared their throat and explained that the meeting would follow its usual format: readings followed by a main share and a feedback session. The main sharer would take around twenty minutes to share their strength, experience, and hope with the group. Afterwards, others could reflect on the main share and check in with how they were feeling today.

As Adam's ears filled with the reassuring rhythm of the meeting, his grip slowly relaxed on the steering wheel, and his heart pounded slightly less fiercely in his chest, offering him a momentary respite from its relentless drumming. His body was still tight with anxiety, but listening to the comforting familiarity of the meeting had an almost instant calming effect.

The main sharer's voice reverberated through the car, clear and steady like a soothing balm for Adam's troubled mind. She spoke passionately about her battles with fear and uncertainty, sharing her hard-won wisdom on confronting inner demons with courage and resilience. As her words washed over him, Adam felt connected and could relate to them, which comforted him. Slowly but surely, the jagged edges of his fears began to soften and melt away under the warmth of her words.

The women's share ended, and participants began responding and sharing their experiences. Adam kept his microphone on mute as he drove on, intently listening to each share. A few people shared similar experiences with threats or intimidation; others spoke about their fears of losing control.

Adam hesitated, his finger hovering over the unmute button for his microphone as he grappled with the words he wanted to say. He couldn't make eye contact with his screen, keeping his eyes fixed on the dark road ahead. Finally, he pressed unmute and spoke, his voice trembling slightly before gaining strength and conviction. He talked about fear and uncertainty, carefully choosing his words not to give away too much. But even in their coded form, they painted a vivid picture of the weight he carried on his shoulders. As Adam verbalised his deepest fears and anxieties, it was as if the weight was lifted off of him. As he finished speaking and pressed mute once again, there was a palpable shift within him, a sense of relief and release. He took a deep breath, feeling a newfound courage coursing through him. The voices of other participants sharing their struggles once again filled the virtual space around him, creating a comforting presence that made him feel less alone in his journey.

As his car pulled into the driveway, Adam could hear the last few words of the closing serenity prayer being led by the meeting host. The flickering streetlights cast an eerie glow on his face as he sat in the darkness for a moment longer, allowing the soothing words and the collective sound of all the participants saying "keep coming back" to wash over him. A newfound calmness settled within him, pushing away the weight of darkness that had threatened to consume him earlier. His thoughts lingered on the looming threats and tomorrow's game, but for now, in this moment, Adam had found a way to keep his fears at bay. The night air was cool and crisp, bringing peace and hope as he stepped out of his car and went inside, ready to face whatever challenges lay ahead with a renewed sense of serenity.

Despite the calming end to the night, sleep remained a distant visitor to Adam. His eyes traced the familiar patterns on his bedroom ceiling as he lay in bed, his body heavy with exhaustion but his mind relentlessly alert. With a deep sigh, he reached for his phone, seeking solace in the hundreds of messages from fans, colleagues, and friends offering their support. As Adam placed his phone back on the bedside table and closed his eyes, he let the room's stillness surround him like a warm blanket. The comforting words and stories shared during the meeting replayed in his mind, bringing a sense of reassurance and peace. His breathing slowed and became more rhythmic until finally, after what felt like an age, sleep crept up on him like a gentle embrace from an old friend.

25

The Final Showdown – Wry

Morning arrived abruptly, the shrill alarm of Adam's phone jolting him awake at six am. The grey light of dawn seeped through the window, casting a ghostly glow around his room. Adam groaned as he dragged himself out of bed, the weight of the day already feeling heavy. It was here, the day he had been dreading and anticipating in equal measure. Moving through his morning routine, showering and dressing into his suit, shirt and tie, Adam found himself in a surreal state of calm acceptance. The anxious thoughts still lingered, but they no longer consumed him completely. As he made his way out into the world, the cool morning air that greeted him as he opened his front door acted as a soothing balm against his nervousness, giving him a glimmer of hope that today might not be as daunting as he feared.

At precisely half past seven, Adam pulled out of his driveway full of determination. The morning sun was beginning to peek over the horizon, casting a warm golden glow on the small town of Swanford. As Adam made his way towards the bustling main street, he knew that his favourite cafe, Coffee Club, would be waiting for him with a hearty breakfast to fuel him for the long day ahead. As he drove past Watson's bakery, he rolled down his window to take in the intoxicating scent of freshly baked bread. It mingled with the crisp morning air, creating a delicious combination that made his stomach growl with hunger. The town was slowly waking up as Adam continued on his journey, passing by familiar landmarks that held special memories for him. But today, his mind was focused solely on the task in hand. There was no room for distraction or reminiscing as he mentally prepared himself for what lay ahead.

Nestled on a quiet corner of Mulberry Street, Coffee Club was a beacon for many in the bustling town. Its rust-coloured exterior exuded an old-world charm that only a historic building could possess. To Adam, it was more than just a cafe. The warm embrace of Barb and the aroma of freshly ground coffee and fried food provided a sense of comfort and familiarity. As Adam pulled into his usual parking spot next to the entrance, the sound of birdsong mingled with the sound of morning traffic. Adam couldn't help but smile as he took in the sights and sounds around him. Stepping inside the cafe, Adam was greeted by the rich scent of coffee and the welcoming atmosphere. Barb, always a constant presence behind the counter, greeted him with her usual smile and friendly banter. In a world that seemed to be constantly changing, Coffee Club remained a comforting oasis for Adam over the past two decades.

"Good morning, lovely," Barb greeted him with a warm smile, "You never mentioned that the job interview was for the new manager of the Swans. You're quite the brave one, aren't you? Will everything be alright today?" she inquired, her concern evident in her voice.

Adam let out a small sigh before responding, "Well, I certainly hope so for all our sakes." Despite his words, he looked far from convinced himself.

Barb furrowed her brow in confusion and asked, "What can I get for you this morning, babes?"

Adam took a moment before replying, "I'll have a full English breakfast, please. The works, but please, no black pudding, and a black coffee as well."

Jotting down his order to pass on to the chef, Barb smiled and replied, "Of course, I remember. Take a seat, and I'll bring it over." The sizzling bacon and brewing coffee aroma filled the air as Adam settled into his seat. Settling into his usual corner table at the cafe, Adam couldn't help but notice a folded newspaper laid out neatly before him. The back page boasted a bold headline. 'Sacked Swanford Manager Mark Booth Speaks Out: A Full Account of Adam Well's Appointment and the Fate of Swanford'.

Intrigued, Adam scanned the words detailing an exclusive interview with the former Swanford manager inside the paper. Adam was disappointed as he realised he was duty-bound to read every word, turning to the designated page inside.

Adam's fingers quivered slightly as he carefully turned the crisp, white pages. The bold, black headline inside caught his eye. 'Booth Blasts Brewer & Wells: An Inside Look at Swanford's Drama'.

With a deep inhale and exhale, Adam began to read the words on the page, each holding immense power over his emotions.

'Adam Wells, an unknown, a video game player, an amateur', Booth began. 'He's undoubtedly got the drive, but he doesn't have the skill or experience. This is my club, and it breaks my heart to say that Swanford are going down. I admire Adam's guts in taking the job for his own personal ambition, but this was a mistake by Scott Brewer and would have never happened under big Don; he'll be spinning in his grave right about now', the article read.

The muscles in Adam's face clenched, and his jaw tightened, grinding his teeth together. The words stabbed at him like sharp knives, cutting deeper than he wanted to admit. As he continued reading, Booth's scathing criticism echoed mockingly in his mind. Each word felt like a slap in the face, bringing back memories of happier times that now seemed impossibly far away.

'I wish the club well', Booth's voice seemed to sneer from the page, 'But I also hope for the sake of Swanford that Adam realises sooner rather than later that managing is more than just picking a team'.

Adam let out a heavy sigh and shifted in his seat as Barb approached. She was carrying a tray with his breakfast on it and a steaming cup of coffee. Her eyes held a deep understanding and sympathy as she placed the tray on the table before him. She had read the interview, too, and knew the burden Adam carried. As she patted his shoulder reassuringly, Barb rolled her eyes and sighed. "Everyone's a critic these days," she muttered before adding with a half-hearted smile, "But you know what they say, babes, tomorrow's chip paper and all that." As she walked away, Adam watched her for a moment. Before leaving the front door, she took off her apron, lit a cigarette, and exhaled the smoke into the crisp morning air, leaning against the wall.

Adam's mouth watered at the sight of his breakfast, a large, sizzling platter filled to the edges with an indulgent spread. Four succulent rashes of bacon laid crisply on one side, while three thick juicy sausages nestled next to them. Two perfectly fried eggs sat on top, their yolks still runny and begging to be devoured. Alongside them was a small helping of fluffy scrambled eggs dotted with specks of herbs for extra flavour. A giant fried mushroom and a plump tomato shared space on the other side of the plate, glistening with butter and seasoning. Two crispy hash browns were tucked in between them, adding a satisfying crunch to each bite. A small serving of baked beans complimented the meal, their rich sauce pooling around the edge of the plate. But that wasn't all; there was also a slice of fried bread and two pieces of toast, cut in half and generously slathered in butter. Adam couldn't wait to use them to mop up every last bit of sauce and juices once he had finished. The only missing element was black pudding, which generally accompanied the hearty breakfast. Adam had chosen to forgo it this time. The thought of what it was made from turned his stomach and threatened to ruin his appetite. The mere thought of Booth's interview made Adam's stomach churn, and he was grateful for the absence of black pudding on his plate.

Adam mechanically picked up his fork and began to eat, focusing on each food item as if it were a task to be completed. The crispy bacon emitted a savoury aroma that soothed his senses, while the tangy beans provided a burst of flavour. From the window, he watched Barb puff away on her cigarette, her wrinkled face conveying weariness and kindness. In that moment, she seemed like a beacon of normality amidst the brewing storm.

Adam savoured the warmth and comfort this meal brought him with each tiny bite. The toast crunch gave way to a buttery, satisfying smoothness on his tongue. As he reached for another piece of toast, his phone buzzed urgently against the wooden table, causing his heart to leap into his throat. Adam's hands shook as he reached for it. He glanced at the screen, and a picture of Scott Brewer popped up, followed by a voicemail notification. Adam's pulse quickened as he listened to the voicemail, Brewer's voice filling his ears.

"Adam, it's Scott," he said, his voice tense and urgent, "Look, I've seen the paper, mate. It's all rubbish." Relief flooded through Adam's body as he heard those words. He had been worried that Brewer would turn on him. "Booth, well, Booth is salty because you got his job," Brewer continued, "Honestly, it lacks class, and to be frank, he couldn't hack it anyway, else I wouldn't have sacked him," Scott explained.

Adam let out a heavy sigh, grateful that at least Brewer was still on his side for now. As he carefully scraped the last remnants of food off his plate with a bread crust, his mind drifted back to the article he had just read. Booth's harsh words reverberated in his head, their sharpness still piercing. Instead of succumbing to feelings of disappointment and defeat, Adam consciously turned them into fuel for motivation. Adam finished his breakfast and gulped down the last bit of coffee, leaving enough money on the table for Barb, who was still standing outside, before heading out of the cafe to make his way to the club.

As Adam opened his car, Barb called, "Good luck today, babes. When you pull it off, your next breakfast is on me." Adam smiled at her politely before climbing into his car. The drive to the stadium was short, but Adam went through a whirlwind of emotions. Doubt, fear, excitement, and anxiety gnawed at him. As he parked in the manager's spot, the time had just turned eight-forty-five-am. Adam glanced at himself in the car's rearview mirror before stepping out and into the madness of the day ahead.

As Adam strode towards the reception doors, his phone rang urgently in his pocket. He fished it out with a sigh; the caller ID was withheld. Suspicion flickered through him as he answered the call.

"Hello, Adam Wells speaking," he said.

"Hi Adam, it's Shane Finn, head of police. Sorry for the timing of the call, given the severity of today's events. Are you alright?" came the voice on the other end.

Adam swallowed back his anxiety and replied, "Yeah, I'm ok. Anxious and busy, but holding up. What's up?" he asked.

"Well, ideally, I'd come and see you and Scott in person," Shane began, his tone serious, "But given today's schedule and the potential risk it presents, I needed to call instead."

Adam's mind raced with possibilities as he replied, "Go on."

"We have an update on the case," Shane explained, "We've made an arrest and have evidence to back it up from a warranted search of the individual's property. We also have a recorded confession. As a result, the CPS has granted us a charge for the death threat and bullet sent, which was supported by the discovery of a matching firearm found on the property of the suspect, which holds a separate charge. Furthermore, we have grounds to charge on an additional conspiracy to pervert the course of justice offence," Shane explained.

A wave of cold dread washed over Adam at Shane's words. This was worse than anything he'd been expecting, "But how, who?" Adam stammered out.

"I'm afraid to say it was Mrs. Sarah Baker-Jones. It would seem that she and former manager Mr Booth have been entwined in an extramarital affair and have been for several years. She was bitter at his dismissal and hoped that scaring you out of the job would result in his re-appointment and the resumption of their affair," Shane explained.

Adam's stomach twisted uncomfortably before he replied, "What do you want us to do about this as a club?" he asked. Adam's voice sounded small and uncertain even to his own ears.

"Well, we have remanded Mrs. Baker-Jones in custody for now, so there won't be a direct risk from her today or in the immediate future. For now, carry on as usual, but be vigilant, Adam. She may have connections," Shane answered.

"Alright," Adam said tightly, trying to keep his voice steady, "Thanks for letting me know."

Adam ended the call and stood momentarily, staring blankly at the phone in his hand before slowly slipping it back into his pocket. His thoughts swirled with fear and disbelief as he turned back towards the reception doors.

"Good morning, Mr Wells. You're early today," the receptionist greeted him with a firm, friendly smile on her face.

"Yep, the early bird and all that," Adam replied, "The players will be arriving shortly, please direct them to the centre circle of the pitch, where I will be waiting for them please," he asked.

"Sure, I will, boss," the receptionist replied.

Walking out onto the pitch, Adam could hardly breathe. The news of the morning was still stinging his mind. The stands were empty, leaving Adam with only the bright grey morning light and the crisp morning air for company.

The stadium, usually pulsing with energy during matches, seemed eerily serene now. Adam stood in the centre circle of the pitch, waiting for his players to arrive. One by one, they appeared and made their way to join Adam in the centre circle, their joyous laughter echoing in the solitude of the vast stadium. They greeted Adam warmly, clapping hands and sharing quick jokes as they gathered around him in the centre circle.

"Alright, lads," Adam smiled, "Here we are, the big day, everything we have worked towards. Today is a day for heroes to prevail through battle. Please sit and listen as I read you a speech I've prepared, after which I'll explain how the next few hours before kick-off will unfold."

The men fell silent, their eyes drawn to Adam's stern face as they sat on the cool, dew-soaked grass. The emerald blades tickled their legs as they settled in, eagerly awaiting what was to come. Adam cleared his throat and pulled a piece of crumpled paper from his pocket. He smoothed it against his knee, his fingers tracing the creases and wrinkles. With a confident stance, he held the paper before him and began reading.

"Gentlemen, I stand before you today with a fire raging inside me. A burning, seething mix of emotions that I can barely contain. We are facing a trial like no other, a test of our strength and resilience, a journey into the depths of hell itself. But make no mistake, we have a choice to make. We can either cower in this darkness or tap into our fierce determination and fight our way back into the light.

But let me be clear, I cannot do this for you. Each of you will be pushed to your limits, but it is up to you to dig deep and find the strength to persevere, not just for yourselves but also for the brothers beside you and the fans who support us.

You must want this victory more than you want to breathe, more than anything you've ever desired in your life. Give it everything you have because average is not good enough in this battle. It's time to unleash our inner beasts and show our enemies that we will not be defeated.

Remember, a person's true character is revealed when they are backed against the wall. No setback is too great for us to overcome. If setbacks come, and they may well come, we must pick ourselves back up, adapt, and rise above them.

The world has doubted and made fun of us, but remember that every successful person was once ridiculed before becoming revered. So let's put on our armour and show them what we are made of.

There is a story I once heard about a lion, the king of the jungle. He lay dormant under a tree while others taunted and mocked him. But when they got too close, he rose and tore them apart in a ferocious display of power and dominance. This fight will be no different. It will be a dogfight until the end. Always remember that everything is impossible until someone achieves it. We must be hungry dogs, ready to run faster and fight harder.

Some of you have been selling yourself short, giving only sixty percent when you have one hundred and twenty percent within you. It's time to unleash that full potential and leave everything on the battlefield.

Believe me, when I say this, we can do this. So let's believe in ourselves, fight with every fiber of our being, and emerge victorious as survivors. This is our time. This is our moment. Let's seize it."

As Adam finished his rousing speech, the players let out a roar of encouragement. Their voices echoed through the empty stadium, filling it with a palpable sense of determination, resolve and passion. Adam could see that his words had hit their mark, stoking a fire in each player as they prepared for the game.

Taking a moment to bask in the collective energy of his team, Adam continued, "So, lads, here's the plan. I want you all to head up to the Donald Brewer suite, where you will share a team brunch. I'll have to join you in a bit as I have some other matters to attend to first, but Mike and Shea will lead you there when I finish speaking." He paused for a moment before adding with a sly grin, "Don't worry, I won't be too far behind. After lunch and some time to relax and prepare mentally, we will reconvene in the briefing room at half past one for a pre-game meeting," Adam announced confidently.

With much excitement, the team dispersed from the pitch, following Mike and Shea up through the tunnel en route to the Donald Brewer suite. The Donald Brewer suite was a testament to luxury and extravagance, its lavish design rivalling the grandeur of the stadium it overlooked. Perched high on the third floor, it boasted panoramic vistas of the sprawling pitch and the towering stands that faced each other across the vast green expanse. The walls were adorned with a gallery of photographs, capturing moments of triumph and glory from the team's illustrious past. Each image was a tribute to their rich and storied history, proudly displayed for all to see.

As the players entered the suite, their senses were immediately overwhelmed by a lavish food display, a feast fit for kings spread out before them on long, ornately decorated tables. The rich aroma of roast chicken and rare beef wafted through the air, intermingling with the smoky scent of salmon and the fresh tang of various salads. Exotic fruits, their colours vibrant against the white tablecloths, added a touch of luxury to the already impressive spread. To their right, tall glass doors led to an expansive balcony where retired players and pundits mingled in the warm late morning sunlight. Mike and Shea led the players first to the tables of food, where they compiled plates of brunch before sitting along two long dining tables that were beautifully laid out. As the players took their seats, hushed conversations filled the room. Many players chatted about Adam's speech and speculated on what lay ahead in their pre-game team meeting, whilst some shared light-hearted banter.

Despite the warm and cosy atmosphere, an underlying tension lingered. It crept into hurried glances and forced smiles, revealing the weight of what was at stake today. This game wasn't just a mere match; it was their shot at becoming legends. The players were acutely aware of this, each feeling pressured to perform and rise to greatness. They were determined to seize this opportunity and make their mark in history.

Meanwhile, Adam's brisk footsteps echoed through an empty hallway as he went to the boardroom to meet with Scott. As Adam entered the room, Scott was already there waiting for him, excitedly, practically bouncing in his seat.

"Good morning, Adam," Scott exclaimed as he jumped up to greet him, "Here we are, ready for our big day?" he asked.

"Indeed, gaffer," Adam replied with a small smile.

Adam and Scott took their seats at the long, polished table that dominated the centre of the room. The solid wood gleamed under the lights. "So, what's the feeling in the camp," Scott asked eagerly, "How have preparations gone?"

"Yeah, all good, boss," Adam replied confidently, "The lads have trained well, and there is a quiet sense of confidence in our abilities to pull this off. It won't be easy, but I think we've got what it takes to win."

Next, Adam felt the need to move on to more pressing matters by asking, "Scott, have you spoken to Shane Finn at all this morning?"

"No, why?" Scott asked curiously.

"Well," Adam began slowly, still trying to wrap his head around the shocking news himself, "He called me. They have made an arrest, and it turns out it was someone within the club after all," he explained.

"Who was it?" Scott asked incredulously.

"Sarah Baker-Jones," Adam revealed with a shake of his head.

"What? Why," Scott asked, clearly shocked by the revelation, "I don't get it. Why would she do something like this?"

"It seems she was having a long-term affair with Mark Booth," Adam explained, "She hoped to scare me off so you would be forced to re-appoint him and they could continue their affair."

Scott let out a disbelieving laugh. "Well, that would never have happened. I would never give Mark another chance after the way he behaved when I sacked him. Plus, he was taking the club backwards. Mark and Sarah in an affair? Shocking. I've heard it all now" he shook his head in disbelief.

As they continued their pre-match meeting, Adam and Scott discussed tactics and strategies for the season's final game. After half an hour, they stood up to leave the boardroom. As they walked out, Scott put a supportive hand on Adam's shoulder, "Whatever happens out there today, know that you have done an outstanding job," he said sincerely, "The whole team has. I'd like to address the lads personally before the match. Would that be ok? When would be best for your schedule?"

"How about at the end of my pre-match meeting at about half two?" Adam suggested.

"Perfect, see you there," Scott replied with a smile before heading off.

With his phone in hand, Adam stood at the top of the grand staircase, occasionally glancing down at the screen as he made his way towards reception. Excitement bubbled within him, knowing he would soon meet with Molly, a devoted fan who had caught his attention on the Sports Radio call-in show. As he descended the regal staircase, his mind was still reeling from the conversation he had just had with Scott and the shocking revelations about Sarah. Just as he reached the bottom step, a loud buzz jolted him back to reality, and a message on his phone from reception informed him that Molly had arrived and was waiting for him. With a deep breath, Adam composed himself before going through a double door to reception to greet her.

Adam entered the reception area and immediately caught sight of someone he presumed was Molly, sitting on a plush leather sofa and waiting for him opposite the reception desk. Molly's face lit up in recognition of him. She was a petite woman, her delicate features framed by cascading chestnut hair. Her hazel eyes sparkled with an evident enthusiasm for football and the club. In her hands, she clutched an old Swanford shirt, its faded fabric a testament to years of devotion.

"Good morning, Molly. It's great to meet you," Adam greeted her amicably, extending his hand towards her.

Molly quickly reciprocated the gesture, her smile widening to reveal a dimple on her left cheek. "It's nice to meet you too, Mr. Wells. I'm so excited to be here today," she exclaimed eagerly.

"And we're glad to have you here," Adam replied warmly.

As they sat on the sleek leather sofa, Adam kept the conversation light yet engaging, steering clear of any potentially sensitive topics related to the upcoming match. He soon discovered that Molly hailed from a family of ardent supporters who had been following the club's journey for generations. Her love for the team ran deep and was intertwined with cherished memories and family traditions. After a pleasant twenty-minute chat filled with shared anecdotes and laughter, Adam asked Molly to follow him for the plans he had in store for her, something which she quickly agreed to with eager anticipation.

Adam led Molly towards the Donald Brewer suite, their steps echoing off the marble floors as they walked up the grand staircase. As they walked, Adam couldn't help but feel a sense of kinship with her. She wore a jersey and scarf in the team's colours, her eyes excitedly bright. Adam could see her love for the club and the game radiating from her. It reminded him of his deep connection to football, a bond that went beyond just a simple sport. Despite the danger surrounding his decision to stay loyal to the team, Molly's enthusiasm reminded him why he had never once regretted it. Football was more than just a game; it united people from all walks of life, and Molly embodied that spirit perfectly.

After a journey up the staircase and through the luxurious corridors of the stadium, they finally arrived at their destination, the legendary Donald Brewer suite. As Adam led Molly inside, he couldn't help but notice her soft gasp of amazement at the suite's grandeur. The view from the window truly took Molly's breath away, a sweeping vista of the pristine pitch below.

Adam's voice rang out, cutting through the players' chatter as he swept a welcoming arm over the luxurious suite. The players turned curiously towards him, their eyes landing on Molly, the woman standing by his side. As Adam introduced her to the team, she could feel their curious gazes on her. She greeted each player with a shy "Hello," star-struck by their presence. Adam was touched by the warmth and kindness of his players as they welcomed Molly into their circle.

After the introductions and some players resuming their meals, Molly was led to the food counter. The aroma of delicious dishes filled her senses as she eagerly selected items for her plate. With her food in hand, she searched for an open seat among the players. Just when she thought she would have to settle for standing, Michael Knight stood up and offered her an extra seat next to him and Shea. Grateful for the invitation, Molly sat and joined the lively conversations. Adam looked on as Molly interacted with the players, a smile spreading across his face. He joined the meal and shared the conversation, revelling in the lively football banter filling the room. This was precisely what the team needed before the big match: relaxation to prevent nerves.

After lunch, it was time for the pre-match meeting, but only after Adam gave Molly another surprise. After declaring, "Right, lads, see you shortly in the briefing room for a half-one start," Adam asked Molly to follow him. He led her down to pitch level and through the player's tunnel. Adam could feel Molly's excitement radiating as he led her into the bright early afternoon sun and onto the pitch. As they stepped onto the pitch, Molly gasped. She stood on the hallowed turf, the same turf many of her heroes had adorned, looking toward empty stands that would soon be filled with cheering fans, goalposts waiting for balls to be kicked into them, and the pitch meticulously groomed for the game.

"You'll be leading us out today," Adam said to Molly, smiling at her stunned reaction.

She blinked at him and then erupted into joyous laughter that echoed across the stadium. "Are you serious?" she asked incredulously.

"Absolutely," Adam affirmed, laughing along with her. Looking toward the old team shirt that Molly was still clutching, Adam asked, "So the shirt? Was that your Granddads?"

"Yes, it was," Molly replied with a tear in her eye.

"Ok, follow me," Adam replied before leading her toward the centre circle, "I want you to lay it down, if you would, over the centre circle. It will remain there until kick-off. Is that ok?"

A choked sob escaped Molly's lips, shattering the stadium's lingering silences. Tears welled up, each one a glistening memory cascading down her cheeks. Once a vibrant symbol of hope, the jersey in her hand now felt heavy with unspoken grief. With trembling fingers and a reverence that hushed the wind itself, Molly laid it on the pitch, a silent message carried skyward to the heavens. Adam's touch on her shoulder was a dam against the torrent of emotions threatening to engulf her. A quiet understanding passed between them as they walked back through the tunnel.

Molly, her face a mask of tear-streaked vulnerability, sniffled back a honking sob, her attempts to wipe away the glistening trails and running mascara a losing battle. Finally, her voice, raw and cracked like a weathered flag, rasped, "Adam, thank you. This means everything to me and will to my family when they find out."

"You are more than welcome," Adam replied.

The players greeted them with excited chatter as they entered the meeting room. Adam reached the front of the room and raised his hand for silence. "Before we begin discussing today's game," he announced, "I want you all to take a moment to listen to some encouragement from Molly. Let her stoke the fire within you."

Adam turned to Molly, a glimmer of mischief in his eyes. "Sorry to put you on the spot, but if you wouldn't mind, I'd love for you to repeat what you said during your phone call to Sports Radio. Especially about your late grandfather. May he rest in peace and be looking down on his beloved Swans today. Is that ok?"

Molly's face registered shock before she composed herself and replied, "Of course, Adam. I'd be honoured." The room fell silent as everyone eagerly awaited her words. Molly calmed herself and cleared her throat before she began. "Hi, thank you, Adam. My family and I have followed Swanford for generations, and I was introduced to the club as a seven-year-old girl when my Granddad brought me to a game. He was a giant of a man, and I clutched his hand with my little one as we walked up to the ground and through the excited match day crowd. I was hooked from the moment we walked through the turnstiles, and I caught a glimpse of the pitch. It was like nowhere else on earth when we were at a game. The crowd's thrill, the pitch's scent, and the sound of our cheers echoing through the stadium were magical. I can't remember how many times my Granddad would lift me onto his shoulders so I could see over the crowd as we shouted and cheered with all our might."

Molly's voice had wavered slightly as she spoke of her grandfather, but she took a deep breath and continued with renewed vigour, "At the age of sixteen, I got my first job and brought my first season ticket to sit beside my Granddad, Dad, Uncle and Brother. I have been a season ticket holder ever since. Some of my fondest memories with my Grandad have been first at the old stadium and then at this new one. As I grew older, our roles reversed. He held my hand tightly when we walked into this grand stadium, and he leaned onto me for support as his frailty grew with age. Even though his body was weak, his spirit was as strong as ever. He'd tell me, 'Molly, this team is more than just players on a pitch. It's a brotherhood. It's unity. It's spirit. And win or lose, it's our heart'. His voice would crack with emotion, but he never let go of my hand."

Pausing slightly to hold back tears, Molly continued, "Even when he got too old and sick to attend the games, I'd visit him in the hospital. I'd sit by his bedside, radio held between us as we listened to how our team was doing. His eyes would glitter with joy whenever Swanford scored. 'That's my team', he'd cheer, raising a frail fist in the air."

Molly continued, "His passion for this game was contagious, infecting every fiber of my being and never letting go. He would proclaim, 'Molly, it's not simply a game. It's a way of life. It's not just about scoring goals, but about the unbreakable bond of teamwork, the relentless drive to succeed, and the unwavering desire to rise from every defeat'. These words are etched into my soul, a constant reminder of his unwavering spirit."

"On Christmas Day, Granddad took his last breath surrounded by us loved ones. His final wish, stated in his will, was for his ashes to be scattered at Swanford, the club he held dear. We stood on that sacred pitch, feeling the wind carry flecks of him across the ground he'd spent countless hours cheering his heroes on. Our tribute didn't end there. We placed a memorial brick outside reception as a constant reminder of his unwavering dedication to this team." Molly's voice trembled as she spoke, her eyes scanning each player in the room, each one captivated by her words and visible emotion, "He believed in this team long before any of you were even born. He repeatedly saw this club rise from the ashes, defying all odds."

Molly paused, her voice fierce and passionate, "And now our community needs you to do it again. This is not just a game. It's the lifeblood of our town. Every fan who lives and breathes Swanford is counting on you to bring home victory today and keep us up." A hush fell over the room, broken only by the soft sounds of sniffling as Molly finished her heartfelt speech. As if they didn't before, the players now knew what was at stake.

Adam finally broke the silence after composing himself and wiping away his tears. "Wow, just wow," he whispered, raising his voice, "What more needs to be said, lads? Please join me in giving a big round of applause for Molly, and let us remember her dear Grandad in our hearts." The room erupted in sorrow, pride, and admiration as they applauded Molly's courage and her grandfather's memory. As the applause died down, the players stood up individually to give Molly warm handshakes and heartfelt hugs. Some whispered words of gratitude, while others offered solemn condolences. Each player was fully aware that they were not just performing for the town of Swanford but also for the legacy of devoted fans like Molly's beloved Granddad.

After each player paid their respects, Adam wrapped Molly in a tight embrace, thanking her for the inspiring words before asking Shea to guide her to the luxurious hospitality suite reserved for her and her family. "We've made sure you have the best seat in the house for today's game," Adam said with a smile, "Let's hope we can secure a win and keep us up for you and your Granddad."

As Molly expressed her gratitude and followed Shea out of the room, Adam's voice rose with authority. "Right, pre-match team meeting. Let's get down to business." The players turned their attention to their manager as a solemn hush fell over the room. Adam shuffled through his notes, ready to lead his team to victory. Together, Adam, his coaches and the players analysed the opposition's strengths and weaknesses, recalling their own past experiences against them and planning how to triumph in the high-stakes match ahead. Everyone contributed their thoughts and ideas, united by a shared belief. It wasn't just about skill and strategy anymore; it was about heart and fight and giving it their all on the pitch. With a final declaration from Adam that Scott, the chairman, who had now entered the room, wanted to speak with them, Adam concluded the meeting by explaining that the players would now be given time to relax and prepare for warm-ups at three o'clock and that they should report to the dressing room for the warm-ups at ten to three.

Scott made his way to the front of the room before speaking. "Lads, if I may have your focus for just a moment," he began, his confidence shining through, "I want to wish you all good luck today. I know in my gut that you can pull this off." With a smile, he added, "As an extra incentive, the player who scores the winning goal today, should it come, will receive a special gift from me, this limited edition collectors watch worth over twenty-thousand pounds that my Dad, Big Don, had commissioned and is therefore totally bespoke and a one-off," Scott explained, holding the glistening timepiece aloft.

The watch wasn't just a timepiece but a supernova trapped on a wrist. Diamonds blazed under the room's soft glow like a thousand captured stars. The band, a cascade of pure gold, shimmered with a warmth that seemed to emanate from within as if Midas himself had dipped his hand and left his mark. But it was the watch face that genuinely captivated. A mesmerising labyrinth of gears and springs lay intricately displayed beneath a flawless sapphire window, a tiny universe ticking with purpose. This wasn't a watch but a trophy, a tangible manifestation of wealth and victory. A collective gasp rippled through the team. In that exquisite timepiece, they didn't just see luxury; they saw a challenge, a glittering promise of the life they craved. The watch wasn't just an object but a spark that ignited a fire within them, a burning desire to reach the pinnacle of success and claim their piece of the glittering prize.

The players appraised the watch with awe and respect, knowing its true value was a measure of Scott's seriousness. Scott's smile pierced through the glances as he added, "Let this be an added motivation for you all," he declared, "Now go out there and get us that win. Our survival depends on it."

The clock struck ten to three as Adam and his team gathered in the dressing room, preparing to don their training gear for warm-ups at three pm. The room was filled with the scent of freshly laundered jerseys and the sound of cleats clicking against the tiled floor. As the players carefully laced up their boots, Adam broke the silence, raising his voice above the noise. "Right, lads, before you go out to warm up, I've just given the media department and referee the team sheet, so listen up, here it is. In goal, Barlow. Across the back, from left to right, Donovan, Kofi, Shea and Turner. The midfielder in the defensive role is Ethan Fox. Midfield Knight and Young. Left-wing, Louis Sims. Right-wing, Davids and up-top Neil Cole.

A recognition spread through the room as the players acknowledged their roles. "Alright, lads, you know your jobs. Remember our formation and tactics," Adam continued, slamming his fist on a nearby locker for emphasis, "We're going up against a tough team today, also fighting for survival. Still, no team can stand in our way if we play our game right. Barlow, I want you to command that penalty area like it's your kingdom. Donovan, Kofi, Shea and Turner, please set up our box like a fortress. Nothing gets through. Fox," he said, locking eyes with Ethan, who was methodically lacing up his boots, "I need you to be everywhere today. Protect our backline and break up their plays. Knight and Young control the tempo of the game. Sims and Davids, speed is key today. Keep their defence on their toes and support Cole up top." "Cole," Adam said finally, turning to the striker already wrapped up in his pre-game rituals, "You're our spearhead. I want intensity and precision from you every minute of this game, and hey, that watch would look superb on your wrist, would it not?" he said, smiling.

As the team nodded in agreement and started pumping each other up for the big match ahead, Adam took a moment to himself. He looked at the clock again; it was five to three. Five more minutes for his boys to mentally prepare before they hit the pitch for warm-ups. Every man in that dressing room was tense yet had unshakeable confidence. They were ready to give everything on the pitch: sweat, blood, and tears if it came down to it. One thing was clear: they were not just playing for themselves or their manager this afternoon; they were playing for every single fan out there, hoping for a victory and survival.

Stepping out of the dressing room and into a cascade of daylight, the team made their way down the tunnel towards the pitch, greeted by a chorus of cheers from early-arriving fans. The crisp grass beneath their feet and the crowd's roar energised them, setting the stage for an intense and exhilarating warm-up session. The crowd and excitement were building within the ground as the players warmed up and went through their fitness, passing and shooting drills. The nerves and anticipation of the upcoming titanic clash amplified every echo. The green canvas of the pitch, meticulously maintained by the ground staff, shone brightly under the afternoon sun, each blade of grass glittering like a precious gem.

The looming stadium clock inched closer to the anticipated quarter to four, signalling for the players to return to the dressing room before kick-off. As they did, adrenaline pumped through their veins as they readied themselves. The low hum of chatter and clanking equipment filled the air, mingling with the scent of freshly laundered kits and sweat. As the clock struck ten to four, Adam commanded the room's attention by raising his voice over that of anything else.

"Right, boys, this is it. I don't have much to say. You know the tactics and what we've worked on. You know the stakes. With that in mind, I won't conduct the team talk. I will let the fans do it. If you look at the TV screen, you'll see that the media team have been out into the pubs and around the ground, gathering messages of luck and encouragement from the fans as they arrived today. Please watch it and let it motivate you. Mike, hit play, please," Adam signalled.

The five-minute video played out like a montage ripped from the heart of Swanford, a tapestry woven from the raw emotions of their most loyal supporters. Weathered faces, etched with the loyalty of decades, creased with hopeful smiles. Youngsters, barely taller than the ball itself, eyes shining with unadulterated belief. The screen pulsed with a kaleidoscope of cheers, tears, chants, and songs, a passionate symphony resonating deep within every player.

An older man, his voice thick with a lifetime of unwavering support, spoke first. "Come on, lads," he rasped, a worn scarf wrapped tightly around his neck, "We've been through the mud together, tasted defeat, but you've always brought us back. Make us proud one more time."

A choked sob escaped a little girl with vibrant pigtails as she held up a hand-drawn sign, its message bold and clear: I love Swanford. "My daddy says if you believe you can win, you will. So believe!" she screamed.

Each message, a shard of hope and expectation, lodged in the players' hearts. The minutes ticked by, each filled with messages of support and motivation until the screen finally went dark.

Adam spoke up one last time before they headed into the tunnel. Gesturing towards the glowing TV screen, he said, "Those people out there, they believe in us," he declared, his gaze shifting back to his team, "They're not just fans, they're family, and we will not let our family down." "Today, we leave it all on the pitch. We give everything we have, even if it means getting hurt in challenges, diving in for balls, or fighting for goal-scoring opportunities." Adam looked at each of his team, willing them to feel the same burning desire within themselves.

"We battle for every inch because that's what this game and survival means to us." With that final remark, all the players rose to their feet simultaneously, ready to enter battle.

They could feel the energy building around them as they made their way into the tunnel, surrounded by shuffling feet and nervous whispers. They lined up beside the Wry players and match officials, their hearts beating as one, ready to face whatever challenges lay ahead. As their feet touched the grassy pitch again, the players were greeted by an overwhelming roar from the ocean of fans in the stands. Each player felt the weight of responsibility on their shoulders, not just for themselves, but for their entire team. The two teams stood in perfect formation, the stadium falling silent as they awaited the piercing sound of the referee's whistle, signalling the start of a fierce battle.

From kick-off, Wry's players played with composure and confidence. Each pass was precise and calculated as if they were playing a chess game on the pitch. With a calm demeanour, they slowly advanced through the Swanford half, weaving their way past defenders and breaking through the line of defence before disaster struck. In the third minute, Wry's winger sent a perfect cross into the eighteen-yard box where their star striker Skarzynski awaited, completely unmarked. He slotted the ball into the back of the net in one swift motion for an effortless goal. The roar of the away fans filled the air as Wry took an early lead against a nervous-looking Swanford side. 0-1.

A stunned silence descended upon the home fans. Their joyous roars were choked back, replaced by a gasp that rippled through the stands. Across the pitch, the away end erupted in a volcanic celebration, their cheers a taunting counterpoint to the sudden hush that had engulfed Swanford's faithful.

Adam, a storm brewing in his eyes, stalked the sideline. When his voice rose above the din, it wasn't laced with encouragement; it crackled with raw fury. These weren't platitudes he barked; they were demands, challenges flung like verbal grenades at his players. The message was clear: this wasn't a setback but a call to arms. They were down, but they weren't out, and by God, they were going to fight their way back.

The players didn't nod. They snarled. A silent promise, a predator's glint in their eyes. Knocked down? Maybe, but defeated? Never. With new resolve, they kicked off to restart play.

With slick movement, Cole passed the ball back to Shea, who passed it to Ethan Fox. The young player took his time on the ball, displaying a calm and collected composure that belied his age. His deliberate pace slowed down the game, allowing his team to regroup and strategise. With a glance at his teammate's attacking runs, Ethan carefully directed a long pass to Louis Sims on the left wing. Anticipating the play, Louis deftly chipped the ball into the area for Neil Cole to receive, completing a fluid diamond passing sequence to breach the Wry defence. With one expert touch to control the ball, Neil effortlessly curled the ball toward goal, only to see Wry's goalkeeper pull off a world-class save. That was close.

The home crowd exploded into a frenzy of cheers and encouragement for their side, their voices merging to create a roar. The sound reverberated through the stadium, bouncing off the walls like crashing waves against jagged cliffs. Swanford continued to grow into the game, looking more and more threatening by the minute. Then, on the half-hour mark, disaster struck again.

Shea cradled the ball, the rhythm of the game pulsing through his veins. Then, silence. A monstrous crack shattered the air as an opposing player lunged with reckless fury. Shea screamed a primal howl that echoed through the stunned stadium. As he crumpled to the ground, his ankle was twisted at an impossible angle, a nightmarish mockery of human anatomy. Ethan was the nearest player to Shea, and as he got closer to him, a horrifying glimpse confirmed his fears. Like a shard of ivory, bone protruded from a crimson gash, a grotesque centrepiece displayed on Shea's leg. The world tilted, and the metallic tang of bile rose in Ethan's throat as he emptied his stomach onto the pristine pitch. A collective gasp rippled through the stands. Swanford players sank to their knees, raw emotion etched on their faces. Tears welled up, blurring the image of the fallen comrade. The game and the competition all faded into insignificance. Through the white-hot pain, Shea displayed a warrior's stoicism. A testament to the steel beneath his skin, he refused to surrender to the scream threatening to erupt.

The perpetrator, the Wry player responsible for the reckless challenge, stood frozen. Horror, raw and dawning, painted his face. Tears streamed down his cheeks, each one a glistening counterpoint to the bone protruding from Shea's leg. His teammates gathered around, unable to do anything but console him as he frantically asked for assurances that Shea was all right, or at least would be.

As treatment continued, Shea was given a gas and air mask for pain relief while a stretcher was prepared. The concern throughout the whole stadium was apparent. Nobody liked to see anyone injured so severely. Rivalries meant nothing in moments like these. After ten minutes of treatment, Shea was stretchered off to make his way to an ambulance, and Reynolds was sent on to replace him. The referee decided the right thing to do would be to send off the Wry player who'd committed the foul, so they were now down to ten men.

The Swanford players were shellshocked as play resumed, and their minds were on nothing other than Shea. Shea had become a leader and a father figure within the camp and was much loved. His injury had distressed the team mentally, and they were struggling to recover. The players may have been on the pitch, but their heads were either replaying the tackle and injury or in the back of the ambulance with Shea. Being absent-minded and lacking focus, just before half-time, Wry carved their way through the unconscious Swanford defence to score again. 0-2. Swanford's hopes of survival were fading fast.

As the referee signalled half-time, Adam rushed his players down the tunnel and into the dressing room, keen to ensure they made the most of every second of the fifteen-minute half-time break to regroup. As the players entered the dressing room, it was filled with an eerie silence, broken only by tired athletes' heavy sighs and murmurs. Amidst it all, one man seized the moment and stood tall: Michael Knight.

"Right, listen up!" he shouted to command the attention of everyone in the room as he began to speak, "We've shown everyone what we're made of lately," Michael started, "We're not here to just play football and make up the numbers, we're here to win. We need to tighten up our defence, shut down Skarzynski's shots, and exploit their weak spots," he said pacing around the room looking each player in the eye, making sure they understood what was at stake. A growing sense of resolve replaced the silence pervading the room. Neil leaned forward, wiping the sweat from his brow with a towel. He knew that Michael was right; victory and safety were still within their grasp if they could produce their very best for this final forty-five minutes of the season.

Watching on in respect and inspiration, Adam began to strategise, thinking of ways to break through the Wry defence and put more pressure on Skarzynski. He watched as his team slowly transformed before his eyes. He nodded approvingly as Michael concluded his speech with, "We've been training for this moment all season. This is our time. Now show them what we've got." Finally, Michael turned to Adam and said, "Gaffer, over to you, lead us into this final throw, what say you?"

Adam nodded with a look of thanks and respect for Michael before saying, "Victory is about belief. I believe in you, your families believe in you, your kids believe your heroes, your mums and dads and youth coaches believed in you, scouts believed in you, this town believes in you, the man who stands beside you believes in you, and I believe in you. Now's the time to believe in yourselves, let's go," he declared with a rallying call.

"Can I just add," Mike interjected, "There is someone else who wants to say something." Mike pointed to the TV, which he'd rigged his phone up to.

As Mike hit play, a familiar face came into view. It was Shea. He had recorded and messaged the video led in the back of the ambulance en route to the hospital. "Lads," Shea began, "From what I've been told, you're after conceding again and failed to recover mentally from my injury. That is not acceptable," he said, "You are professionals, and the show must go on. Listen, I'm alright. I've already had a drop of the Irish god's finest black stuff in the back of this wagon, and I've been assured there's some whiskey on tap at the hospital; I'll be grand. Forget about me. Play your game in that second half and get the win. The best thing any of you can do for me right now is show me why I think you are the best bunch of players in the world, ones who I love," he concluded.

The message buoyed up the players as they gave out a thunderous roar of intent. On cue, the referee's bell rang, and it was time to line up in the tunnel beside Wry and the match officials, ready to walk down the tunnel and onto the pitch for the final forty-five minutes of battle in a long and tiring season.

The roars of a feverish crowd echoed through the concrete walls, each cheer, jeer and chant forming a tangible wall of sound that seemed to vibrate through the players' bones. Both teams emerged into the arena and stepped onto the pristine green pitch. With just forty-five minutes on the clock, their dreams hung in the balance, waiting to be etched into history or become mere footnotes under it. The enormity of it all was both crushing and empowering, a reminder of the immense pressure and opportunity on their shoulders.

Adam strode purposefully up the touchline. As he neared the dugout, he spotted two figures standing there: the stadium announcer and a camera operator. Without hesitation, Adam requested the announcer's microphone and the live camera be put on him. His request was quickly granted. As the teams lined up for the second half, Adam's passion-filled face was projected onto the giant screens around the stadium, catching the attention of thousands of fans.

"Swanford, we need you," he declared into the microphone, his voice streaming through the speakers, "This is our moment, our chance to make history. We need your support now more than ever. So be loud, be proud, and be our twelfth man!" The emotional call to action echoed throughout the stadium, igniting a unified roar from the Swanford faithful that seemed to shake the very foundations of the stadium.

Adam stood in his dugout, ready for the start of the second half, eyes sweeping over the players on the pitch. They looked back at him, their expressions filled with a fierce thirst for victory. They seemed to draw strength from his words and the fire that ignited in the crowd's hearts as if driven by some unseen force. The opposing team watched in shock, their previous confidence wavering as they faced this sudden shift in atmosphere. It was as if an ancient battle cry had been sounded, awakening each Swanford player's primordial instinct to fight, win, and survive at all costs.

The referee's whistle pierced through the air, signalling the beginning of the second half. The once pristine and perfectly manicured pitch now resembled a battlefield marked by cleat imprints and patches of torn grass. As the second half began, each Swanford player fought for every inch of ground, every tackle, and each pass held immense significance. They battled like fearless warriors, fiercely defending their territory, knowing one misstep could spell disaster.

Intense emotion rippled through the Swanford team as Adam raised his arms in a commanding gesture from the touchline. His eyes gleamed with an unyielding desire, urging his players to give everything they had. And they did. They dug deep, finding reservoirs of strength and willpower they never knew existed. With each step forward, they pushed past their limits and broke through barriers of doubt, fuelled by a fierce desire to succeed. The first ten minutes of the half was a duel; both teams were evenly matched and did not want to make a wrong move or mistake, given the magnitude of defeat.

As the game reached its crucial hour mark, Swanford launched another well-carved attack using their diamond passes before Neil Cole got hold of the ball twenty-five yards from goal and rifled it past the goalkeeper into the top left-hand corner of the goal. 1-2. Game on.

As the last fifteen minutes of the game approached, a sense of resignation seemed to settle over the Swanford team as they couldn't find another goal to level the game. Shoulders began to sag, and the players' movements became noticeably slower. Adam watched on, a gnawing helplessness creeping over him. He looked frantically at the scoreboard, which reminded everyone of their impending doom. The numbers seemed to mock him, a cruel reminder of how close they were to losing everything.

As the game clock ticked down and defeat seemed inevitable, energy crackled through the stadium. The once silent home crowd erupted into a desperate chant, "Swan-ford, Swan-ford!" they cried out, their voices a rallying plea for victory. It started as a whisper, barely audible over the roar of the opposing team's fans, but it grew in strength and intensity until it thundered around the entire stadium. Then, in one glorious moment of unity between man and ball, Kofi Adams stepped up in the club's hour of need. From almost the halfway line, he spotted the Wry goalkeeper off his line and, with all his might, drove the ball into the top right corner of the goal. The crowd erupted into loud cheers and applause as they watched in awe at the sheer force behind his shot. 2-2. The score was now tied, and Swanford were back in the fight. As if awakened from a slumber, the once solemn fans found their voices again and roared on with renewed hope. They were now only one goal from safety.

The whistle shrieked, but the roar of the Swanford faithful drowned out the echo. From the kick-off, they weren't a team; they were a storm surge crashing against the Wry defence. Survival was in their grasp against all odds, predictions, and logic.

A minute in, Neil Cole became a whirlwind of desperate fury. He hounded a nervous Wry defender, a predator stalking wounded prey. With a surge of power, he broke free, entering the box with a lethal grace. The net seemed to beckon, a gaping maw promising salvation. Then, a butcher's challenge. A Wry defender slid in, a challenge to halt Cole's momentum. The referee's whistle pierced the tension like a bolt of lightning. Penalty. A gasp rippled through the Wry supporters, replaced by a thunderous roar from the Swanford side. This wasn't just a chance at goal; it was a lifeline, an opportunity to defy the inevitable.

The sudden turn of events seemed surreal. The noise in the stadium reached deafening levels as thousands of hearts pounded with hope. The home crowd, who had fallen in silence following their team's earlier mistakes, were now on their feet, every pair of eyes locked on the penalty spot. Adam stood on the sideline, barely able to watch, doing so through his fingers. He watched as Michael Knight took the ball and vowed to take this crucial penalty. Was this to be Michael's moment of redemption?

The Wry goalkeeper paced back and forth inside the box, his nerves evident as he fixated on Knight. The stadium fell eerily silent, with even the away fans holding their breath in anticipation. Every pair of eyes was glued to the scene unfolding before them, knowing that the next few seconds could determine the fate of their team. Knight placed the ball on the white-chalked spot, his eyes unwaveringly fixed on the goal before him. Taking a deep breath, he stepped back and then, with a sudden burst of energy, he sprinted forward and struck the ball with all his might. The world seemed to slow down as everyone watched the ball soar through the air, curling past the outstretched arms of Wry's desperate goalkeeper. A collective gasp resonated through the stadium, followed by complete silence as they waited with bated breath for the outcome of this crucial moment.

Suddenly, a roar erupted from the stadium, a cacophony of cheers and screams as the ball soared into the back of the net. The Swanford fans leapt for the air, their voices blending in a jubilant thunderstorm. In the midst of it all was Michael Knight, his arms raised triumphantly as he soaked in the crowd's adoration. Against all the drama and conflict, despite all fears and failures, he had single-handedly revived Swanford's faltering dream with his perfectly executed penalty kick. He ran off to celebrate with Adam on the sideline, only to be tackled by his teammates, who swarmed him with unbridled joy and delight. 3-2.

With only eight minutes left in the match, plus any added time from the referee, Wry were quick to kick the game back to life and ensure their survival. The stakes were simple for them. A draw would secure their safety from relegation, as they started the day with a one-point lead over Swanford.

Eager and focused like a greyhound chasing its prey, Wry wasted no time in making their move towards the Swanford box. Swanford seemed caught off guard, still reeling from the high of taking the lead, causing their concentration levels to slip. A perfectly executed cross was floated into the box, and Skarzynski's head was found. The force of his header drove the ball straight into the back of the net, completing an impressive hat trick for him. 3-3.

The once rowdy and passionate Swanford fans were once again stunned into silence, their cheers silenced as they hung their heads with defeat. In the same way a boxer falls to the cold canvas of the ring; they, too, found themselves lying on the ground, feeling unable to beat the ten count. The players on the pitch mirrored this dejection, their shoulders slumped and faces showing the harsh reality sinking in. Meanwhile, Wry erupted into wild jubilation, players embracing each other in joy and pumping their fists triumphantly, knowing they were now safe if they could focus and see the game through to full-time. Skarzynski's sweat-dusted face beamed with fierce joy as the devoted Wry fans in the away section roared in approval, their cheers echoing through every corner of the silent stadium.

The sound of the referee's whistle pierced through the intense atmosphere, signalling the resumption of the game. On the sideline, the assistant referee held up an electronic board displaying five minutes of added-on time. Swanford pressed frantically, their players dashing after every pass, desperately attempting to gain possession and launch an attack. Somehow, they still believed. Sensing the situation's urgency, they managed to take advantage of an intercepted pass in midfield and mounted another swift counterattack. This was their last chance to turn the game around, and there was no room for error. Michael, who had won possession, quickly passed the ball to David's on the right wing. He sped towards Wry's defence before spotting Louis Sims in vast open space on the left wing. David's lofted a perfectly placed ball across the pitch towards Louis's waiting foot.

With hunger in his eyes, Louis charged towards Wry's right back. Upon realising he couldn't beat him, he selflessly passed the ball to Neil Cole, who had made a run through the middle and approached the outside of the box. With impressive footwork, Neil beat one defender, then another on his way into the box before unleashing a powerful shot towards goal. The Wry goalkeeper dived to his right desperately to save it, but it was too late. The ball thundered into the net, securing Neil

Cole's brace and giving Swanford the lead. Neil's teammates rushed towards him in celebration. It was a goal that would go down in history as one of his most outstanding achievements, marking a significant turning point in his promising career as a football star. 4-3.

Unreal and unexpected, the unthinkable had happened. The once-quiet stadium was now bursting with life as the Swanford fans screamed and hugged each other in a frenzy of celebration. Amidst the chaos, a few overzealous fans jumped onto the pitch, only to be quickly escorted off by vigilant stewards.

As the clock ticked down, Swanford fought with every last ounce of energy they had to maintain possession of the ball. In the final moments, they managed to get the ball into the corner and held on for dear life as their opponents desperately attempted to take it back. Every muscle strained, and every heart raced as they defended their lead until the very last second, as if their lives depended on it.

Finally, after what felt like an age, the blast of the referee's whistle pierced through the air, signalling the end of the match and the season. The Wry players, now relegated, collapsed in disbelief and tears. Meanwhile, the once pristine pitch was quickly swallowed up by a sea of jubilant Swanford fans, flooding onto the pitch to celebrate their team's miraculous last-minute survival against all odds. Amidst the chaos and commotion, the Wry players were quickly ushered off the pitch for their safety. In contrast, the victorious Swanford players soaked it up, revelling in their hard-fought victory with their ecstatic fans.

Amidst it all, Adam stood still, his heart pounding excitedly as he suddenly heard an unexpected chant rising above the crowd's roar: "Adam Wells' black and white army!" A grin spread across his face as he turned to look up at the corporate seats in the stand above, pumping his fists in exhilaration towards chairman Scott Brewer and Molly and her family, who were watching on with beaming Cheshire cat smiles. Then his gaze shifted back to the pitch, and he couldn't help but feel overwhelmed with emotion as he looked towards the sky and thought of his late Granddad. Tears pricked at his eyes as he dropped to his knees and uttered a triumphant yell of, "Yessssss."

Available worldwide online
and from all good bookstores

Michael Terence
Publishing

www.mtp.agency

www.facebook.com/mtp.agency

@mtp_agency

Printed in Great Britain
by Amazon

56926913R00142